explanation then of the likely unfolding of events is closer to what is happening right now than any other commentator present or past."

—Bill Bonner, quoting a reader from Australia, *Bits of News*

"The chapter on real estate was particularly prescient [in explaining] the games played by banks, mortgage brokers and property appraisers—the no-money down loans, the juiced up home valuations, the home equity withdrawals that were bigger than properties were worth—that made the credit binge possible. And there was this warning: Financial institutions that invest in mortgage-backed securities will 'surely regret' it....

"The good news—if you can call it that—is that when the economy, the stock market and real estate finally hit bottom, there's going to be one heck of a buying opportunity. Even Mr. Prechter agrees on that. So it wouldn't hurt to keep some cash on hand, just in case he turns out to be right."

—John Heinzl, *Globe and Mail*

"Prechter is a stock market technician who analyzes historical stock prices and patterns using the Elliott Wave Theory....In 2002 he wrote a book titled *Conquer the Crash: You Can Survive and Prosper in a Deflationary Depression*. In it he correctly forecast a huge credit contraction, brought on by all the mortgage debt issues that we're now facing.

"Reading this book today, it seems as if Prechter had a crystal ball. That's why his current view of the market is so compelling....He says the 'credit implosion' is not finished. Much like Japan, he predicts, we'll have to live through a long period of declining assets, summed up in one word: deflation."

—Terry Savage, *Chicago Sun Times*

"I looked into Robert Prechter's forecasts once I learned that early 2007 is when he positioned his subscribers for a stock market top. I read *Conquer the Crash*, and I have never been so riveted with a non-fiction book in my entire life. He describes things that had already begun to happen, and he wrote this book in 2002! *Conquer the Crash* describes how we get to, what will happen, and how to survive a deflationary depression."

—David Brown (blog)

"I have to shut my mouth around people who have lost 50% while I have gained 100% in one account. Do yourself a favor and read *Conquer the Crash* without delay."

—Biotechmgr (blog)

"Call him the ultimate contrarian. He is one man who did not flinch in the face of overwhelming majority of market commentators who predicted soaring inflation following the credit-awash policy central banks chose to drown the world in. Instead, he was steadfast in his belief that the outcome would be far more dangerous, i.e. deflation. The script he laid out in his book *Conquer the Crash* in 2002 has vividly played out since August 2007 as the credit implosion finally reared its ugly head."

Outlook PROFIT

"I like the book *Conquer the Crash* by Bob Prechter and have been recommending it to people for years. Rooted in decades of serious research, published in 2002, this book was a frighteningly accurate predictor of the 2008 crash. It explains the 'big picture' of how economic conditions ebb and flow over time, how to profit from them and how to avoid getting caught in the inevitable squeezes that wipe out the unwary (i.e. 99% of the world.)"

—Ken McCarthy, *Independence Day Blueprint*

"Six years from his being a voice in the wilderness on deflation, most has come to pass now. It is frightening, even for the 'prepared.'"

—Tom McGraw, email

"I recently had the good fortune to attend a lecture given by Bob Prechter—his purpose was to update his 2002 book, *Conquer the Crash*....Prechter's brilliant insight is to note that the laws of supply and demand cannot be properly applied to the financial markets because there are no producers to provide the supply curve required for establishing price equilibrium.

"Neither prophets nor intellectual iconoclasts are often honored in their own time....Fortunately, as befits a man focused upon the future, Prechter has responded to this challenge by laying a solid, methodological foundation which can readily be built upon by others interested in following in his footsteps."

—Vox Day, *WorldNetDaily*

"Robert Prechter of Elliott Wave International and the leading proponent of socionomics (social mood determines events, rather than the other way around) has been, in my mind, one of the only analysts/pundits/economists out there who has legitimately called both the deflationary credit crisis and the ensuing rally that we are in now. His unique method tracks the stock market as a barometer of social mood which patterns itself in distinct formations representing fear and greed. The reason I believe that Prechter has been nailing the tops and bottoms of the last few years is because of his con-trary position as to the causal nature of social and economic events."

—Matt Stiles, *Futronomics*

Reviews Published with Original Edition

"Bob Prechter's new book, *Conquer the Crash*, provides a wealth of self-help do's and don'ts. It's a must-read book, which I'm personally putting on my gift list for friends and loved ones."

— Martin D. Weiss, Ph.D.
author of the national best seller,
The Ultimate Safe Money Guide

"This is the most crucial financial period in your life. This book explains why. It also tells you what you should do about it. If you want to preserve your wealth, I urge you to follow Prechter's advice. You will be grateful that you did."

—Ian Gordon
The Long Wave Analyst

"*Conquer the Crash* provides disciplined investors with a map, compass and survival guide. Don't leave home without it."

—Henry Van der Eb
President, Gabelli Mathers Fund

"A compelling exposition of how both the mechanics and the psychology of the business cycle can be encapsulated in market analysis."

—Sean Corrigan
Capital-Insight.com

"Prechter knows the facts like few others. Read his forceful argument carefully. It can save you from financial loss."

—James R. Cook
President, Investment Rarities

CONQUER THE CRASH

CONQUER the *CRASH*
You Can Survive and Prosper in a Deflationary Depression

Robert R. Prechter, Jr.

JOHN WILEY & SONS, LTD

For general information on our other products and services or for technical support, please contact our Customer Care Department within the United States at (800) 762-2974, outside the United States at (317) 572-3993 or fax (317) 572-4002.

Wiley also publishes its books in a variety of electronic formats. Some content that appears in print may not be available in electronic books. For more information about Wiley products, visit our web site at www.wiley.com.

ISBN-13 978-0-470-56797-5

Printed in the United States of America

10 9 8 7 6 5 4 3 2 1

Dedication

This book is dedicated to all my friends and colleagues at Elliott Wave International, who put up with three months of my single-mindedness in producing this book.

Acknowledgments

In putting together this volume, I had invaluable help from Robert Prechter Sr., Lou Crandall, Pete Kendall and Jean-Pierre Louvet, who provided expert information that enhanced certain chapters in this book. Rachel Webb, Sally Webb and Angela Hall did the charts and formatting, and Robin Machcinski and Darrell King designed the jacket.

Contents

Book Three

Added for the 2009 edition

Note: The Foreword and the first 262 pages of this book are identical to the first edition. Readers of the prior edition should begin with Book Three on page 263.

Foreword

"Look out! Look out! Look out! Look out!"
— Barry, Greenwich and Morton,
via The Shangri-Las

My first book, *Elliott Wave Principle*, which I wrote with A.J. Frost, was very bullish. It came out in November 1978, with the Dow at 790. Today the outlook is much different. Now is not the time to take financial risks. It's time to batten the hatches so you can emerge safe from the storm.

As you can see by this book's title, I am once again calling for events that few expect. But this time, I feel more trepidation about doing so. Deflation and depression are exceedingly rare. Sustained deflation hasn't occurred for 70 years, and the last one was so brief that it lasted less than 3 years. During the past two centuries, there have been just two periods that historians unanimously identify as depressions. The 19th century had one, and the 20th century had one. Predicting such extraordinary events is a complex and challenging task. Everyone who has tried it in the past fifty years has failed. Amidst today's social psychology, merely addressing the ideas of deflation and depression is considered something akin to heresy or lunacy. Survey after survey shows that most economists believe that depression and deflation, considered together or separately, are utterly impossible now if not *ever*. Most believe that the U.S. economy is in a rising trend of perpetual prosperity with moderate inflation and that if any interruptions do happen along the way, they will be mild and brief.

Despite this overwhelming consensus, I am resolute. Book One tells you why, and Book Two tells you what to do if you agree with my conclusions.

If by some bizarre circumstance you are already convinced that preparing for deflation and depression is your desired course of action, you can turn to Book Two right now. If not, then you need Book One. Before you can take steps to protect yourself against a deflationary crash and depression, you have to understand what they are, believe that they are possible, and then agree that they are *likely*. Guiding you to that point is Book One's goal. After you assimilate those ideas, you will be primed to act confidently to insure your survival and prosperity, as outlined in Book Two.

Warning

I've been wrong before. The biggest mistake of my career was in the stock market. After identifying the start of the great bull market and later forecasting, "Investor mass psychology should reach manic proportions," even I never imagined that the stock mania would last as long or go as high as it did. So I jumped off the train too early. Regardless, I think my *basic interpretation* of the long-term financial picture, which we will explore in Chapter 4, is correct. It has never been a matter of whether we would experience a tremendous bull market followed by a historic bear, only a matter of timing and extent.

The reason that I remain willing to express my unconventional view is that I believe that my ideas of finance and macroeconomics are correct and the conventional ones are wrong. True, wave analysts make mistakes, but they also make stunningly accurate long-term forecasts. In contrast, those who do not understand waves can't make any useful social predictions at all.

It may seem to you that the prospect of taking actions that are contrary to the beliefs of a vast array of experts is a big risk to take. But a practical point virtually eliminates that risk:

If you follow the advice in this book and no financial crisis occurs, you cannot get hurt. In fact, you should profit nicely from most of these suggestions. Even if my outlook proves incorrect, the worst case is that your money will earn less than it otherwise may have. Compare these outcomes to the opposing scenario: If conventional economists, who in the aggregate have a perfect record of failing to predict economic contractions, are wrong again, you will lose everything that you have worked so hard to obtain. You will also blow the chance to make a fortune beginning at the next major bottom.

Here's a bonus: If you end up missing out on some of the investment profits that a decade of prosperity can provide, I hereby truly apologize; I know what it feels like to miss an opportunity, and I will regret that I influenced you to do so. By contrast, if you get destroyed financially by following the bullish advice of economists, money managers, brokers, media experts and the like, they will not apologize. They will claim that the future was unforeseeable, so *the rock-hard convictions and platitudes that they cavalierly expressed, the ones that you relied upon to plan your financial future*, were wrong through no fault of their own.

There is one catch: I refuse to offer you an excuse to disclaim all responsibility. If you lose your money, your house, your income and your pension in a deflation and depression, at least you can blame the experts for it. You can cry, "I did what they all told me to do!" If you take action after reading this book, I insist that you do so because you agree with my case, not because you are blindly following my conclusions. To be successful in life, or at least to learn something along the way, you have to think for yourself.

—*Robert Prechter, March 2002*

BOOK ONE

WHY A STOCK MARKET CRASH, MONETARY DEFLATION AND ECONOMIC DEPRESSION ARE LIKELY TO OCCUR SOON

PART I

THE CASE FOR CRASH AND DEPRESSION

Uncomfortable woman in car: "I'm sitting on something!"
W.C. Fields: "I lost mine in the stock market."
                                                —*International House* (1933)

Chapter 1:

A Myth Exposed

How many times over the past decade have you heard glowing reports about the "New Economy"? Hundreds, maybe thousands of times, right? Those of you who have been living on a desert island or who are reading this book fifty years from now can experience the same thing vicariously through Figure 1-1, which displays the accelerating frequency with which the global media have been referring to the "New Economy" year after year. It's been everywhere. Economists celebrate the broadening "service economy" and proclaim that economic growth in the new Information Age has been "unprecedented" in its vibrancy, resilience and scope. Rhetoric is cheap. Evidence is something else.

What would you say if you discovered that we have not had anything near a New Economy, that all that talk is a lie? This chapter is going to show you that the vaunted economic expansion of recent decades in the world's leading economic power, the United States — much less the rest of the world — is far less impressive than you are being led to believe.

First take a look at Figure 1-2, which depicts the U.S. stock market from its low in 1932 during the Great Depression all the way to the present. This graph delineates five phases — or "waves" — of rise and fall.

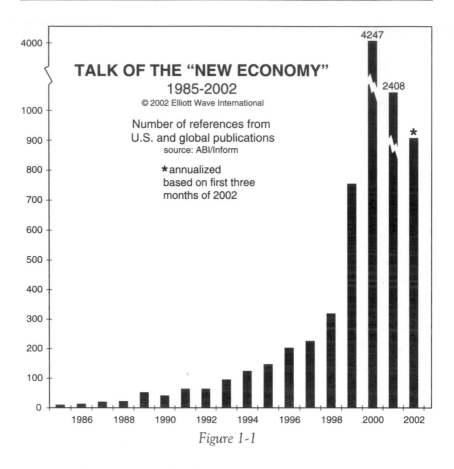

Figure 1-1

The notes on the chart summarize a shocking fact: The economic expansion during the latest phase, wave V, which lasted from 1974 to 2000, was demonstrably weaker than that during the preceding rising phase, wave III, which lasted from 1942 to 1966. Both periods sported a persistent bull market in stocks that lasted about a quarter century, so in that sense, they are quite similar. One noticeable difference is that the DJIA gained only 971 percent during wave III but a remarkable 1930 percent during wave V, twice the amount. This tremendous bull market in stocks in wave V is the great "boom" that people feel in their bones. Yet as you are about to see, the economic vigor

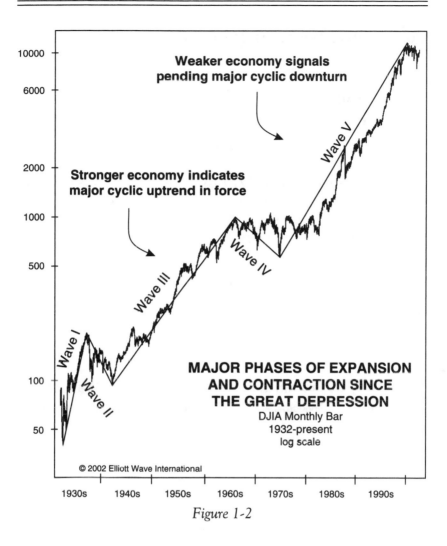

Figure 1-2

and financial health of wave V, the one that has received so much radiant press, failed to measure up to those of wave III by every meaningful comparison.

Please go through the following citations one by one. (Economists do not have all the data from the 1940s, so in some cases, our data for wave III begin later.) After you absorb this information, we will set to the task of finding out what it means.

Comparative Measures of Economic Health

(see Figure 1-3)

Gross Domestic Product

> • In wave III, from 1942 to 1966, the average annual real GDP growth rate was **4.5** percent.

> • In wave V, from 1975 through 1999, it was only **3.2** percent.

Industrial Production

> • In wave III, the average annual gain in industrial production was **5.3** percent.

> • In wave V, it was only **3.4** percent.

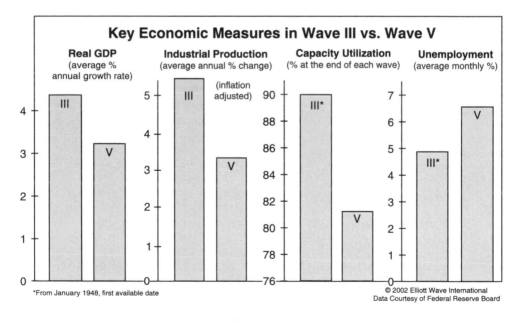

Figure 1-3

Combining GDP and industrial production figures, we may generalize from the reported data that the economic power of wave V was one-third less than that of wave III.

Capacity Utilization

Factories' capacity utilization depicts the energy of an economic expansion compared to the infrastructure's ability to handle it.

- In wave III from 1948 (when figures became available), capacity utilization rose 22 percent to **91.5** percent in June 1966 and stayed high through the late 1960s.

- In wave V, capacity utilization was net flat, peaking in January 1995 at **84.4** percent. U.S. plants were producing at only 82.7 percent of capacity at the ensuing peak in June 2000.

Unemployment Rate

This is an economic measure of *ill* health.
- In wave III from 1948 (when data became available), the monthly average of the unemployment rate was 4.9 percent.

- In wave V, it was 6.6 percent.

Comparative Measures of Debt, Deficits and Liquidity

(see Figure 1-4)

To grasp the full measure of the underlying weakness of wave V's "fundamentals," one must look beyond economic figures to the corporate, household and government balance sheets that underlie those results.

Balance Sheet Items at the End of Wave III vs. Wave V
(scales at left)

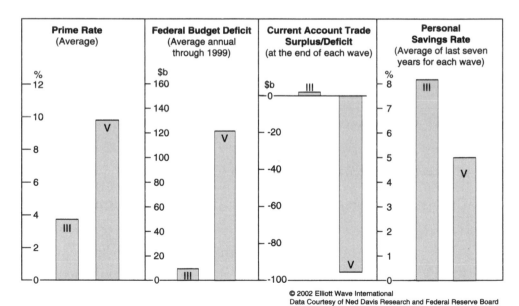

© 2002 Elliott Wave International
Data Courtesy of Ned Davis Research and Federal Reserve Board

Figure 1-4

Households' Liquid Assets

> • At the end of wave III, households' liquid assets were **161** percent of liabilities.

> • At the end of wave V, households' liquid assets were **93** percent of liabilities, meaning that they had *less cash on hand than they had liabilities.*

Federal Debt

> • At the end of wave III, federal debt was **43.9** percent of GDP.

> • At the end of wave V, it was **58.6** percent.

Consumer Debt

> • At the end of wave III, consumer debt was **64** percent of annual disposable personal income.

> • At the end of wave V, it was **97** percent.

Total Debt as a Percent of GDP

> • During wave III, from 1949 to 1966, total credit market debt as a percentage of GDP slipped slightly from **151** percent to **148** percent.

> • In wave V, it rose from **172** percent to **269** percent.

Prime Rate

> • In wave III, the prime rate of interest, the cost of money for the highest quality corporate borrowers, averaged **3.74** percent.

> • In wave V, it averaged 9.66 percent, nearly three times as high.

Federal Budget Deficit

> • In wave III, federal budget deficits were not sustained. The only consecutive years of deficits were in the war years of 1942-1946. The average annual federal deficit was less than **$9** billion.

> • In wave V, the annual federal deficit averaged **$127** billion, which is far greater even when adjusted for inflation.

Current Account Trade Figures

> • At the end of wave III, the U.S. showed a net Current Account trade *surplus* of **$1.3** billion.

> • At the end of wave V, the Current Account showed a record *deficit* of **$96.2** billion.

Personal Savings Rate

> • In wave III, the personal savings rate followed a fairly flat trend, bottoming at **6.5** percent of disposable personal income in February 1969.

> • In wave V, the personal savings rate dropped persistently, falling to a record low of **0.5** percent in March 2000.

U.S. Balance Sheet (not shown)

> • At the end of wave III, the U.S. was a net **creditor**.

> • At the end of wave V, the U.S. was a net **debtor**, owing a record $2 trillion more to foreigners than it is owed.

These figures, dramatic as they are, do not reveal the full extent of wave V's inferior relative performance because both the government's economic reports and corporate accounting methods changed during wave V in such a way as to overstate wave V's economic vigor. If we adjusted for those cosmetic alterations, most of these figures would reveal an even greater dichotomy between the two periods. If we begin wave V's figures in 1982 to put the expansion in the best possible light, they change little and in a few cases are worse. If the Dow were to manage a new high in coming months, we would have to add the weak economic and financial figures of the past two years to wave V's average performance, which would drag it down even more. So you see, *it has not been a New Economy after all* but rather a comparatively lackluster one.

Economic Deterioration During the Final Decade of Wave V

The economic expansion waned not only on a long-term basis but also on a near-term basis, within wave V. While real GDP stayed fairly steady throughout the bull market, some measures showed a subtle but persistent slowdown in economic vibrancy. For example, average annual corporate profit growth fell from **10.8** percent in the first 15 years of the bull market to **8.8** percent in the 1990s, a decline of about **20** percent. From the stock market's low in September/October 1998 through the third quarter of 2000 (the peak of economic performance for that period), profit growth averaged only **4.6** percent, revealing further slowing as wave V crested.

Portent of Reversal?

Collectively, these statistics reveal that the economic advance in the United States has been slowing *at multiple degrees of scale*, a trend that is still manifest today. A continuation of this trend will mean that the expansion that resumed in October 2001 will be the briefest and weakest yet.

The persistent deceleration in the U.S. economy is vitally important because, in my opinion, it portends a major reversal from economic expansion to economic contraction. Chapter 5 will expand upon the reasons for this conclusion. As we are about to see, though, we need not rely on hypothesis alone. The 20th century provides two great precursors to the current situation.

The U.S. in the 1920s

If you recall your economic history, you know that a phrase in vogue in the 1920s was that the economy had entered a "New Era." Economists of the day, as President Hoover ruefully recalled in his memoirs, gushed over the wonderful economy, just as they are doing today. Were the Roaring 'Twenties truly a New Era, or was such talk a spate of hype spurred by the good feelings associated with a soaring stock market?

According to data from Professor Mark Siegler of Williams College (MA), from 1872 through 1880, the annual inflation-adjusted Gross National Product of the United States rose from $98 billion to $172 billion, a **68** percent gain. From 1898 to 1906, real GNP rose from $228.8 billion to $403.7 billion, a 56 percent gain. In contrast, from 1921 through 1929, during the Roaring 'Twenties, GNP in the supposed "New Era" rose from $554.8 billion to $822.2 billion, only a **48** percent gain. This latter performance was particularly poor given that the stock market enjoyed a greater percentage rise from 1921 to 1929 than it had done in any equivalent time in U.S. history.

Similarly to today, the economy of that time failed to keep pace with the advance in stock prices and under-performed the prior expansion. The aftermath was the Great Depression.

The Japanese Experience and Its Implications

If you are over 20 years old, you surely remember the "Japanese Miracle" of the 1980s. The country's products were the best in the world. Its corporate managers lectured and wrote books on how they did it, and the world's CEOs flocked to emulate their style. The Japanese Nikkei stock average soared, and foreign investors poured into the "sure thing." Was the Japanese economy truly miraculous, or once again were economists ignoring economic statistics and simply expressing the good feelings associated with its stampeding stock market?

Figure 1-5 shows real GDP growth in Japan from 1955 to the present. Notice that Japan's growth from 1955 through 1973 was extremely powerful, averaging **9.4** percent per year. But its economic growth from 1975 through 1989 averaged only

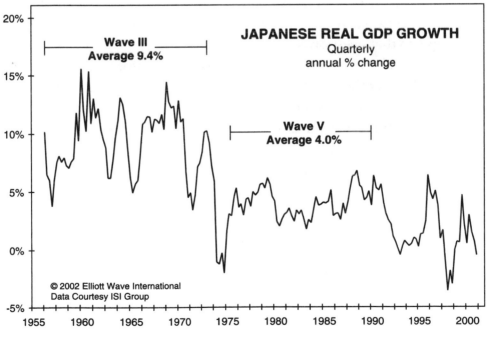

Figure 1-5

4.0 percent per year. This relatively poor economic performance coincided with a record-breaking stock market boom. Just as in the U.S. in the 1920s, the economy in Japan's celebrated years failed to keep pace with the advance in its Nikkei stock index and under-performed the prior expansion. This double dichotomy signaled an approaching reversal of multi-decade importance in both stock prices and the economy. Since the top of its own "wave V," the Nikkei stock index has plunged 70 percent, the economy has had three recessions in a dozen years, and the banking system has become deeply stressed. As we will see in Chapter 8, this downtrend isn't over yet.

A Naked Emperor

The "New Era" of the 1920s ended in a bust. The "Japanese Miracle" of the 1980s ended in a bust. Is that what will happen to today's "New Economy"? We have already gotten a hint of the answer. The next seven chapters will provide a definitive reply to that question.

When historians return to this time, I suspect that they will discover the slow but persistent regression in both U.S. and worldwide growth over the decades in the latter half of the twentieth century and wonder why so few recognized it as a signal of the coming change.

Chapter 2:

When Do Depressions Occur?

Depressions are not just an academic matter. In the Great Depression of 1929-1933, many people lost their investments, their homes, their retirement plans, their bank balances, their businesses — in short, their fortunes. Revered financial professionals lost their reputations, and some businessmen and speculators even took their own lives. The next depression will have the same effects. To avoid any such experience, you need to be able to foresee depression. Let's see if such a thing is possible.

Defining Depression

An economic contraction begins with a deficiency of total demand for goods and services in relation to their total production, valued at current prices. When such a deficiency develops, prices for goods and services fall. Falling prices are a signal to producers to cut back production. In response, total production declines.

Economic contractions come in different sizes. Economists specify only two, which they label "recession" and "depression."

Based on how economists have applied these labels in the past, we may conclude that a recession is a moderate decline in total production lasting from a few months to two years. A depression is a decline in total production that is too deep or prolonged to be labeled merely a recession. As you can see, these terms are quantitative yet utterly imprecise. They cannot be made precise, either, despite misguided attempts to do so (more on that later).

For the purposes of this book, all you need to know is that the degree of the economic contraction that I anticipate is far too large to be labeled a "recession" such as our economy has experienced eleven times since 1933. If my outlook is correct, by the time the contraction is over, no economist will hesitate to call it a depression.

Depressions and the Stock Market

Our investigation into the question of forecasting begins with a key observation: Major stock market declines lead directly to depressions. Figure 2-1 displays the entire available history of aggregate English and American stock price records, which go back over 300 years. It shows that depression has accompanied every stock market decline that is deep enough to stand out on this long-term graph. There are three such declines, which occurred from 1720 to 1784, 1835 to 1842 and 1929 to 1932.

To begin to orient you to my way of thinking, I would like to explain Figure 2-1's title. The stock market is modern society's most sensitive meter of social mood. An increasingly optimistic populace buys stocks and increases its productive endeavors. An increasingly pessimistic populace sells stocks and reduces its productive endeavors. Economic trends lag stock market trends because the consequences of economic decisions made at the peaks and nadirs of social mood take some time to play out. The Great Depression, for example, bottomed in February 1933, seven months after the stock market low of July 1932. So psychological trends create economic trends. This causal relationship between psychology and the economy is the opposite of what virtually everyone presumes, so do not be alarmed if you find it counter-intuitive. Chapter 3 will elaborate on this theme.

If you study Figure 2-1, you will see that the largest stock-market collapses appear not after lengthy periods of market deterioration indicating a slow process of long-term change but quite suddenly after long periods of rising stock prices and economic expansion. A depression begins, then, with the seemingly unpredictable reversal of a persistently, indeed often rapidly, rising stock market. The abrupt change from increasing optimism to increasing pessimism initiates the economic contraction.

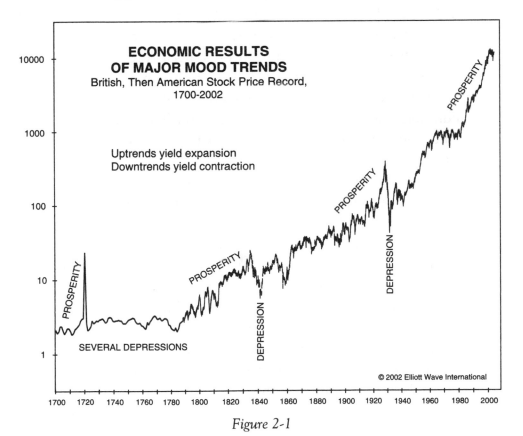

Figure 2-1

The graph shows that these reversals do not appear after every period of rising stock prices but only after some of them. If you are guessing that maybe one of the hints of reversal is a slowing economy in the face of such advances, you're right. We'll learn even more about this factor in Chapters 3 and 5.

Hierarchy in Finance and Economics

You might be interested to know that almost every smaller stock market decline observable in Figure 2-1 also led to an economic contraction. The severity of each contraction is related to the size of the associated stock market decline.

Unfortunately, this hierarchy in economic trends is difficult to display because conventional quantitative definitions of recession get in the way. Sometimes the economy just fails to breach the arbitrary definition of "official recession" that economists use, so their graphs show no recession when in fact the economy contracts, corporate earnings fall, and economic indicators weaken. In some cases of brief or small stock market declines, the economy simply slows down without actually having a "negative" month or quarter, but an effect occurs nevertheless.

Modern attempts to quantify the term "recession" by absolute size are flawed. It would be as if botanists decided to define "branch" or "twig" by length and width. The result may denote an "official" branch or twig, but the definition would obscure the actual continuum of sizes attending parts of trees. Likewise, attempted quantifications of the term "recession" derive from and foster misunderstanding with respect to the hierarchical nature of economic expansion and contraction. It would be far better for economists to adopt the perspective of the Wave Principle, a model of hierarchically patterned financial market change, which we are about to encounter in the next chapter.

All We Need

Such discussions aside, Figure 2-1 is all we need for our purposes. It shows that the biggest stock market declines follow long periods of advance of like degree. They lead to economic contractions so dramatic that nothing gets in the way of their being noticed and recorded as "depressions." Now let's see if we have the means to anticipate their arrival.

Chapter 3:

When Do Stock Markets Turn from Up to Down?

We see that depressions accompany major stock market declines. So if we can predict those rare and dramatic bear markets, we can predict depressions. Can we do that?

The Stock Market Is Patterned

In a series of books and articles published from 1938 to 1946 (available in *R.N. Elliott's Masterworks*, 1994), Ralph Nelson Elliott described the stock market as a fractal. A fractal is an object that is similarly shaped at different scales.

A classic example of a self-identical fractal is nested squares. One square is surrounded by eight squares of the same size, which forms a larger square, which is surrounded by eight squares of that larger size, and so on.

A classic example of an indefinite self-similar fractal is the line that delineates a seacoast. When viewed from space, a seacoast has certain irregularity of contour. If we were to drop to ten miles above the earth, we would see only a portion of the seacoast, but the irregularity of contour of that portion would resemble that of the whole. From a hundred feet up in a balloon, the same thing would be true. These ideas are elucidated in Benoit Mandelbrot's *The Fractal Geometry of Nature* (1982) and numerous publications since.

Scientists recognize financial markets' price records as fractals, but they presume them to be of the indefinite variety. Elliott undertook a meticulous investigation of financial market behavior and found something different. He described the record of stock market prices as a specifically patterned fractal yet with variances in its quantitative expression. I call this type of fractal — which has properties of both self-identical and indefinite fractals — a "robust fractal." Robust fractals permeate life forms. Trees, for example, are branching robust fractals, as are animals' circulatory systems, bronchial systems and nervous systems. The stock market record belongs in the category of life forms since it is a product of human social interaction.

How Is the Stock Market Patterned?

Figure 3-1 shows Elliott's idea of how the stock market is patterned. If you study this depiction, you will see that each component, or "wave," within the overall structure subdivides in a specific way. If the wave is heading in the same direction as the wave of one larger degree, then it subdivides into five waves. If the wave is heading in the *opposite* direction as the wave of one larger degree, then it subdivides into three waves (or a variation). Each of these waves adheres to specific traits and tendencies of construction, as described in *Elliott Wave Principle* (1978).

Waves subdivide this way down to the smallest observable scale, and the entire process continues to develop larger and larger waves as time progresses. Each wave's degree may be identified numerically by relative size on a sort of social Richter scale, but to keep things simple, this book's brief references to specific degrees use their traditional names.

Figure 3-2 shows a rising wave in a manner more consistent with Elliott's detailed observations about typical real-world development. Observe, for example, that waves 2 and 4 in each case take a slightly different shape.

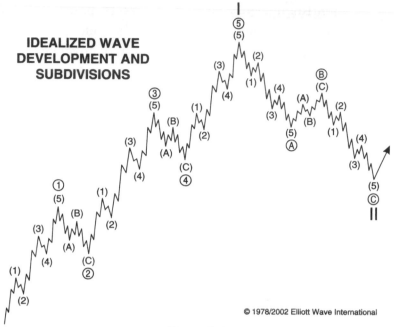

**IDEALIZED WAVE
DEVELOPMENT AND
SUBDIVISIONS**

© 1978/2002 Elliott Wave International

Figure 3-1

**A MORE REALISTIC
WAVE DEPICTION**

© 1999 Elliott Wave International

Figure 3-2

Understanding how the market progresses at all degrees of trend gives you an invaluable perspective. No longer do you have to sift through the latest economic data as if they were tea leaves. You gain a condensed view of the whole panorama of essential trends in human social mood and activity, as far back as the data can take you.

Why Is the Stock Market Patterned?

For the most part, consumers judge prices for bread and shoes consciously and reasonably according to their needs and means. When human beings value financial assets, they must contend with a debilitating lack of knowledge and feelings of uncertainty. They contend with these obstacles to a great degree by forming judgments in sympathy with or in reaction to the opinions and behavior of others. This surrender of responsibility makes them participants in a collective, which is not a reasoning entity. The fact that price changes are patterned proves that the collective's net valuations are not reasoned, but it also shows that they are not random, either. The remaining option is that they are unconsciously determined. Indeed, shared mood trends and collective behavior appear to derive from a herding impulse governed by the phylogenetically ancient, pre-reasoning portions of the brain. This emotionally charged mental drive developed through evolution to help animals survive, but it is maladaptive to forming successful expectations concerning future financial valuation. The only way for an individual to temper the consequences of the herding impulse and to gain independence from it is to understand that it exists. For some evidence of these conclusions, please see *The Wave Principle of Human Social Behavior* (1999).

Examples of Real-World Waves

Figures 3-3 through 3-6 display advancing waves in various financial markets. As you can see, they all sport five waves

SAMPLE ELLIOTT WAVES

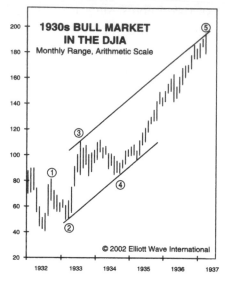

Figure 3-3   Figure 3-4

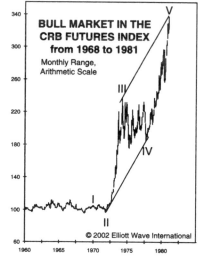

Figure 3-5   Figure 3-6

up. These five-wave patterns proceeded relentlessly, ignoring news of every imaginable variety, including Prohibition, a crash in Florida land values, Roosevelt's seizure of Americans' gold, Hitler's rise to power and the end of the Vietnam war.

I chose these examples because they display one of Elliott's guidelines, which is that bull market waves often end after reaching the upper parallel line of a trend channel. In most cases, the market creates channels in which the lower line touches the bottom of waves 2 and 4, while the upper line touches the top of wave 3 and, later, wave 5.

A Quiz

OK, now you try it. Figure 3-7 shows an actual price record. Does this record depict two, three, four or five completed waves? Based on your answer, what would you call for next?

Figure 3-7

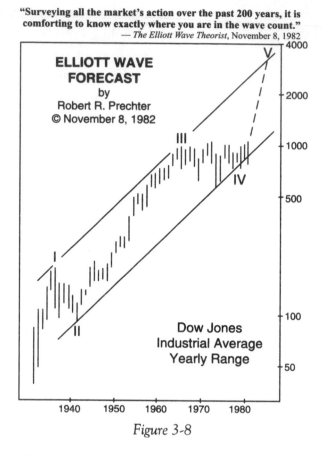

"Surveying all the market's action over the past 200 years, it is comforting to know exactly where you are in the wave count."
— *The Elliott Wave Theorist*, November 8, 1982

ELLIOTT WAVE
FORECAST
by
Robert R. Prechter
© November 8, 1982

Dow Jones
Industrial Average
Yearly Range

Figure 3-8

Let's compare your answer with mine. *The Elliott Wave Theorist* in September 1982 called for the Dow to quintuple to nearly 4000 and on October 6 announced, "Super bull market underway!" The November 8 issue then graphed the forecast for the expected fifth wave up, as you can see in Figure 3-8.

I have purposely kept this example as simple as possible. To view the detailed labeling and real-time analysis that fully justified the prediction made in Figure 3-8, please see the discussions attending the Appendix and Figure 5-5 and 8-3 in *Elliott Wave Principle*.

As you can see, Elliott waves are clear not only in retrospect. They are often — particularly at turning points — quite clear in prospect. I could fill a book describing other triumphs (and failures) of applying the Wave Principle, but I hope this one example conveys its occasionally immense value for forecasting.

What Are the Signs of a Topping Stock Market?

Simply stated, a stock market uptrend ends when five waves of a specific construction are complete. The larger the degree of those five waves, the larger will be the ensuing partial retracement of their progress.

The real world is not as tidy as an idealized depiction of a wave, just as real trees are not as tidy as any single summary depiction of a tree in general. Often third waves are long, with distinct subdivisions. Sometimes first or fifth waves extend in the same manner. Using price patterns alone, there can often be some doubt as to whether one is accurately identifying a fifth wave or whether it might be part of another wave's extension.

To help overcome difficulty in real-world application, I recorded certain traits that waves seem always to display. Figure 3-9 illustrates some of these traits.

For the purposes of this book, the most crucial description is the one attending wave 5: "Market breadth and the economy improve, *but not to the levels of wave 3*. Optimism creates lofty valuation." These observations, which I formulated in 1980 after studying myriad fifth waves, tell us four things to look for any time we presume that the stock market is in a major *fifth* wave rather than a first or third wave:

(1) A fifth wave must have narrower "breadth" than the corresponding third wave, i.e., there must be fewer stocks advancing on the average day in a fifth wave than in the preceding third wave of the same degree.

Elliott Wave Characteristics
© 1980/2002 Elliott Wave International

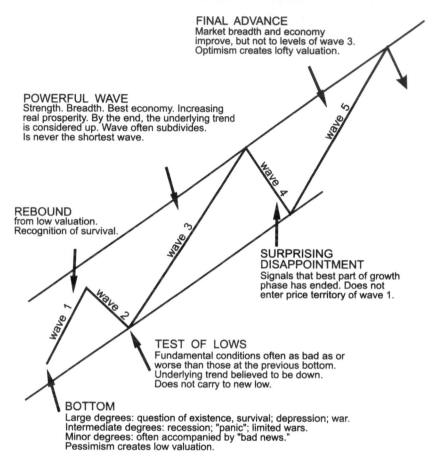

FINAL ADVANCE
Market breadth and economy
improve, but not to levels of wave 3.
Optimism creates lofty valuation.

POWERFUL WAVE
Strength. Breadth. Best economy. Increasing
real prosperity. By the end, the underlying trend
is considered up. Wave often subdivides.
Is never the shortest wave.

REBOUND
from low valuation.
Recognition of survival.

**SURPRISING
DISAPPOINTMENT**
Signals that best part of growth
phase has ended. Does not
enter price territory of wave 1.

TEST OF LOWS
Fundamental conditions often as bad as or
worse than those at the previous bottom.
Underlying trend believed to be down.
Does not carry to new low.

BOTTOM
Large degrees: question of existence, survival; depression; war.
Intermediate degrees: recession; "panic"; limited wars.
Minor degrees: often accompanied by "bad news."
Pessimism creates low valuation.

Figure 3-9

(2) In a fifth wave, there must be a lesser expansion in the economy and weaker financial conditions than occurred during the corresponding third wave.

(3) Stocks must attain high valuations based on their historic relationship to related data.

(4) There must be evidence of optimism among investors.

While we have already learned something along these lines in Chapter 1, Chapters 5 through 7 will discuss each of these aspects in detail, one at a time, with respect to today's stock market.

These distinctions, helpful though they are, do not eliminate uncertainty in interpretation. For example, sometimes fifth waves are quite brief, and other times they go on and on. Their own five-wave subdivisions will in turn display the proper characteristics of waves, of course, helping us to assess the picture. But because these wave characteristics are relative, there can always be more development that still reflects these guidelines even after the market has already met the minimum criteria.

That being said, we can often be certain of important things. For example, using the above criteria, we can *know* that a certain wave is — or is not — a fifth wave. The bigger it is, and the longer it has lasted, the more important that information becomes. Early in the process, we can anticipate the ultimate reversal; later in the process, we can begin to assert boldly that a downturn is imminent.

The reason that identifying the end of a fifth wave is so important is that when a fifth wave ends, a correspondingly large bear market ensues. That's what happened after each one of the bull markets shown in Figures 3-3 through 3-6. At this point, we have enough knowledge to figure out the position of the stock market in its wave pattern *right now*.

Chapter 4:

The Position of the Stock Market Today

Figures 4-1 through 4-3 display my interpretation of the stock market's wave position today at three degrees of trend. Once again, I am keeping these illustrations and explanations as simple as I can. Many fascinating nuances attend these structures, and you will be well rewarded for taking the time to study them via Elliott Wave International's publications if you are so inclined. Suffice it for now to say that the foregoing conclusions are consistent with the analysis of the main wave practitioners of the past century: R.N. Elliott (1871-1948), Charles J. Collins (1894-1982), A. Hamilton Bolton (1914-1967) and A.J. Frost (1908-1999). Their published works on the subject — along with my own — are available in their entirety (aside from a handful of Elliott's lost "market letters") for review at elliottwave.com/books.

Figure 4-1 shows the uptrend of a postulated "Grand Supercycle" wave Ⅲ from 1784 (plus or minus a decade; records are sketchy) to the present. As you can see, its broad strokes seem to trace out a five-wave structure. I have left the preceding bear market of 64 years in British stock prices on the chart to show that the advance arose from the ashes of a bear market of corresponding degree, wave Ⅱ.

Figure 4-2 shows the detail of the fifth wave from Figure 4-1, "Supercycle" wave (V), which was born in 1932 at the bottom of the biggest bear market since the 1700s. As you can see,

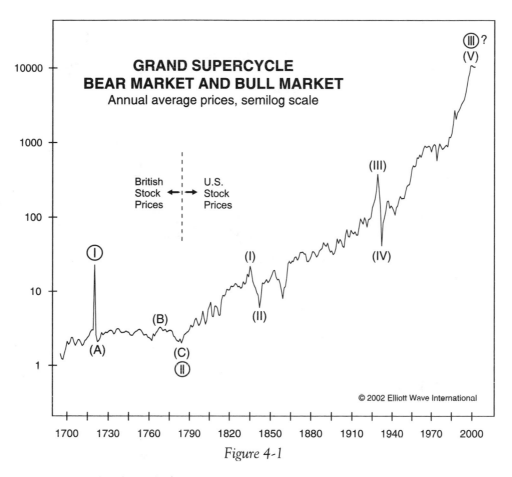

Figure 4-1

it is easily identified as a five-wave structure, which emerged from the ashes of a bear market of corresponding degree, wave (IV). As Chapters 5 through 7 will show, this labeling is definitive.

Figure 4-3 shows the detail of the fifth wave from Figure 4-2, "Cycle" wave V, which began in 1974 at the bottom of wave IV, the biggest bear market since the one that ended in 1942. As you can see, the rise can be labeled as five completed waves, and in this case, they form a trend channel. Although I would like to be able to assert that Figure 4-3 is definitive, certain nuances of wave identification allow a slight chance that the Dow could make another new high within Cycle wave V. In that case, the final rally, currently underway, will be brief and short.

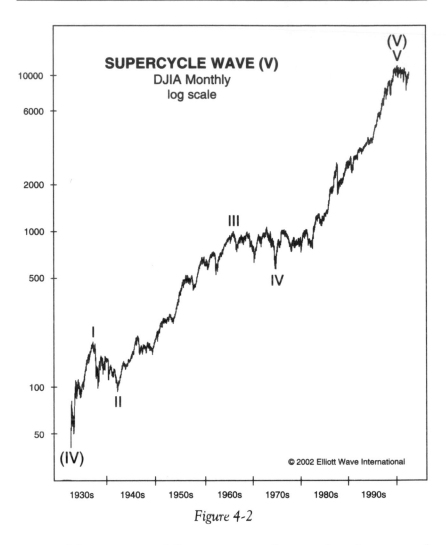

Figure 4-2

My summary of these pictures, then, is that the uptrend from around 1784 is probably five waves, the uptrend from 1932 is definitely five waves, and the uptrend from 1974 is very probably a completed five waves. To conclude, then, here is what we have: A bull market that has endured since the time of the Great Depression is definitely ending, and its termination could well mark the end of an uptrend of one degree larger, which has endured since the founding of the Republic.

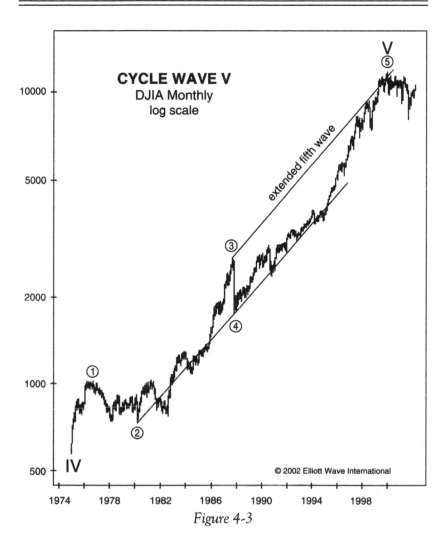

Figure 4-3

Specific Renditions of the Stock Market Fractal

The last time that the stock market formed a fifth wave of Cycle degree was in the 1920s. That's why Elliott wave forecasts from November 1978 and September 1982 specifically called for the emerging bull market to "parallel the 1920s." (See *Elliott Wave Principle*, Chapter 8 and Appendix.) Although the two waves in Figure 4-4 are quite different quantitatively in terms of both duration (8.05 vs. 25.1 years) and extent (596.5% vs.

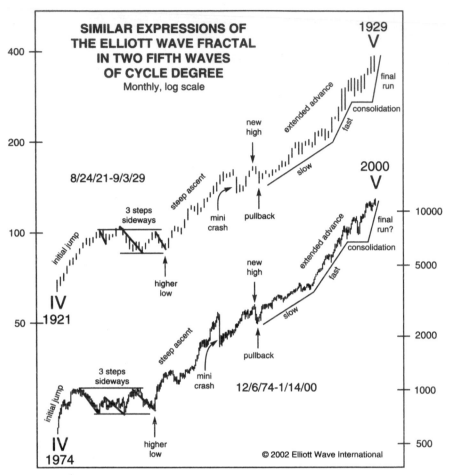

Figure 4-4

1929.6%), you can see that their forms are strikingly similar.
If you apply your calculator to the figures just quoted, you will
also discover that the lower graph rises 3.2 times the percentage
gain of the upper graph in 3.1 times the time. In other words,
their overall rates of ascent are essentially identical. If someone
had showed you these two data series — unmarked — under the
guise that they were concurrent, wouldn't you agree that they
were correlated? In my opinion, the similarities between the
two advances are not coincidental. This form is an expression of
how mass psychology progresses in Cycle degree fifth waves that

contain extended fifth sub-waves, apparently an ideal setting for an investment mania.

Worldwide Stock Values

The long-term Elliott wave position and outlook are hardly confined to the United States. The World Stock Index, which reflects the total value of stocks worldwide, also shows five waves up from 1974 and portends a major decline. The wave labeling in Figure 4-5 is slightly more detailed, showing Intermediate and Primary degree subdivisions.

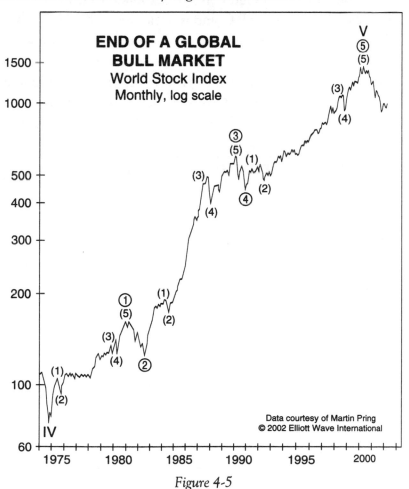

Figure 4-5

A Final Selling Opportunity in the Making

Immediately after the terrorist attack of September 11, 2001, the U.S. stock market was shut down. The entire country, not just the investment community, was in a panic. That day, my publication, *The Elliott Wave Theorist*, issued a forecast diagram of the Standard & Poor's 500 Composite Index. It called for the index to fall just a bit further and then begin the largest rally since it topped in March 2000. Six trading days later, the stock market bottomed and turned up.

You can see in Figure 4-6 why I made that forecast. In September 2001, the S&P Composite (along with the Wilshire 5000 and other indexes) was clearly finishing five waves down. If you re-examine Figure 3-1, you will see that a pattern of five waves down from a bull-market high always calls for a bear-market rally in an up-down-up pattern and then a resumption of the larger downtrend. The S&P's five waves down, then, called for

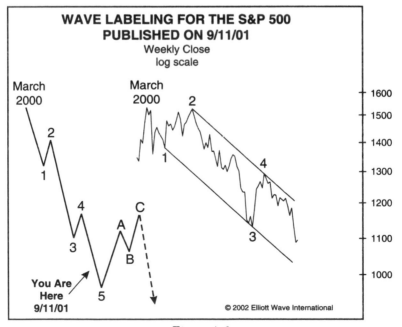

Figure 4-6

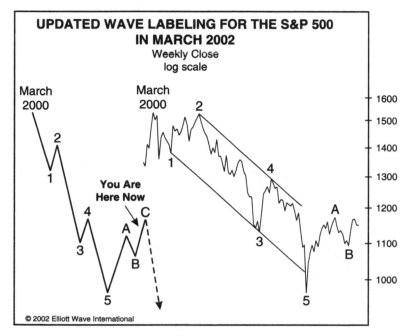

Figure 4-7

a corresponding three-wave rally, which began on September 21, six days after the market re-opened.

Most segments of the market are still advancing here near the end of the first quarter of 2002 as I put the final touches on this book. The S&P and the Wilshire 5000 indexes have continued to follow the expected path, as you can see in the updated graph of the S&P in Figure 4-7, and the Dow has climbed back above 10,000.

This rally has been strong enough in selected secondary issues to propel two stock averages, which are constructed so as to reflect this bias, to new all-time highs, as you can see in Figure 4-8. While the first quarter of 2000 presented a whale of a selling opportunity for the S&P and the NASDAQ, the current rally is creating one just as good for many sectors of the market. Releasing this book into the heat of this rally should provide maximum benefit to you.

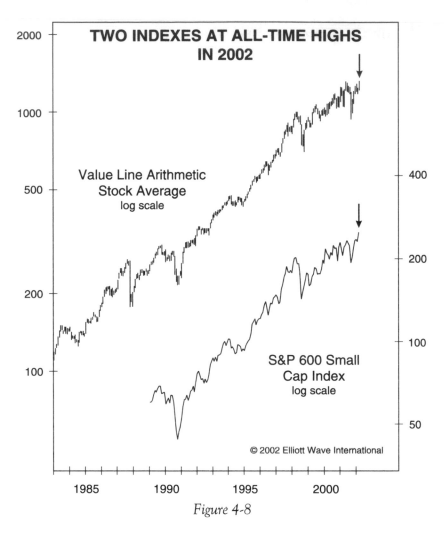

Figure 4-8

Further upside potential is nothing more than a near-term consideration. What you need to care about is the major reversal that is about to impact your financial health dramatically. The following three chapters demonstrate the extremely high probability that the larger advancing wave depicted in Figure 4-2 — the one that began seven decades ago — has run its course.

Chapter 5:

Evidence from Stock Participation and Economic Performance

Now let's conduct two key investigations to help answer the question of whether the advance from 1974 was truly a fifth wave. First we will examine the breadth of the market, and then we will confirm the value of our economic analysis in Chapter 1.

Stock Selectivity in Wave V

Elliott Wave Principle notes, "Fifth waves in stocks are always less dynamic than third waves in terms of breadth." In other words, if the advance from 1974 to 2000 is truly a fifth wave, then it must have been more selective than the third wave in terms of the number of stocks participating in the uptrend. Let's find out if wave V performed as expected compared to wave III.

Figure 5-1 shows the entire available history of what market analysts call the "advance-decline line." It is a cumulative sum of the daily ratio of the number of stocks advancing minus the number declining, the net then divided by the total number of changed issues. The resulting graph, for which the data begins in 1926, shows the tendency for all stocks traded to advance or decline on a daily basis. As you can see by the trend of this line, for most of waves I, III and V, when the overall trend of the Dow was up, more stocks advanced on the average day than declined,

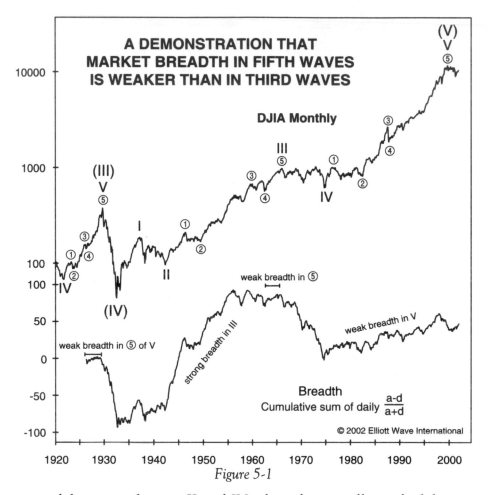

Figure 5-1

and for most of waves II and IV, when the overall trend of the Dow was down or sideways, more stocks declined on the average day than advanced.

Look more closely at the details of the line. Notice that during the stock market advance from 1926 to 1929, which was a fifth wave within a fifth wave, the advance-decline line made almost no upside progress. Observe that near the end of wave III, when subwave ⑤ was in force, the advance-decline line was not rising as dynamically as it was during the earlier wave ③. This is the breadth guideline of Figure 3-9 in action.

Now look at the dramatic difference between the behavior of this line from 1974 to 2000 and how it performed from 1942 to 1966. Despite what pundits myopically call "the greatest bull market in history," the advance-decline line over 26 long years of bull market was so weak that it could not even retrace what it lost in the bear market of 1966-1974, a mere eight years!

Anecdotal evidence dramatizes the difference. Here is R.N. Elliott's 1946 description of one stunning consequence of the overwhelming breadth of wave ① of III:

> The first wave, from 1942 to 1945, disclosed inflationary characteristics. Low-priced stocks of questionable value surged ahead at the expense of the "blue chips." The New York Sun selected ninety-six stocks that advanced phenomenally. Every stock started at some figure below $2 per share. The highest rate of advance was 13,300 percent. The lowest rate of advance was 433 percent. The average for the group was 2,776 percent.

Contrast that performance with the briar patch of the 1990s. In *The Wall Street Journal*'s stock-picking contests, for example, the pros beat the Dow only a little over half the time. Here are sample reports from some of the rougher periods:

July 13, 1994: **Darts Beat Pros but Losses Are the Rule**

> Four stocks chosen by a random throw of darts fell an average 8.7 percent between Jan. 10 and June 30, compared with an average loss of 13 percent for stocks selected by a team of four investment professionals. The Dow Jones Industrial Average, meanwhile, declined 6.2 percent.

July 10, 1996: **Pros Lose Out to Chance, Industrials**

> The stocks chosen by the four pros declined an average 9.2 percent, while four stocks selected by flinging darts at the stock tables fell 5.3 percent. But the industrial average rose a tidy 10.2 percent.

February 11, 1997: **Investment Pros Defeat Darts, but Can't**
Top Surging Market

> Four investment professionals' stock picks posted an average
> gain of 7.7 percent in just under six months as of Jan. 31,
> 1997, a full three percentage points better than the Wall
> Street Journal staffers' dart board choices. However, the
> Dow's gain for the period was 19.6 percent.

April 9, 1997: **Pros Beat Darts, but in a Losing Contest**

> Four stocks selected by the pros all lost money in the period
> from last Oct. 8 through March 31, declining an average 10
> percent. They still did better than the forces of chance. Four
> stocks chosen by flinging darts at the stock tables dropped
> an average 16.9 percent. The Dow Jones Industrial Average,
> meanwhile, rose 9.6 percent during the same period.

May 13, 1998: **Pros Beat Darts, but Picks Trail Dow Jones**
Industrials

> Investment professionals walloped the [darts] but still
> couldn't keep up with the surging Dow Jones Industrial
> Average. The four pros racked up a 17.4 percent gain in
> the period from Nov. 12, 1997 to April 30, compared with
> an average loss of 10.5 percent for four stocks selected by
> Wall Street Journal staffers flinging darts at the stock tables.
> Meanwhile, the industrial average gained 22.5 percent.

November 5, 1998: **Darts Draw Blood as Pro Losses Far Exceed**
Those of Industrials

> If you have been having trouble picking winning stocks in
> recent months, you aren't alone. A team of four investment
> professionals posted an average investment loss of 23.6
> percent in this column's latest stock-picking contest, from
> May 12 through Friday. A portfolio of four stocks chosen
> by Wall Street Journal staffers flinging darts at the stock
> tables did only slightly better, with an average loss of 21.5
> percent in the period. The Dow Jones Industrial Average
> slid 6.2 percent.

Stock market investors in the early 1940s, rare though they were in the beginning years of the wave (V) uptrend, must have felt like geniuses. Whatever method they used to pick stocks would have worked. Fund managers and stockbrokers in the 1980s and 1990s had no such luxury. Every other month, their clients would demand to know why their selections were not keeping up with the Dow, S&P and NASDAQ indexes. As the averages were soaring skyward in 1998, one brokerage firm manager confided to me, "I'm more depressed than I have ever been in my whole life." The key to his misery is that aside from a breathtaking "Internet stock" frenzy in 1999, the blue-chip components of the Dow, S&P and NASDAQ were the heart of the mania. Few stock pickers, money managers or stockbrokers could outperform them because the number of other stocks participating in the bull market was relatively small.

The Wave Principle not only provides a basis for understanding this breadth dichotomy but also a model for predicting it. The observation in Figure 3-9 and the simple labels "IV" and "V" in Figure 3-8 portended relative selectivity in the forecasted bull market, which is exactly what we got.

It is crucial to observe that all fifth waves feature a sharp deterioration in breadth. At stock market tops, when the "fifth of the fifth" wave is in force, the advance/decline line is typically already heading down. For example, in wave V of the 1920s, the advance-decline line peaked in May 1928, 16 months before the final high in the Dow. It trended down while the Dow traced out its final wave (5) of ⑤. Similarly, in the latest wave V, the advance-decline line peaked in April 1998, 21 months before the Dow's high in January 2000. During wave (5) of ⑤, which began in late 1998, breadth was so weak that the advance-decline line went down not only as the Dow and S&P market averages went to a new high but also as the NASDAQ nearly quadrupled! This is one reason why I am fairly confident that the labeling of the sub-waves in Figures 4-3 and 4-5 is correct, which means that the time is right to undertake the safeguards outlined in the second half of this book.

Economic Weakness in Wave V

As noted in Figure 3-9, if the advance from 1974 is truly a fifth and final wave, then it must also display weaker economic performance and financial conditions than did the preceding third wave, the one that lasted from 1942 to 1966. As you saw in Chapter 1, that's exactly what it did, by every pertinent measure. Chapter 1 also described two precedents, the U.S. experience of the 1920s and the Japanese experience of 1974-1989, in which economic performance seriously lagged both the stock market and the economic expansion of the previous comparable period. Now we see that the Elliott wave model both supports the implication of these analogies to the current situation and explains them: All three cases involve a major fifth wave; in fact, they were all of Cycle degree, labeled wave V under the Wave Principle.

Observe the similarity between the trends of the economic data summarized in Figure 1-2 and the advance/decline line of Figure 5-1. Both sets of statistics show weakness in wave V relative to wave III as well as deterioration in the latter portion of wave V as compared to the earlier portion. These two sets of data reveal a parallelism between the "technical" and "fundamental" aspects of waves, i.e., the psychology of waves and their product.

The Value of Knowing the Difference

Economists do not even comment upon the blatant long-term deterioration in economic performance over the last half-century. Now you know that there is an approach to macro-economic forecasting that actually *predicted* it.

In fact, the idea that there is a difference between economic performance during a third wave and that during a fifth wave has been a part of the Wave Principle for over twenty years. Frost's and my 1978 book *Elliott Wave Principle* describes third waves as "wonders to behold" as they bring about "increasingly favorable fundamentals." In contrast, "the fifth of the fifth [wave] will lack the dynamism that preceded it." By labeling the 1942 to 1966 bull market as "wave III," we established the economic growth rate of the 1950s and 1960s as a standard that the new bull market would not surpass. In an August 1983 report on the developing "Super Bull Market," *The Elliott Wave Theorist* reiterated the expected relationship between the two periods, adding, "This fifth wave will be built more on unfounded hopes than on soundly improving fundamentals such as the U.S. experienced in the 1950s and early 1960s."

These descriptions and forecasts were issued years before the data became available for wave V. Can you imagine any such perspective from conventional macroeconomics? I believe that wave analysts were able to anticipate the difference because we understand the dynamics that were set up to produce it.

Furthermore, we did not wait for recession to be in force before presenting this crucial data to business people who had to plan well ahead of the 2001 recession's arrival (which economists now date back to March 2001). In September 1998, five months after the top in the advance/decline line and 16 months before the top of wave V, we published "Wave V Fundamentals and Their Implications," which laid out the case (reprinted in *View from the Top of the Grand Supercycle* and recapped here in Chapter 1) for an approaching major reversal in the economy. Anyone who read that article was given the opportunity to begin positioning his business dealings for the approaching trend change while everyone else was becoming overly extended speculating on the New Economy. The good news is that there is still time to take advantage of the opportunity, well before anyone else knows what's happening.

The Reason for Narrowness and Deceleration

Why does stock participation narrow and why does the economy expand more slowly in fifth waves? The simple answer to this question is that stock market advances and economic cycles must get weaker before they reverse. The final rise is where that weakness must be evident. Advances come in five waves, so the fifth wave is where the relative weakness manifests.

The mechanism of that difference, I believe, is the immense optimism of major fifth waves, which encourages the populace to engage in financial speculation. Third waves are built upon muscle and brains. Fifth waves are built upon cleverness and dreams. During third waves, people focus on production to get rich. During fifth waves, they focus on finance to get rich. Manipulating money is not very productive. The entire enterprise costs a fortune in transaction costs, personnel and time. Extensive borrowing for speculation also requires extensive interest payments, and the rising cost of interest burdens the entire process of production. In a production-oriented economy, most enterprises benefit. In a finance-oriented economy, comparatively few entities benefit. These differences show up blatantly in the advance/decline line and more subtly in overall economic performance figures.

A prime symbol of the deterioration in wave (V) of (III) (for orientation, see Figure 4-1) is the Federal Reserve System. Its manipulation of money and credit for the past 89 years (see Chapter 10) has been so destabilizing that it has transformed America from a production powerhouse into a society obsessed with dodging inflation and manipulating money and credit. These preoccupations have so burdened the productive capacity of the United States that even the major expansion of the 20th century, wave (V), has experienced a slowing in the rate of real growth relative to the major expansion of the 19th century, wave (III).

A prime symbol of the deterioration in wave V of (V) is General Electric, the oldest name in the Dow Jones Industrial Average. Through wave III ending in 1966, GE was one of the finest engineering and manufacturing concerns in the world. Its goods lasted for decades. In wave V, accountants took over the company and transformed it from a manufacturing concern into a financial concern. Today, its manufactured goods are often mediocre and its vaunted company a cardboard edifice of credit services. It is the United States in microcosm.

It's a Fifth Wave

The latter half of the last sixty years has seen deterioration both in the breadth of stock participation in the market's advance and in the long-term rate of economic progress. The degree of slowing — covering decades — confirms that the advance since 1974 is a *fifth wave*, which supports the wave labeling of Figure 4-2.

Chapter 6:

The Significance of Historically High Stock Market Valuation

Recall that fifth waves produce "lofty valuation" for stocks. The evidence that wave V in the global bull market has produced historically high valuations for corporate shares could fill two books. Let's look at the primary data for U.S. valuations to verify this point.

Dividend Yield

The "yield" of the Dow Jones Industrial Average is the annual dividends that the 30 companies listed in the Dow pay out to shareholders as a percentage of their stock prices. If you study Figure 6-1, you will see that investors accept low dividends at market tops and demand high dividends at market bottoms. It is easy to understand why. At tops, they believe that stocks will go up much more, providing a huge capital gain, so who needs dividends? At bottoms, they believe that stocks will fall much more, providing a capital loss, so they demand high dividends to offset their perceived risk.

Of course, this thinking is backwards and makes investors lose money. It nevertheless must be this way because if they acted otherwise, markets would not be continually forming tops and bottoms.

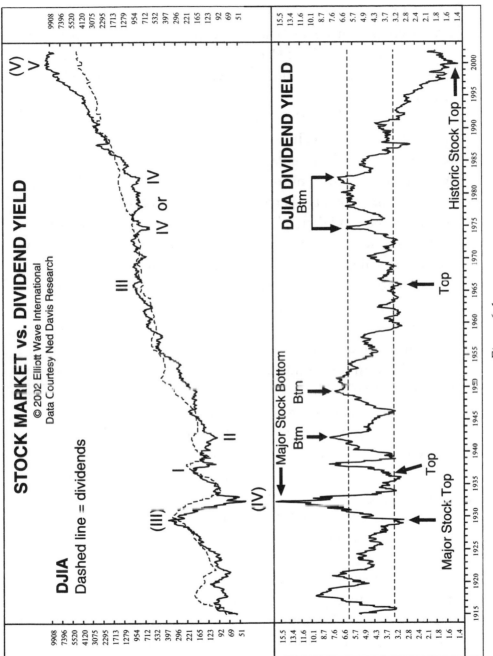

Figure 6-1

Observe that the DJIA's dividend yield tends to be around 6.5 percent near moderate bear market bottoms. It went far higher at the bottom of the Great Depression. Conversely, the dividend yield has tended to be around 3 percent at major tops, including the historic top of 1929.

In 2000, the Dow's dividend yield did something that it had never done before. It reached 1.5 percent. A larger index of industrial stocks, the Standard & Poor's 400 Industrials, yielded only 1 percent. This is historically high valuation.

It takes about 1 percent of the value of a stock for an investor to buy and then sell it. The dividend payout in the year 2000, then, was enough to cover transactions costs *if* you were to buy and sell no more than once a year. If you own shares of a mutual fund, the managers take 1 percent annually for fees. At 1 percent, then, stocks effectively have no yield. What's more, the DJIA represents the best of the country's blue-chip stocks. Most companies listed on the NASDAQ exchange pay no dividends at all. Throw in transaction costs or management fees, and they have a negative yield.

Today, optimists argue that dividends "don't matter." They claim that "investors want companies to plow money back into the company" so that the company will be more profitable and the stock price will go up more. These are excuses and rationalizations. If no dividend is ever paid, of what value is a share of stock? Do you really want to own a share of a super-successful enterprise that handsomely pays everyone involved in it except you, an owner?

The few optimists who still think that dividends matter declare that stock prices need not fall because our "unprecedented economy" eventually will generate enough corporate income to pay those higher dividends. Yet after two decades of nearly uninterrupted economic growth, it hasn't happened.

Given the evidence in this book, it isn't about to happen, either. The economy will be unprecedented, all right, but in the other direction.

The inevitable fluctuations of mass psychology assure that at some time in the future, the dividend yields on the Dow and other major stock indexes will be far higher than they are today. Unfortunately, the change is not going to come about with a simple adjustment downward in stock prices. The reason is that when stock prices fall substantially, the result is almost always a weaker economy. The degree of the currently developing downturn is so large that the economy will undoubtedly become extremely weak, and that trend in turn will put pressure on companies to *decrease* dividends. Falling dividends will follow falling stock prices, and falling stock prices will chase falling dividends, making it difficult for the stock market to return to an attractive yield typical of major bottoms. Stock indexes have a *long way down to go* before their yields return to levels that reflect investor pessimism.

Book Value

If a company has to value itself for liquidation, it does so on the basis of the market value of its assets. A company's "book value" comes close to reflecting that value.

As we are about to see, stock prices today reflect the most expensive valuation of corporate assets in recorded history. Today's stock prices are not just historically high compared to book values; they are amazingly, outrageously high.

How did they get that way? One of investors' requirements for buying expensive stock during the 1990s was that the associated company continually report higher earnings per share. Such an achievement is meaningless in isolation, because the real question is *what are the earnings relative to the size of the company* and *relative to the price of the stock,* questions no one has been asking. As you can see, we are not dealing with reason here but with rationalization. The last time investors adopted this guideline was the late 1920s. (For more on that point, see Graham & Dodd's comments in Chapter 14 of *Market Analysis for the New Millennium,* 2002.) Because investors adopted this guideline, "aggressive" accounting methods sprang up during wave V to help companies repeatedly perform the feat of reporting higher earnings per share. Achieving that goal often meant diluting the true underlying value of the company, for example by using company assets to buy back the company's own shares. As we will see in a moment, today's book values reflect this dilution.

A Composite Measure of Valuation

A low dividend yield might be acceptable if there were no other yields available, but there are. They come from bonds, and investors can choose between the two sources. To compare their valuations, we must ask, what is the relative yield between the best stocks and the best bonds?

Figure 6-2 combines two of our benchmarks. The vertical axis reports the price-to-book value of the S&P 400 Industrials index. The horizontal axis reports the yield from top-grade corporate bonds relative to the yield of these top-grade S&P 500 stocks. The rectangular box on the chart delineates the range of values that has held for most of the 20th century. Additional figures from prior years show that year-end bond yield/stock yield ratios were well to the left side of this box at least back to 1870.

Until 1987, only five years since 1927 (where our graph begins) ended with values outside that box, and only two of those were on the high-valuation side. These five readings indicated historic extremes of either pessimism or optimism and therefore a likely major turning point in the stock market.

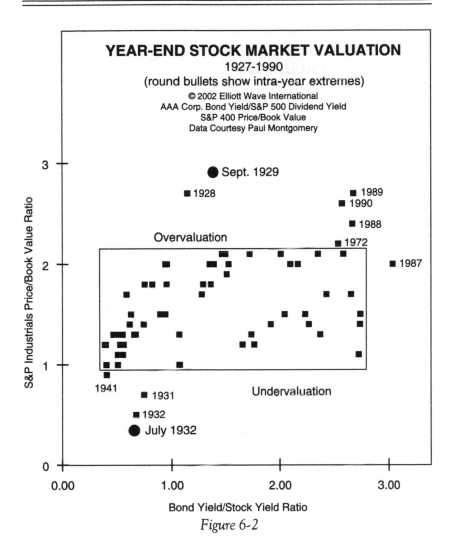

Figure 6-2

Do you see anything missing from Figure 6-2? If you look closely, you will see that it is lacking a crucial set of data points, namely, all of the year-end values for the past 11 years!

Now look at Figure 6-3, which includes the year-end valuations from 1991 to the present. The bullet denoting valuations in March 2000 looks like Pluto in a picture of our solar system, doesn't it?

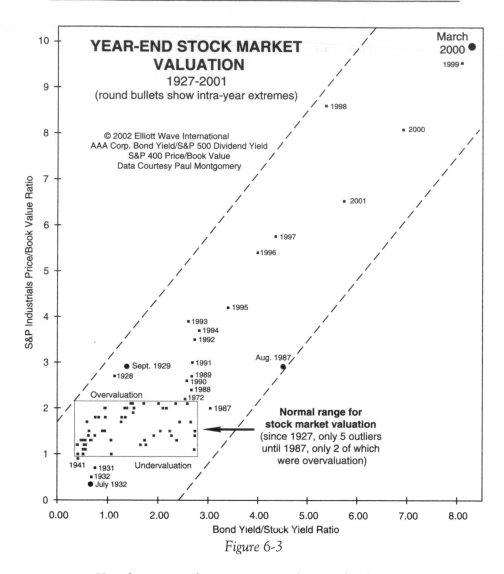

Figure 6-3

You do not need to investigate the worth of any argument that purports to justify these stock values. All you need is eyes.

The squares representing values at the end of 2000 and 2001 indicate that the trend has reversed. Rest assured that sometime soon, annual valuations will be back in that box. In fact, if investors follow their usual pattern, the decline will not end until there is at least one bullet below and/or to the left of the box.

The Price/Earnings Ratio

The price/earnings ratio is the only popular market valuation indicator on Wall Street. It is also the least valuable except in rare cases.

The P/E is the ratio between the price of stocks and the value of their associated companies' annual earnings per share. Sometimes the ratio's compilers use *projected* earnings, which is what brokerage house analysts think that earnings *will* be. Needless to say, earnings estimators are repeatedly too pessimistic at bottoms and too optimistic at tops, just when you most need the indicator to tell the truth. Therefore, our graph will compare stock prices to *actual* earnings for the preceding year.

Corporate earnings cycle with the stock market but with a 2-month to 2-year lag. Earnings do not begin to rise until well after stock prices have turned up from a bottom, and they do not begin to fall until well after stock prices turn down from a top. For this reason, the two trends often oppose each other. In contrast, book values and dividend payouts tend to be much steadier, cycling only on a very long-term basis with the largest economic trends, therefore providing a steady benchmark against which to compare stock prices to obtain a reliable relative valuation measure. There usually is little point in comparing stock prices to corporate earnings because the two opposing cycles push and pull on the ratio in such a way as to render most current readings nearly meaningless for market timing purposes. Most of the time, you could divide stock prices by the price of pickles and have a more reliable indicator.

There is one exception to this general objection. *After* the stock market has made a turn of *major* import, the earnings cycle comes into play with investor psychology in a most interesting way.

Usually, investors (erroneously) welcome rising earnings as bullish. There is one time that they don't, which (naturally) makes them wrong again.

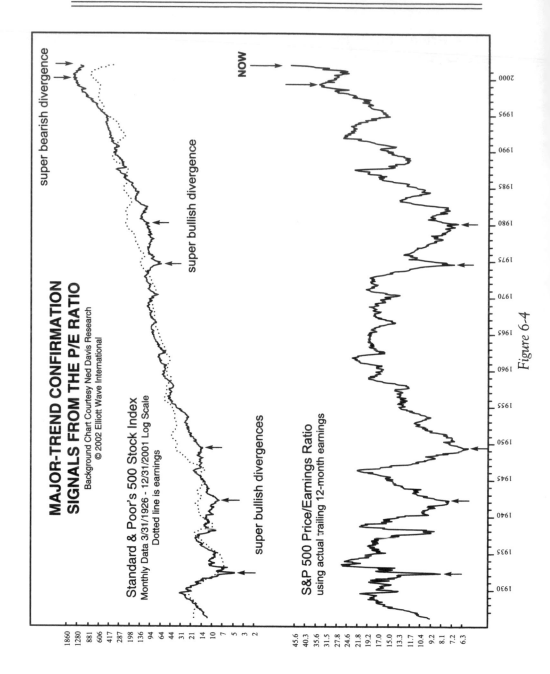

MAJOR-TREND CONFIRMATION SIGNALS FROM THE P/E RATIO

Background Chart Courtesy Ned Davis Research
© 2002 Elliott Wave International

Standard & Poor's 500 Stock Index
Monthly Data 3/31/1926 - 12/31/2001 Log Scale
Dotted line is earnings

S&P 500 Price/Earnings Ratio
using actual trailing 12-month earnings

super bearish divergence

super bullish divergence

super bullish divergences

NOW

Figure 6-4

Go back to Figure 3-9 and note the characteristics of "wave 2." That's when people believe fervently that the larger trend is down, *even though it isn't.* An excellent example of this proclivity is the fact that a New York Stock Exchange survey conducted in 1952 found that a paltry 4 percent of eligible Americans owned stocks! The other 96 percent apparently believed that holding stock was foolish and risky. Of course, the market was in the early years of a multi-decade uptrend; that's when people think this way.

Figure 6-4 displays the P/E ratio for the S&P 500 Composite index from the mid-1920s to the present. Study the first set of arrows toward the left of the graph. Generally speaking, earnings were dutifully following the stock market upward after the major bottom of 1932. Nevertheless, in 1942 and again in 1949, investors' pessimism was so strong that it pushed the P/E ratio *below its level at the preceding lower stock market bottom.* These readings indicated *deep pessimism in the face of rising stock prices and an expanding economy* and therefore an immense psychological potential to drive stock prices higher. The middle set of arrows marks a second occurrence of this phenomenon in 1980, when stocks had a lower P/E ratio than they did at the preceding lower stock market bottom in 1974. In each of these cases, stocks had already launched a huge long-term advance, and most of it lay ahead.

Today, for the first time in the history of the figures, we have the opposite situation, with the opposite implication. When stock prices decline from a major top, commercial activity decreases, and lower earnings follow. Last year, earnings fell faster than the S&P did, so the P/E ratio rose despite lower stock prices. In fact, it rose so strongly that the P/E ratio at the end of December was 46, the highest ever. The P/E ratio on the S&P 400 Industrials was 53. P/E ratios for the S&P 500 have ranged from around 7 at bear market bottoms to the low-to-mid 20s at bull market tops. So the S&P's P/E ratio today is twice what it is at a typical bull-market top and *six to seven times* what it is at a typical bear-market bottom. In other words, the S&P would have to fall about 85 percent to get its P/E to normal bottom levels, *and that's if earnings fall no further.* Earnings *will* fall in a bear market that size, so today's P/E ratios portend the same stock price debacle that is implied by the stock market's wave structure, the low dividend payout, overpriced book values and the high bond yield/stock yield ratio.

Today's record P/E ratios alone are enough to command attention (the stock/pickles price ratio is near the highest ever, too), but what matters more is the P/E ratio *relative* to the action of the market and the economy. Examine the third set of arrows, toward the right of Figure 6-4. Although earnings have been dutifully following the stock market downward since shortly after the top in the first quarter of 2000, investors' optimism remains so strong that it has pushed the P/E ratio to *above its level at the preceding higher stock market top.* This dramatic rise to an all-time record indicates *entrenched optimism in the face of falling stock prices and a weakening economy* and therefore an immense psychological potential to drive stock prices lower. The implication of this divergence is that blue-chip stocks have already launched a bear market with much more ahead of it than lies behind.

Why does this phenomenon occur? Early in major uptrends, investors remain deeply scarred psychologically by their experiences in the preceding bear market and economic contraction. Though the downtrends and contractions are over, the fear of them remains. The P/E ratio reaches an extreme low because people believe that the rise in earnings is temporary and that the economy will collapse back downward, justifying low stock valuations. The second arrow in the final set (marked "NOW") reflects investors' diametrically opposing attitudes today. Though the trend of stocks has been sideways to down for two years and the economy has receded, the presumption that the old uptrend and expansion are the natural order of things remains as firm as ever. Investors anticipate — directly opposing their counterparts of the 1940s — more glory days ahead. People think that earnings will begin rising again, and they want to own as much stock as they can before that happens.

The first problem with this idea is that investors have priced stocks so high that to get them bear-market cheap again, earnings would have to soar 600 percent, and that's if the S&P does not budge a single point higher than it is today! The second problem is that the extended economic expansion that so many expect almost certainly is not going to happen. If my interpretation of the P/E disparity is accurate, it has not been a stock market "correction" in the S&P; it's a bear market, which means that the economic contraction is not merely a "mild, brief recession," it's the first contraction in a developing depression.

Obfuscation and Rationalization

As I write this chapter, the "watchdog" of earnings, Standard & Poor's, has just bowed to pressure to change the basis of its earnings reports to "operating earnings" rather than total company earnings. As a result, the reported P/E ratio has suddenly changed to about half of what it really is. Analysts are expected to tack these ratios onto the old ratio's eighty-year history as if they are the same thing. Operating earnings omit several items, the main one being "non-recurring expenses." *Hello!* All expenses affect a company's performance. A creative accountant can drive a truck through that loophole and manipulate operating expenses to almost any desired level. Yet another proposal, to report only "core earnings," will exclude gains or losses due to companies' pension fund obligations. If my outlook is right, these obligations will soon be killing the profitability of industry. Leaving potentially massive drains on capital out of the earnings calculation is like leaving torture equipment out of a description of a dungeon. Real investors want real numbers, and these changes provide the opposite. The desperation within the financial world to avoid reporting "bad news" (i.e., the truth) is obviously immense.

How do so many public and professional investors justify holding such expensive stocks today? The latest issue of Money magazine (March 2002) quotes a manager at one of the largest stock mutual funds in the world: "You have to trust them. To some degree they become faith stocks." Money concurs, "Investors must rely as much on gut instinct as on objective analysis. Sometimes an extra-large helping of hope is required." One could hardly utter a worse guide to life, much less to the assumption of financial risk. Those of us dedicated to objective financial analysis aren't always right. But those who rely on extra-large helpings of trust, faith, hope and "gut instinct" always regret it.

Chapter 7:

The Significance of Historically Optimistic Psychology

The engine of high stock market valuation is widely shared optimism. The greater the degree of the advance that is ending, the greater the optimism at its peak. Optimism also tends to remain strong in the early stages of a bear market (waves "A" down and "B" up, in wave parlance). Bull markets, they say, climb a "Wall of Worry." I like to add, "and bear markets slide down a Slope of Hope."

Today, are investors optimistic or pessimistic, and to what degree? The answer is that measures of optimism in early 2000 reached awesome, historic levels, and they remain just below — and in some cases even above — those levels today. As you are about to see, psychology is a long way from the shared deep pessimism that produces a buying opportunity.

Psychology of Academics

In about 1997, professors, PhDs and decorated economists at universities and think-tanks began peppering the media with articles that essentially put before the public the idea that macroeconomic science has lent its sanction to the historic extremes in stock values generated by the great asset mania of the 1980s and 1990s. In *The Wall Street Journal* alone, we have read bullish essays and learned of bullish studies by two Nobel laureates, a

former Fed Governor and scholars at the American Enterprise
Institute, the University of Pennsylvania, the Massachusetts
Institute of Technology, the Brookings Institution, the Wharton
School, the University of Rochester, Princeton University, New
York University, Bear Stearns, Credit Suisse First Boston, the
Federal Reserve Banks of Dallas and Philadelphia, the Hoover
Institution, the Discovery Institute and the Graduate School of
Business of the University of Chicago, to list just the ones with the
most prominent credentials. These articles were most abundant
between March 1998 and April 2000, though they still appear
today. Not one bases its conclusions on an analytical method that
has any forecasting history at all, and others contradict ones that
do. During the period that the quotations below appeared, only
one academic made a passionate case for investor caution in the
WSJ, in two articles published in April 1999 and March 2000.

As you look at the dates of the following quotes from some
of these professorial essays, keep in mind that the Value Line
Geometric stock average and the advance/decline line peaked
in April 1998, the Dow and S&P in gold and commodity terms
topped in July 1999, and the nominal highs in the S&P and
NASDAQ (and probably the Dow as well) took place in the first
quarter of 2000. Here is what the experts have told us:

•March 30, 1998: "Pundits who claim the market is
overvalued are foolish."

• July 30, 1998: "This expansion will run forever."

• February 3, 1999: "We have at last arrived in a new-era
economy."

• March 19, 1999: "A perfectly reasonable level for the
Dow would be 36,000 — tomorrow, not 10 or 20 years
from now. The risk premium is headed for its proper level:
zero."

• August 30, 1999: "The recent dramatic upswing represents a rosy estimate about growth in future profits for
the economy."

• September 18, 1999: "Researchers have found compelling evidence that conventional accounting understates the earning power of today's companies."

• January 1, 2000: "In much the way Albert Einstein's theory of relativity transformed the time-space grid of classical physics at the beginning of the twentieth century, the Einsteins of Internet communications are now transforming the time-space grid of the global economy."

• April 18, 2000: "Don't be fooled. Historical forces continue to point toward a Great Prosperity that could carry the Dow Jones Industrial Average to 35,000 by the end of the decade and 100,000 by 2020."

If this one-sided outpouring of scholarly judgment proves to be anything other than a manifestation of the prevailing optimistic mass psychology that crystallized after 7 decades of mostly rising stock prices and 2½ decades of dramatically rising stock prices, I will be mightily surprised.

Psychology of Economists

Two years ago, as most major U.S. stock indexes reached their all-time highs, *The Wall Street Journal* observed, "Economists are downright euphoric." Of 54 economists surveyed, all but two were bullish for 2000. One year later, when the Dow, S&P and NASDAQ were down 8 percent, 15 percent and 51 percent from their respective highs and the onset of recession was just weeks away, the consensus for continued growth was even stronger. Only one economist out of 54 surveyed called for a recession in 2001. On New Year's Day, January 2002, although the economy had been slumping for nearly a year, economists managed to achieve an even greater optimistic consensus, thanks surely to the Dow's rally back above 10,000. Not one of the 55 economists surveyed for *The Wall Street Journal*'s 2002 forecast expects the recent contraction to develop into a serious decline. All predict that the economy will expand this year if it hasn't begun to do so already. The recent stock-market rally — reflecting an improving social mood — has naturally led to an improvement in a number of economic indicators. These changes have induced economists to keep up the drumbeat. Here are just three excerpts out of hundreds:

The Atlanta Journal-Constitution, February 22, 2002: "Economists Optimistic: Survey Says Recession Likely Is Already Over"

> The U.S. recession has probably ended, according to a survey by the National Association for Business Economics that projects growth of at least 3.5 percent in the second half of 2002 and in 2003.

USA Today, February 28, 2002: "'Recessionette' Might Be at an End"

> Bank One's chief economist calls it a "recessionette," and the U.S. Chamber of Commerce's chief economist insists the current slump is no recession at all.

Fortune, March 18, 2002, adds that such is "the opinion of virtually every economic forecaster out there."

Obviously, economists of all stripes, from theoreticians to practitioners, have been bullish throughout the past two years, right past the top in most stocks, right past the onset of the 2001 recession (which may or may not be "officially" recognized) and right through today. You no longer need guess at the source of those "New Economy" quotes tallied in Figure 1-1.

Economists as a group have an unbroken record of failing to predict economic contraction. Most of the time, ill-timed optimism is harmless because most of the time, recessions are indeed mild and brief. The reason is that the fluctuations in the economy are a hierarchical fractal, as described in Chapter 3. Small, mild retrenchments occur more frequently than large ones, so forecasting errors are only mildly damaging. Yet rarity does not equate to impossibility. It is wrong to assume, after a long period of prosperity with only mild recessions, that the large economic contractions will never occur again. Yet that belief invariably materializes at such times. Why is that?

Economists' forecasts always seem to be little different from a description of the present, tempered or augmented by the forward-weighted trends of the past. That's how human nature works. People — including professionals who should know better — generally accept recent experience as "normal," no matter what it is. Economists would serve their clients much better if the trends and extremities of their opinions were the opposite of what they are.

Psychology of Brokerage Strategists

Professional brokerage-house equity-allocation strategists tend to recommend a heavy weighting in stocks just before

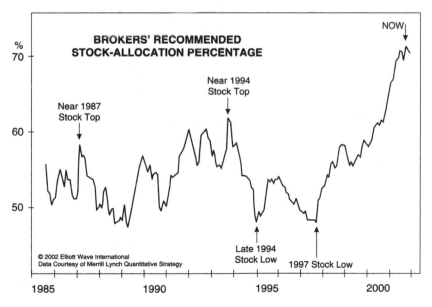

Figure 7-1

the market falls and a lighter weighting just before the market advances. This is normal behavior, which itself helps to set the market's highs and lows.

Figure 7-1 shows fifteen years of average weighting recommendations by brokers. Look at their current average opinion: a *record* high weighting recommendation of 71 percent! This is how advisors felt during the rally of early 1930, as well. Their advice was not profitable. Nor should it have been. A consensus this strong means that people are about as invested as they can get. It is bearish.

Psychology of Money Managers

In the aggregate, money managers are always most invested in stocks at tops and least invested at bottoms. Figure 7-2 shows how pension funds and insurance companies increased their percentage of stock holdings from 7 percent of total assets in 1952 to 53 percent on New Year's Day, 2000. Figure 7-3 shows the percentage of cash that stock mutual funds hold in their portfolios. Again, they usually hold lots of cash at bottoms and little at tops. Needless to say, it would benefit their clients if they did the opposite. Needless to say, it can be no different.

Managers' optimism today is stunningly one-sided not only in the U.S. but throughout the Western world. Canadian polling firm Towers Perrin reports that among 48 Canadian and 23 foreign investment firms, *not a single one* expects negative returns from their stock investments in 2002. Nor are they just mildly optimistic. As Toronto's *Globe and Mail* (1/10/02) summarizes the survey, "Money managers are looking for *double-digit returns* from Canadian, U.S. and international equity markets this year." Although the analysis in this book focuses primarily on the U.S. equity market, similar conditions attend all stock markets around the globe that have held near their highs.

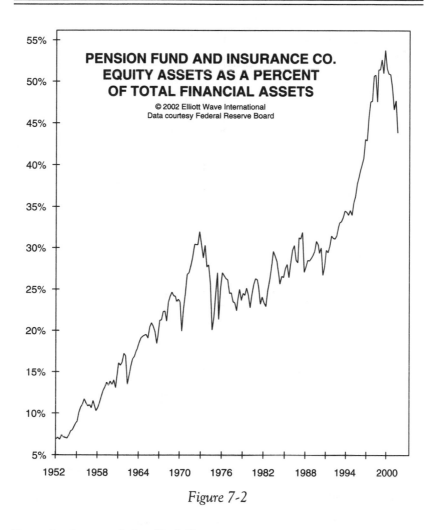

Figure 7-2

Psychology of the Public

The public agrees with the experts. Figure 7-4 shows that investors' margin debt, a paltry $3 billion in late 1974, topped $250 billion in early 2000. In just 25 years, investors multiplied by over 80 times the amount of money that they borrowed from brokers to buy stocks. Figures 7-5 and 7-6 are long-term measures of the public's attitude toward stocks. It took decades, but in the 1990s, the public became, by these measures, more bullish than it was at the two biggest tops of the past century: 1968 and 1929.

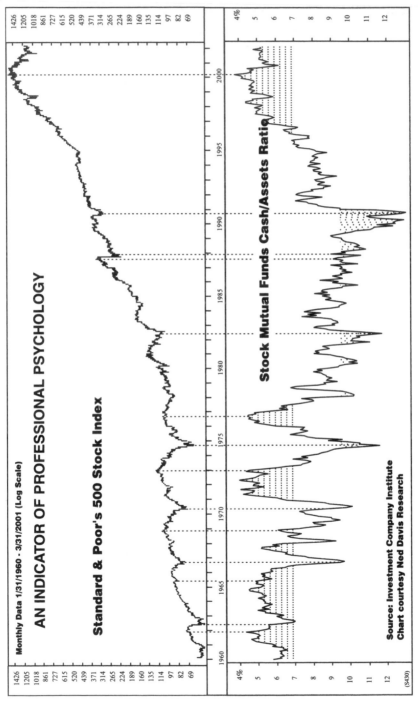

Monthly Data 1/31/1960 - 3/31/2001 (Log Scale)

AN INDICATOR OF PROFESSIONAL PSYCHOLOGY

Standard & Poor's 500 Stock Index

Stock Mutual Funds Cash/Assets Ratio

Source: Investment Company Institute
Chart courtesy Ned Davis Research

(S430)

Figure 7-3

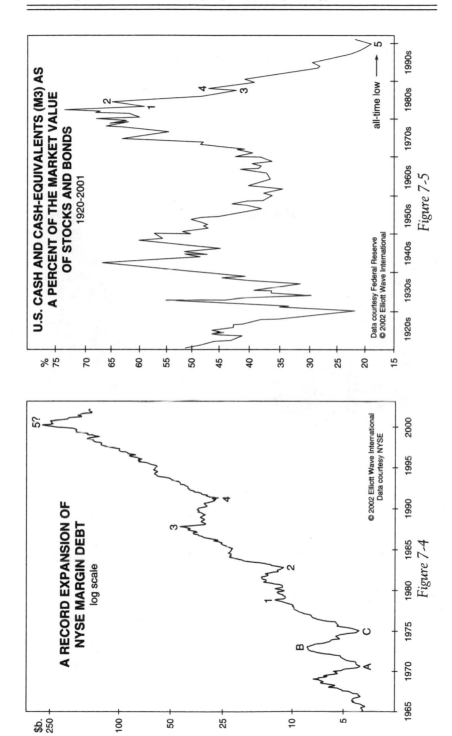

A RECORD EXPANSION OF NYSE MARGIN DEBT
log scale

© 2002 Elliott Wave International
Data courtesy NYSE

Figure 7-4

U.S. CASH AND CASH-EQUIVALENTS (M3) AS A PERCENT OF THE MARKET VALUE OF STOCKS AND BONDS
1920-2001

Data courtesy Federal Reserve
© 2002 Elliott Wave International

Figure 7-5

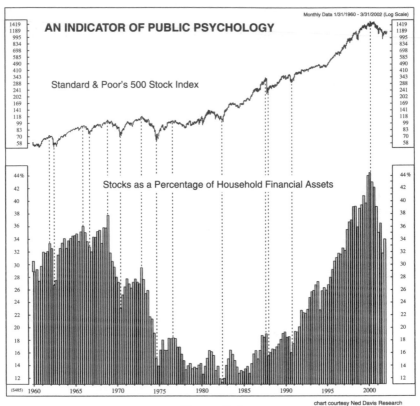

Figure 7-6

In utter contrast to their underinvested counterparts of the early 1950s, over half of American families, which must mean most families that actually have money to invest, are invested in the stock market. These readings make investors' level of excitement during the Roaring Twenties look like ennui. For more graphs of this type, please see Appendix D of *At the Crest of the Tidal Wave* (1995).

P/E ratios and brokerage strategists' allocations are not the only market psychology indicators at all-time highs. Here in the first quarter of 2002, the weekly survey of futures contract ownership shows that "small traders," i.e., the most naïve market players, have just reached an all-time record in their holdings of "long" futures contracts. The "commercials," i.e., the most sophisticated market players, have held record and near-record levels of *short* futures contracts since mid-2000. Figure 7-7 displays 13 years of history showing that commercials during that time were most bullish at the stock market bottoms of 1990 and 1994 and were most bearish recently; in other words, they tend to be right. Conversely, the public was most bearish in early 1995, as the market was blasting off for a record five-year run. As you can see, the public is generally wrong.

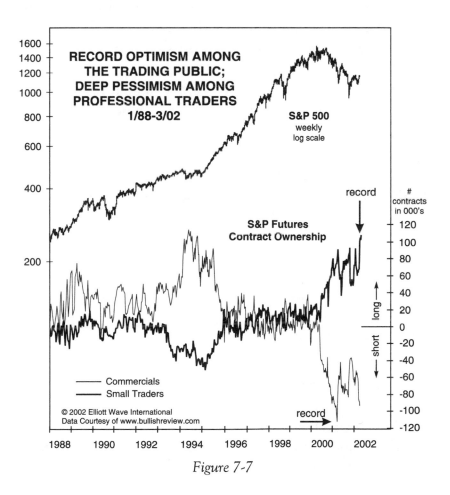

Figure 7-7

Becoming more bullish at lower prices is highly unusual behavior on the part of investors generally speaking, but, like the P/E phenomenon, *it is normal behavior shortly after a major top in stock prices.* As *Elliott Wave Principle* explained in 1978, "During the A wave of a bear market, the investment world is generally convinced that this reaction is just a pullback pursuant to the next leg of advance. The public surges to the buy side despite the first really technically damaging cracks in individual stock patterns." The B-wave rallies that follow exhibit "aggressive euphoria and denial." The past two years fit these descriptions. As with other indicators presented in this book, Figure 7-7 provides assurance that a major bear market is in force and that the bulk of it lies ahead.

The New York Times reports today (March 12) on a study of "newly optimistic" investor attitudes. It shows that an amazing 90 *percent* of individuals polled say that the stock market will continue to advance over the next 12 months. This revival of optimism is emerging *six months after* the proper time to have been near-term optimistic, six months after *The Elliott Wave Theorist* forecasted the largest rally in the S&P since the all-time high, six months after the bottom of wave A. The article concludes, "The optimism of individuals...suggests that the coming year could be a good one for stocks." This claim reflects a bizarre incognizance of the multi-decade history of stock market sentiment indicators.

Psychology of the Media

As you can see by the graphs in this chapter, there is no question that optimism is entrenched horizontally throughout the nation and vertically through all strata of expertise. This overwhelming consensus has engendered an outpouring of elation from the nation's magazine covers and newspapers' front pages here in the first quarter of 2002. "Positive Reports Hint at Swift

Recovery," says *The New York Times*. "Better Times Coming," announces the Minneapolis *Star*. "Hope Soars in U.S." adds Denver's *Rocky Mountain News*. *The New York Post* enthuses, "Recovery at Last." *USA Today* announces, "Fed Chief Declares Recession at an End." *U.S. News and World Report* shows us "How to Cash In." The President himself assures us that 2002 will be a "Great Year."

The newspaper clippings on the following pages show that optimism permeates both local and national news reporting. (In case you can't see the one magazine cover clearly, that's Abraham Lincoln advising, "Buy!") Most of these headlines are from the cover of the magazine or page 1 of the newspaper in which they appeared, which means that editors deem the sentiments worthy of the strongest highlight. It's unfortunate, because such ideas expressed at the wrong time kill people financially and, in extreme cases, physically as well.

The Next Psychological Trend

When the stock market turns back down, academics, economists, advisors, money managers and media commentators will begin to turn bearish. Bad news will begin pouring out of the newspapers as a consequence of the emerging negative-mood trend. The more the market falls, the higher the number of bears will become, because enough time will go by that the trends not only of the present but also of the recent past will be down. The largest number of bears, public and professional, will be at the bottom.

Poll: Americans optimistic

Positive Reports Hint at Swift Recovery
—New York Times, December 29, 2001

President says 2002 will be 'a great year'

DECEMBER 31, 2001   **BARRON'S**

The Case for a "Super-V"

Three stimulating economic factors may come together in 2002

According to various surveys, strategists look for about a 9 percent gain by the Dow Jones industrial average next year, 12 percent for Standard & Poor's 500-stock index and 13 percent for the Nasdaq composite.

As 2001 bows out, economy looks up
—The Atlanta Journal-Constitution, December 29, 2001

American consumers are ending a frightening year in a cheery mood, more confident about the future.

Forecast For Growth: Even More
—The Atlanta Journal-Constitution, December 29, 2001

Confidence in economy on the rise
—The Atlanta Journal-Constitution, December 29, 2001

Consumer spending the key to forecasts for a rebound
—The Atlanta Journal-Constitution, December 29, 2001

Forecasters smell a recovery

STRONG RECOVERY FOR STOCKS
—Financial Times, Jan 2, 2002

BANKS FORECAST A

Economy shows signs of year-end comeback
Recession threatening North America is yesterday's story,' chief economist says
—Globe and Mail, December 29, 2001

SMALL CHANGE / THE YEAR'S HOT / WORKING IN / ANNUAL
MANAGE FREE / NEW TECH FLOWS / NETWORKING / FORECAST
AIR TRAVEL / MONDO & SUMMING / ISSUE / GUIDE

SmartMoney
THE WALL STREET JOURNAL MAGAZINE OF PERSONAL BUSINESS

THE
Best
Investments
FOR **2002**

As our economy rebounds, these 10 stocks and 6 mutual funds will make you big money. Honest.

Buy!

Hope Soars in U.S.
Consumer confidence hits unexpected high
—Rocky Mountain News, December 29, 2001

Market raises new year hopes

Yes, There Are Still Optimists in Japan
—New York Times, Dec 30, 2001

City optimistic after two years of sliding equities

Recession May Have Bottomed
Factors seem in place to end market's two-year losing streak

Economy, consumer confidence, home sales and other indicators suggest early recovery.
—Los Angles Times, December 29, 2001

"It's clear that we've started the next leg-up."

Economists Declare Recovery
—*USA Today*

"Everything that could be going right for the recovery is going right." Indeed, from manufacturing and consumer spending to construction, almost every report for January and February has beaten expectations. Not only, in the words of one Federal Reserve insider, could the first half "be gangbusters," the momentum may well be sustainable.
—*BusinessWeek*, March 18, 2002

The upbeat trend had economists upwardly revising their quarterly growth forecasts and fund managers enthusiastically reinvesting in the equity markets.

What Recession?
—*Christian Science Monitor*, Mar 12, 2002

BusinessWeek

THE SURPRISE ECONOMY

Officials Question if Recession Was Real
—*Reuters*, March 4, 2002

Rallying Cry from the US
The US Economy Is Greeting the Arrival of Spring With a Host Of Golden Indicators
—*Financial Times*, Mar 9, 2002

recent data shows that the economy is not only on the mend, but that expectations are also rising for a more robust recovery than previously thought.

Business Outlook
GET READY FOR REBOUNDING PROFITS
—*Business Week*, March 25, 2002

TALIBAN HOLDOUTS • BE...
U.S.News & WORLD REPORT

2002 ECONOMIC REPORT

Business Bounces Back

Growing signs of a recovery
How to cash in

Mood on Wall St. Is 'Euphoria'
—*The Record*, Mar 5, 2002

Traders say new buyers are stepping into the market because/no one wants to miss the next leg-up in the rally.

FOR MANY, RECESSION PROVED BARELY VISIBLE
—*Boston Globe*, Mar 11, 2002

With evidence now overwhelming that the recession has ended, some economists argue the decline in output was so mild it didn't qualify as a recession at all.
—*The Wall Street Journal*, March 11, 2002

Chapter 8:

Implications for the Stock Market and the Economy

If the analysis in the preceding chapters is correct, the U.S. stock market, and by extension most stock indexes worldwide, is rounding the cusp of a trend change of at least Supercycle degree. The DJIA has completed (or is completing) five waves up that will lead to a three-step partial retracement of corresponding degree. This means that the decline will not be a moderate setback such as the market has undergone from time to time since 1932. It will be at least large enough to complete the downside portion of Figure 3-1 if we label its start "1932" and its peak "2000." That is a large setback. We may even have to label its start "1784," in which case the bear market will be the largest since that of the 1700s. In other words, the stock market is embarking upon its biggest bear market assuredly since that of 1929-1932 and possibly since that of 1720-1784. If any such bear market occurs, then as we saw in Chapter 2, the economy will experience a depression.

How Far Will the Market Fall?

As implied in Figure 3-2, stock market corrections tend to bottom in the area of the fourth wave of the largest immediately preceding five-wave structure. Study the actual record, and you will see this guideline fulfilled often. Note, for example, in Figure 4-2, that wave II bottomed in the price area of the 1934 low, and wave IV bottomed in the price area of the 1962 low, which ended fourth waves within waves I and III respectively. Way back in 1978, *Elliott Wave Principle* said that when the great bull market expected for wave V was over, the DJIA would fall back to the area of the preceding fourth wave, which is at least to the 577 to 1051 range of wave IV (see Figure 4-2) and possibly down to the 41-381 range of wave (IV) (see Figure 4-1). To summarize, though my outlook may sound impossible, I am quite comfortable saying that the DJIA will fall from *quintuple* digits, where it is today, to *triple* digits, an unprecedented amount.

What I cannot say with quite as much conviction is which wave of the bear market will carry the Dow to that area. Odds are very strong that it will happen on the first major decline, a potential that the next section supports. Otherwise, it will do so on another decline decades hence. For more on such nuances, please see Chapter 5 of *At the Crest of the Tidal Wave*.

Studies of Manias Bear Out This Downside Potential

In 1997, I undertook a study of financial manias. Manias are episodes of relentless financial speculation that involve substantial infusions of credit, wide public participation, and which drive values to unprecedented levels. For the full study, please see the first essay in *View from the Top*.

A pertinent observation with respect to our current concern is that a mania is always followed by a collapse so severe that it brings values to *below* where they were when the mania began. The apparent reason for this outcome is that so many ordinary people entrust their fortunes to the mania that its reversal brings widespread financial distress, which feeds on itself to force an immense liquidation of investment media.

Famous Market Manias
And Their Aftermaths, 1600-2001

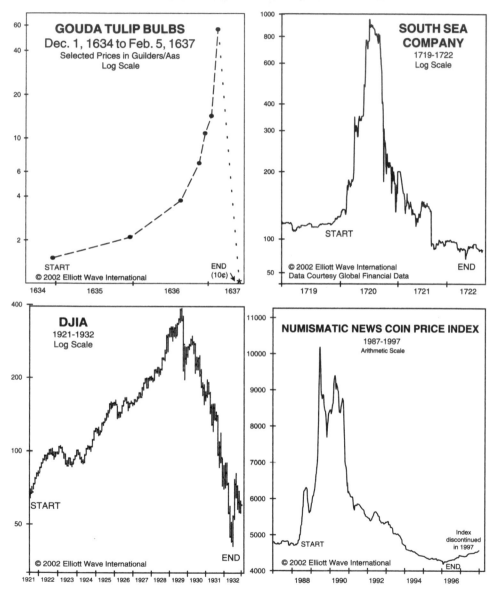

Figure 8-1 through 8-4

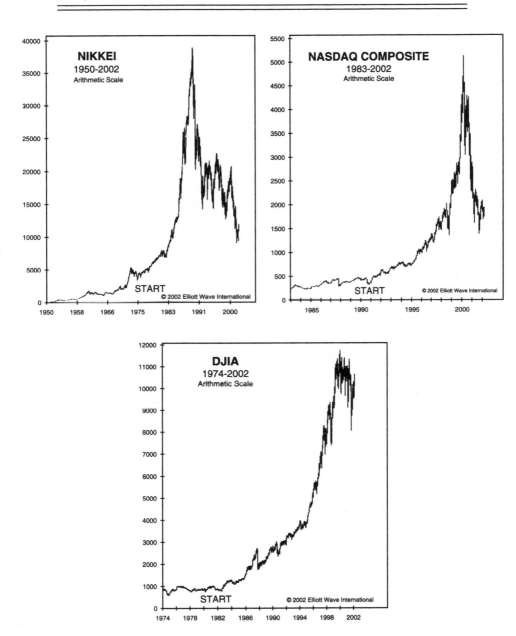

Figure 8-5 through 8-7

Figures 8-1 through 8-7 show the record to date of seven manias. The first four of them are far enough in the past to show the ultimate outcome in which values fell below what they were at the mania's start. The fifth graph is Japan's Nikkei stock index, which topped out on the last trading day of 1989. Its consequences have not fully played out yet, but the relentless fall has already wiped out 80 percent of the Nikkei's peak value and should, if the mania model holds, ultimately carry to or below the values of 1974. The sixth graph is the NASDAQ index, which topped in March 2000. It fell 75 percent into September 2001 and is recovering. Optimists believe that the bear market is over, but it has a long way down to go before erasing the entire mania. The final graph displays the U.S. blue-chip stock mania of the 1980s and 1990s as represented by the DJIA, which remains near its all-time high. If this index behaves like the others, the Dow should fall to below the starting point of its mania. That level is 777, the August 1982 low. So as you can see, the downside potential on this basis is compatible with that indicated by my interpretation of the market's position under the Wave Principle.

Implications for the Economy

If the stock market is going to fall far enough to retrace a substantial portion of the uptrend from at least 1932 and to retrace the price advance that it has undergone during its mania, then it will fall far enough to cause a significant contraction in the economy. How deep will the contraction ultimately become?

The termination of wave III in 1966/68 led to a string of four recessions between 1970 and 1982. Because wave V has had a weaker economic background, and because of the great imbalance between today's sky-high expectations and the decreasingly robust economy, the contraction resulting from this bear market will unquestionably be more severe than any of the contractions following wave III.

Re-examine Figures 2-1 and 4-1. Notice that the last two depressions marked on Figure 2-1 immediately followed the Supercycle degree labels (I) and (III), as shown in Figure 4-1. As you can see in Figure 4-1, we have a new label, wave (V), in place. Notice that the first depression marked on Figure 2-1 immediately followed the Grand Supercycle degree label Ⓘ in 1720. In Figure 4-1, we also tentatively have a label ⒾⒾ in place. These labels, if they are correct, are precursors of a tremendous stock-market crash and a deep depression.

The proper models for the developing economic experience are those that accompanied the stock market setbacks of 1720-1722 in England, 1835-1842 and 1929-1932 in the United States and from 1990 forward in Japan. In two of those cases (1720-1722 and 1929-1932), the contraction was a relentless, acute, brief, all-out depression. In the other two cases (1835-1842 and 1990 to date), the economy contracted over a longer period in two or more steps, with recoveries in between. Either style of progression could happen now.

Japan's retrenchment has been long and slow because most of the rest of the world's economies continued their investment manias and economic growth, allowing vigorous trade to provide support during the first decade of its economic decline. When the rest of the world's economies falter, they will lack a group of healthy trading partners to mitigate the speed of their contractions. For this reason, the developing contraction in the U.S. and around the globe will likely be far swifter than Japan's experience to date.

For the purposes of this book, these observations are all the evidence we need to form at least a general idea of the downside potential in the stock market and the economy in the U.S., and by extension, the rest of the world as well. If you would like more specifics on the details of how the bear market is likely to play out in terms of pattern, time and target levels, please read Chapter 5 of At the Crest of the Tidal Wave (1995).

No Alternative Scenarios

Given the evidence, I think it would be financially sui-
cidal to bet on an extension of the bull market and a requirement
of even moderate prudence to prepare for a major reversal. Aside
from a near-term nuance allowed for the Dow in Chapter 4, I
have no other long-term interpretations of the wave status and
the economy and *no alternative scenarios* at the three illustrated
degrees. The evidence as I see it is too one-sided for me to be
anything now but a one-armed economist. If I turn out wrong,
so be it.

PART II

THE CASE FOR DEFLATION

"Pay no attention to that man behind the curtain."
—*The Wizard of Oz*

Chapter 9:

When Does Deflation Occur?

Defining Inflation and Deflation

Webster's says, "Inflation is an increase in the volume of money and credit relative to available goods," and "Deflation is a contraction in the volume of money and credit relative to available goods." To understand inflation and deflation, we have to understand the terms money and credit.

Defining Money and Credit

Money is a socially accepted medium of exchange, value storage and final payment. A specified amount of that medium also serves as a unit of account.

According to its two financial definitions, *credit* may be summarized as *a right to access money*. Credit can be held by the owner of the money, in the form of a warehouse receipt for a money deposit, which today is a checking account at a bank. Credit can also be *transferred* by the owner or by the owner's custodial institution to a borrower in exchange for a fee or fees — called interest — as specified in a repayment contract called a bond, note, bill or just plain IOU, which is *debt*. In today's economy, most credit is lent, so people often use the terms "credit" and "debt" interchangeably, as money lent by one entity is simultaneously money borrowed by another.

Price Effects of Inflation and Deflation

When the volume of money and credit *rises* relative to the volume of goods available, the relative value of each unit of money falls, making prices for goods generally rise. When the volume of money and credit *falls* relative to the volume of goods available, the relative value of each unit of money rises, making prices of goods generally fall. Though many people find it difficult to do, the proper way to conceive of these changes is that the value of units of *money* are rising and falling, not the values of goods.

The most common misunderstanding about inflation and deflation — echoed even by some renowned economists — is the idea that inflation is rising prices and deflation is falling prices. General price changes, though, are simply *effects*.

The price effects of inflation can occur in goods, which most people recognize as relating to inflation, or in investment assets, which people do not generally recognize as relating to inflation. The inflation of the 1970s induced dramatic price rises in gold, silver and commodities. The inflation of the 1980s and 1990s induced dramatic price rises in stock certificates and real estate. This difference in effect is due to differences in the social psychology that accompanies inflation and disinflation, respectively, as we will discuss briefly in Chapter 12.

The price effects of deflation are simpler. They tend to occur across the board, in goods and investment assets simultaneously.

The Primary Precondition of Deflation

Deflation requires a precondition: a major societal buildup in the extension of credit (and its flip side, the assumption of debt). Austrian economists Ludwig von Mises and Friedrich Hayek warned of the consequences of credit expansion, as have a handful of other economists, who today are mostly ignored. Bank credit and Elliott wave expert Hamilton Bolton, in his February 11, 1957 letter, summarized his observations this way:

> In reading a history of major depressions in the U.S. from 1830 on, I was impressed with the following:
>
> (a) All were set off by a deflation of excess credit. This was the one factor in common.
>
> (b) Sometimes the excess-of-credit situation seemed to last years before the bubble broke.
>
> (c) Some outside event, such as a major failure, brought the thing to a head, but the signs were visible many months, and in some cases years, in advance.
>
> (d) None was ever quite like the last, so that the public was always fooled thereby.
>
> (e) Some panics occurred under great government surpluses of revenue (1837, for instance) and some under great government deficits.
>
> (f) Credit is credit, whether non-self-liquidating or self-liquidating.
>
> (g) Deflation of non-self-liquidating credit usually produces the greater slumps.

Self-liquidating credit is a loan that is paid back, with interest, in a moderately short time from production. Production facilitated by the loan—for business start-up or expansion, for example—generates the financial return that makes repayment possible. The full transaction adds value to the economy.

Non-self-liquidating credit is a loan that is not tied to production and tends to stay in the system. When financial institutions lend for consumer purchases such as cars, boats or homes, or for speculations such as the purchase of stock certificates, no production effort is tied to the loan. Interest payments on such loans stress some other source of income. Contrary to nearly ubiquitous belief, such lending is almost always counter-productive; it adds *costs* to the economy, *not value*. If someone needs a cheap car to get to work, then a loan to buy it adds value to the economy; if someone wants a new SUV to consume, then a loan to buy it does not add value to the economy. Advocates claim that such loans "stimulate production," but they ignore the cost of the required debt service, which burdens production. They also ignore the subtle deterioration in the quality of spending choices due to the shift of buying power from people who have demonstrated a superior ability to invest or produce (creditors) to those who have demonstrated primarily a superior ability to consume (debtors).

Near the end of a major expansion, few creditors expect default, which is why they lend freely to weak borrowers. Few borrowers expect their fortunes to change, which is why they borrow freely. Deflation involves a substantial amount of *invol-untary* debt liquidation because almost no one expects deflation before it starts.

What Triggers the Change to Deflation

A trend of credit expansion has two components: the general willingness to lend and borrow and the general *ability* of borrowers to pay interest and principal. These components depend respectively upon (1) the trend of people's confidence, i.e., whether both creditors and debtors think that debtors will be able to pay, and (2) the trend of production, which makes it either easier or harder *in actuality* for debtors to pay. So as long as confidence and production increase, the supply of credit tends to expand. The expansion of credit ends when the desire or ability to sustain the trend can no longer be maintained. As confidence and production decrease, the supply of credit contracts.

The psychological aspect of deflation and depression cannot be overstated. When the social mood trend changes from optimism to pessimism, creditors, debtors, producers and consumers change their primary orientation from *expansion* to *conservation*. As creditors become more conservative, they slow their lending. As debtors and potential debtors become more conservative, they borrow less or not at all. As producers become more conservative, they reduce expansion plans. As consumers become more conservative, they save more and spend less. These behaviors reduce the "velocity" of money, i.e., the speed with which it circulates to make purchases, thus putting downside pressure on prices. These forces reverse the former trend.

The structural aspect of deflation and depression is also crucial. The ability of the financial system to sustain increasing levels of credit rests upon a vibrant economy. At some point, a rising debt level requires so much energy to sustain — in terms of meeting interest payments, monitoring credit ratings, chasing delinquent borrowers and writing off bad loans — that it slows overall economic performance. A high-debt situation becomes unsustainable when the rate of economic growth falls beneath the prevailing rate of interest on money owed and creditors refuse to underwrite the interest payments with more credit.

When the burden becomes too great for the economy to support and the trend reverses, reductions in lending, spending and production cause debtors to earn less money with which to pay off their debts, so defaults rise. Default and fear of default exacerbate the new trend in psychology, which in turn causes creditors to reduce lending further. A downward "spiral" begins, feeding on pessimism just as the previous boom fed on optimism. The resulting cascade of debt liquidation is a deflationary crash. Debts are retired by paying them off, "restructuring" or default. In the first case, no value is lost; in the second, some value; in the third, all value. In desperately trying to raise cash to pay off loans, borrowers bring all kinds of assets to market, including stocks, bonds, commodities and real estate, causing their prices to plummet. The process ends only after the supply of credit falls to a level at which it is collateralized acceptably to the surviving creditors.

Why Deflationary Crashes and Depressions Go Together

A deflationary crash is characterized in part by a persistent, sustained, deep, general decline in people's desire and ability to lend and borrow. A depression is characterized in part by a persistent, sustained, deep, general decline in production. Since a decline in production reduces debtors' means to repay and service debt, a depression supports deflation. Since a decline in credit reduces new investment in economic activity, deflation supports depression. Because both credit and production support prices for investment assets, their prices fall in a deflationary depression. As asset prices fall, people lose wealth, which reduces their ability to offer credit, service debt and support production. This mix of forces is self-reinforcing.

The U.S. has experienced two major deflationary depressions, which lasted from 1835 to 1842 and from 1929 to 1932 respectively. Each one followed a period of substantial credit expansion. Credit expansion schemes have always ended in bust. The credit expansion scheme fostered by worldwide central banking (see Chapter 10) is the greatest ever. The bust, however long it takes, will be commensurate. If my outlook is correct, the deflationary crash that lies ahead will be even bigger than the two largest such episodes of the past 200 years.

Financial Values Can Disappear

People seem to take for granted that financial values can be created endlessly seemingly out of nowhere and pile up to the moon. Turn the direction around and mention that financial values can disappear into nowhere, and they insist that it is not possible. "The money has to go *somewhere*...It just moves from stocks to bonds to money funds...It never goes away...For every buyer, there is a seller, so the money just changes hands." That is true of the money, just as it was all the way up, but it's not true of the *values*, which *changed* all the way up.

Asset prices rise not because of "buying" *per se*, because indeed for every buyer, there is a seller. They rise because those transacting agree that their prices should be higher. All that everyone else — including those who own some of that asset and those who do not — need do is *nothing*. Conversely, for prices of assets to fall, it takes only *one* seller and *one* buyer who agree that the former value of an asset was too high. If no other bids are competing with that buyer's, then the value of the asset falls, *and it falls for everyone who owns it.* If a million other people own it, then their net worth goes down even though they did nothing. Two investors made it happen by transacting, and the rest of the investors made it happen by choosing not to disagree with their price. Financial values can disappear through a decrease in prices for any type of investment asset, including bonds, stocks and land.

Anyone who watches the stock or commodity markets closely has seen this phenomenon on a small scale many times. Whenever a market "gaps" up or down on an opening, it simply registers a new value *on the first trade*, which can be conducted by as few as two people. It did not take everyone's action to make it happen, just most people's inaction on the other side. In financial market "explosions" and panics, there are prices at which assets do not trade at all as they cascade from one trade to the next in great leaps.

A similar dynamic holds in the creation and destruction of credit. Let's suppose that a lender starts with a million dollars and the borrower starts with zero. Upon extending the loan, the borrower possesses the million dollars, yet the lender feels that he still owns the million dollars that he lent out. If anyone asks the lender what he is worth, he says, "a million dollars," and shows the note to prove it. Because of this conviction, there is, in the minds of the debtor and the creditor combined, two million dollars worth of value where before there was only one. When the lender calls in the debt and the borrower pays it, he gets back his million dollars. If the borrower can't pay it, the value of the note goes to zero. Either way, the extra value disappears. If the original lender sold his note for cash, then someone else down the line loses. In an actively traded bond market, the result of a sudden default is like a game of "hot potato": whoever holds it last loses. When the volume of credit is large, investors can perceive vast sums of money and value where in fact there are only repayment contracts, which are financial assets dependent upon consensus valuation and the ability of debtors to pay. IOUs can be issued indefinitely, but they have value only as long as their debtors can live up to them and only to the extent that people believe that they will.

The dynamics of value expansion and contraction explain why a bear market can bankrupt millions of people. At the peak of a credit expansion or a bull market, assets have been valued upward, and all participants are wealthy — both the people who sold the assets and the people who hold the assets. The latter group is far larger than the former, because the total supply of money has been relatively stable while the total value of financial assets has ballooned. When the market turns down, the dynamic goes into reverse. Only a very few owners of a collapsing financial asset trade it for money at 90 percent of peak value. Some others may get out at 80 percent, 50 percent or 30 percent of peak value. In each case, sellers are simply transforming the remaining future value losses to someone else. In a bear market, the vast, vast majority does nothing and gets stuck holding assets with low or non-existent valuations. The "million dollars" that a wealthy investor might have thought he had in his bond portfolio or at a stock's peak value can quite rapidly become $50,000 or $5000 or $50. *The rest of it just disappears.* You see, he never really had a million dollars; all he had was IOUs or stock certificates. The idea that it had a certain *financial value* was in his head and the heads of others who agreed. When the point of agreement changed, so did the value. Poof! Gone in a flash of aggregated neurons. This is exactly what happens to most investment assets in a period of deflation.

A Global Story

The next four chapters present a discussion that will allow you to understand today's money and credit situation and why deflation is due. I have chosen to focus on the history and conditions of the United States because (1) I have more knowledge of them, (2) the U.S. provides the world's reserve currency, making its story the most important, (3) the U.S. has issued more credit than any other nation and is the world's biggest debtor, and (4) to discuss other countries' financial details would be superfluous. If you understand one country's currency, banking and credit history, to a significant degree you understand them all. Make no mistake about it: It's a global story. Wherever you live, you will benefit from this knowledge.

Chapter 10:

Money, Credit and the Federal Reserve Banking System

An argument for deflation is not to be offered lightly because, given the nature of today's money, certain aspects of money and credit creation cannot be forecast, only surmised. Before we can discuss these issues, we have to understand how money and credit come into being. This is a difficult chapter, but if you can assimilate what it says, you will have knowledge of the banking system that not one person in 10,000 has.

The Origin of Intangible Money

Originally, money was a *tangible good* freely chosen by society. For millennia, gold or silver provided this function, although sometimes other tangible goods (such as copper, brass and seashells) did. Originally, credit was the right to access that tangible money, whether by an ownership certificate or by borrowing.

Today, almost all money is *intangible*. It is not, nor does it even represent, a physical good. How it got that way is a long, complicated, disturbing story, which would take a full book to relate properly. It began about 300 years ago, when an English financier conceived the idea of a national central bank. Governments have often outlawed free-market determinations of what constitutes money and imposed their own versions upon society by law, but earlier schemes usually involved coinage. Under central banking, a government forces its citizens to accept its *debt* as the only form of legal tender. The Federal Reserve System assumed this monopoly role in the United States in 1913.

What Is a Dollar?

Originally, a dollar was defined as a certain amount of gold. Dollar bills and notes were promises to pay lawful money, which was gold. Anyone could present dollars to a bank and receive gold in exchange, and banks could get gold from the U.S. Treasury for dollar bills.

In 1933, President Roosevelt and Congress outlawed U.S. gold ownership and nullified and prohibited all domestic contracts denoted in gold, making Federal Reserve notes the legal tender of the land. In 1971, President Nixon halted gold payments from the U.S. Treasury to foreigners in exchange for dollars. Today, the Treasury will not give anyone anything tangible in exchange for a dollar. Even though Federal Reserve notes are defined as "obligations of the United States," they are not obligations to *do* anything. Although a dollar is labeled a "note," which means a debt contract, it is not a note *for* anything.

Congress claims that the dollar is "legally" 1/42.22 of an ounce of gold. Can you buy gold for $42.22 an ounce? No. This definition is bogus, and everyone knows it. If you bring a dollar to the U.S. Treasury, you will not collect any tangible good, much less 1/42.22 of an ounce of gold. You will be sent home.

Some authorities were quietly amazed that when the government progressively removed the tangible backing for the dollar, the currency continued to function. If you bring a dollar to the marketplace, you can still buy goods with it because the government says (by "fiat") that it is money and because its long history of use has lulled people into accepting it as such. The volume of goods you can buy with it fluctuates according to the total

volume of dollars — in both cash and credit — and their holders'
level of confidence that those values will remain intact.

Exactly what a dollar is and what *backs* it are difficult questions to answer because no official entity will provide a satisfying
answer. It has *no simultaneous actuality and definition*. It may be
defined as 1/42.22 of an ounce of gold, but it is not *actually* that.
Whatever it actually is (if anything) may not be definable. To the
extent that its physical backing, if any, may be officially definable
in actuality, no one is talking.

Let's attempt to define what gives the dollar objective
value. As we will see in the next section, the dollar is "backed"
primarily by government bonds, which are promises to pay dollars. So today, *the dollar is a promise backed by a promise to pay
an identical promise*. What is the nature of each promise? If the
Treasury will not give you anything tangible for your dollar, then
the dollar is a promise to pay *nothing*. The Treasury should have
no trouble keeping this promise.

In Chapter 9, I called the dollar "money." By the definition given there, it is. I used that definition and explanation
because it makes the whole picture comprehensible. But the truth
is that since the dollar is backed by *debt*, it is actually a *credit*, not
money. It is a credit against what the government owes, denoted
in dollars and backed by nothing. So although we may use the
term "money" in referring to dollars, there is no longer any real
money in the U.S. financial system; there is nothing but credit
and debt.

As you can see, defining the dollar, and therefore the
terms money, credit, inflation and deflation, today is a challenge,
to say the least. Despite that challenge, we can still use these
terms because people's minds have conferred meaning and value
upon these ethereal concepts. Understanding this fact, we will
now proceed with a discussion of how money and credit expand
in today's financial system.

How the Federal Reserve System Manufactures Money

Over the years, the Federal Reserve Bank has transferred purchasing power from all other dollar holders primarily to the U.S. Treasury by a complex series of machinations. The U.S. Treasury borrows money by selling bonds in the open market. The Fed is said to "buy" the Treasury's bonds from banks and other financial institutions, but in actuality, it is allowed by law simply to fabricate a new checking account for the seller in exchange for the bonds. It holds the Treasury's bonds as assets against — as "backing" for — that new money. Now the seller is whole (he was just a middleman), the Fed has the bonds, and the Treasury has the new money. This transactional train is a long route to a simple alchemy (called "monetizing" the debt) in which the Fed turns government bonds into money. The net result is as if the government had simply fabricated its own checking account, although it pays the Fed a portion of the bonds' interest for providing the service surreptitiously. To date, the Fed has monetized about $600 billion worth of Treasury obligations. This process expands the supply of *money*.

In 1980, Congress gave the Fed the legal authority to monetize any agency's debt. In other words, it can exchange the bonds of a government, bank or other institution for a checking account denominated in dollars. This mechanism gives the President, through the Treasury, a mechanism for "bailing out" debt-troubled governments, banks or other institutions that can no longer get financing anywhere else. Such decisions are made for political reasons, and the Fed can go along or refuse, at least as the relationship currently stands. Today, the Fed has about $36 billion worth of foreign debt on its books. The power to grant or refuse such largesse is unprecedented.

Each new Fed account denominated in dollars is new money, but contrary to common inference, it is not new value.

The new account *has* value, but that value comes from a *reduction* in the value of all other outstanding accounts denominated in dollars. That reduction takes place as the favored institution spends the newly credited dollars, driving up the dollar-denominated demand for goods and thus their prices. All other dollar holders still hold the same *number* of dollars, but now there are more dollars in circulation, and each one purchases less in the way of goods and services. The old dollars *lose* value to the extent that the new account *gains* value. The net result is a transfer of value to the receiver's account from those of all other dollar holders. This fact is not readily obvious because the *unit of account* throughout the financial system does not change even though its *value* changes.

It is important to understand exactly what the Fed has the power to do in this context: It has legal permission to transfer wealth from dollar savers to certain debtors *without the permission of the savers*. The effect on the money supply is exactly the same as if the money had been counterfeited and slipped into circulation.

In the old days, governments would inflate the money supply by diluting their coins with base metal or printing notes directly. Now the same old game is much less obvious. On the other hand, there is also far more to it. This section has described the Fed's *secondary* role. The Fed's main occupation is not creating money but *facilitating credit*. This crucial difference will eventually bring us to why deflation is possible.

How the Federal Reserve Has Encouraged the Growth of Credit

Congress authorized the Fed not only to create money for the government but also to "smooth out" the economy by manipulating credit (which also happens to be a re-election tool for incumbents). Politics being what they are, this manipulation has been almost exclusively in the direction of making credit easy to obtain. The Fed used to make more credit available to the banking system by monetizing federal debt, that is, by creating money. Under the structure of our "fractional reserve" system, banks were authorized to employ that new money as "reserves" against which they could make new loans. Thus, new money meant new credit.

It meant a lot of new credit because banks were allowed by regulation to lend out 90 percent of their deposits, which meant that banks had to keep 10 percent of deposits on hand ("in reserve") to cover withdrawals. When the Fed increased a bank's reserves, that bank could lend 90 percent of *those* new dollars. Those dollars, in turn, would make their way to other banks as new deposits. Those other banks could lend 90 percent of *those* deposits, and so on. The expansion of reserves and deposits throughout the banking system this way is called the "multiplier effect." This process expanded the supply of *credit* well beyond the supply of money.

Because of competition from money market funds, banks began using fancy financial manipulation to get around reserve requirements. In the early 1990s, the Federal Reserve Board under Chairman Alan Greenspan took a controversial step and removed banks' reserve requirements almost entirely. To do so, it first lowered to zero the reserve requirement on all accounts other than checking accounts. Then it let banks pretend that they have almost no checking account balances by allowing them to "sweep" those deposits into various savings accounts and money market funds at the end of each business day. Magically, when monitors check the banks' balances at night, they find the value of checking accounts artificially understated by hundreds of billions of dollars. The net result is that banks today conveniently meet their nominally required reserves (currently about $45b.) with the cash in their vaults that they need to hold for everyday transactions anyway.

By this change in regulation, the Fed essentially removed itself from the businesses of requiring banks to hold reserves and of manipulating the level of those reserves. This move took place during a recession and while S&P earnings per share were undergoing their biggest drop since the 1940s. The temporary cure for that economic contraction was the ultimate in "easy money."

We still have a fractional reserve system on the books, but we do not have one in actuality. Now banks can lend out virtually all of their deposits. In fact, they can lend out *more* than all of their deposits, because banks' parent companies can issue stock, bonds, commercial paper or any financial instrument and lend the proceeds to their subsidiary banks, upon which assets the banks can make new loans. In other words, to a limited degree, banks can arrange to create their own new money for lending purposes. Today, U.S. banks have extended 25 percent more total credit than they have in total deposits ($5.4 trillion vs. $4.3 trillion). Since all banks do not engage in this practice, others must be quite aggressive at it. For more on this theme, see Chapter 19.

Recall that when banks lend money, it gets deposited in other banks, which can lend it out again. Without a reserve requirement, the multiplier effect is no longer restricted to ten times deposits; it is virtually unlimited. Every new dollar deposited can be lent over and over throughout the system: A deposit becomes a loan becomes a deposit becomes a loan, and so on.

As you can see, the fiat money system has encouraged inflation via both money creation and the expansion of credit. This dual growth has been the monetary engine of the historic uptrend of stock prices in wave (V) from 1932. The stupendous growth in bank credit since 1975 (see graphs in Chapter 11) has provided the monetary fuel for its final advance, wave V. The effective elimination of reserve requirements a decade ago extended that trend to one of historic proportion.

The Net Effect of Monetization

Although the Fed has almost wholly withdrawn from the role of holding book-entry reserves for banks, it has not retired its holdings of Treasury bonds. Because the Fed is legally bound to back its notes (greenback currency) with government securities, today almost all of the Fed's Treasury bond assets are held as reserves against a nearly equal dollar value of Federal Reserve notes in circulation around the world. Thus, the net result of the Fed's 89 years of money inflating is that the Fed has turned $600 billion worth of U.S. Treasury and foreign obligations into Federal Reserve notes.

Today the Fed's production of currency is passive, in response to orders from domestic and foreign banks, which in turn respond to demand from the public. Under current policy, banks must pay for that currency with any remaining reserve balances. If they don't have any, they borrow to cover the cost and pay back that loan as they collect interest on their own loans. Thus, as things stand, the Fed no longer considers itself in the business of "printing money" for the government. Rather, it facilitates the expansion of credit to satisfy the lending policies of government and banks.

If banks and the Treasury were to become strapped for cash in a monetary crisis, policies could change. The unencumbered production of banknotes could become deliberate Fed or government policy, as we have seen happen in other countries throughout history. At this point, there is no indication that the Fed has entertained any such policy. Nevertheless, Chapters 13 and 22 address this possibility.

For Information

There is much information available on the Fed's activities, but nowhere have I found a concise summary such as presented in this chapter. If you would like to learn more, I can start you off on your search. For a positive spin on the Fed's value, contact the Fed itself or any conventional economist. For a less rosy view, contact the Foundation for the Advancement of Monetary Education or join the Ludwig von Mises Institute and order a copy of their 150-page paperback, *The Case Against the Fed*, by Murray N. Rothbard, which is just $5 plus shipping from www.mises.org/catalog.asp. The most knowledgeable source that I have found with respect to the workings of the Federal Reserve System is Lou Crandall of Wrightson Associates, publisher of *The Money Market Observer*, a service for traders. Contact information is as follows:

> *The Money Market Observer*
> Wrightson Associates
> Website: www.wrightson.com
> Email: sales@wrightson.com
> Address: 560 Washington St., New York, NY 10014
> Phone: 212-815-6540
> Fax: 212-341-9253
> Editor: Lou Crandall
>
> Federal Reserve
> Website: www.federalreserve.gov
> Phone: 202-452-3819
>
> Ludwig von Mises Institute
> Website: www.mises.org
> Email: mail@mises.org
> Address: 518 West Magnolia Avenue, Auburn, AL 36832
> Phone: 334-321-2100
> Fax: 334-321-2119
> Book catalog: www.mises.org/catalog.asp
>
> Foundation for the Advancement of Monetary Education
> Website: www.fame.org
> Email: info@fame.org
> Address: Box 625, FDR Station., New York, NY 10150
> Phone: (212)818-1206
> Fax: (212) 818-1197

Chapter 11:

What Makes Deflation Likely Today?

Following the Great Depression, the Fed and the U.S. government embarked on a program, sometimes consciously and sometimes not, both of increasing the creation of new money and credit and of fostering the confidence of lenders and borrowers so as to facilitate the expansion of credit. These policies both accommodated and encouraged the expansionary trend of the 'Teens and 1920s, which ended in bust, and the far larger expansionary trend that began in 1932 and which has accelerated over the past half-century.

Other governments and central banks have followed similar policies. The International Monetary Fund, the World Bank and similar institutions, funded mostly by the U.S. taxpayer, have extended immense credit around the globe. Their policies have supported nearly continuous worldwide inflation, particularly over the past thirty years. As a result, the global financial system is gorged with non-self-liquidating credit.

Conventional economists excuse and praise this system under the erroneous belief that expanding money and credit promotes economic growth, which is terribly false. It appears to do so for a while, but in the long run, the swollen mass of debt collapses of its own weight, which is deflation, and destroys the economy. Only the Austrian school understands this fact. A devastated economy, moreover, encourages radical politics, which is even worse. We will address this topic in Chapter 26.

A House of (Credit) Cards

The value of credit that has been extended worldwide is unprecedented. *At the Crest of the Tidal Wave* reported in 1995 that United States entities of all types owed a total of $17.1 trillion dollars. I thought it was a big number. That figure has soared to $29.5 trillion at the end of 2001, so it should be $30 trillion by the time this book is printed. That figure represents three times the annual Gross Domestic Product, the highest ratio ever.

Worse, most of this debt is the non-self-liquidating type. Much of it comprises loans to governments, investment loans for buying stock and real estate, and loans for everyday consumer items and services, none of which has any production tied to it. Even a lot of corporate debt is non-self-liquidating, since so much of corporate activity these days is related to finance rather than production. The Fed's aggressive easy-money policy of recent months has cruelly enticed even more marginal borrowers into the ring, particularly in the area of mortgages.

This $30 trillion figure, moreover, does not include government guarantees such as bank deposit insurance, unfunded Social Security obligations, and so on, which could add another $20 trillion or so to that figure, depending upon what estimates we accept. It also does not take into account U.S. banks' holdings of $50 trillion worth of derivatives at representative value (equaling five full years' worth of U.S. GDP), which could turn into IOUs for more money than their issuers imagine. Then there is the problem of major coporations' unfunded pension plan liabilities. Companies have promised billions of dollars in fixed-income pensions, but their plan assets will fall so much in value that they will have to fund those pensions from their operating budgets. How much of those liabilities will turn into debt is unknown, but the risk is large and real. Is it not appropriate that you are now reading Chapter 11?

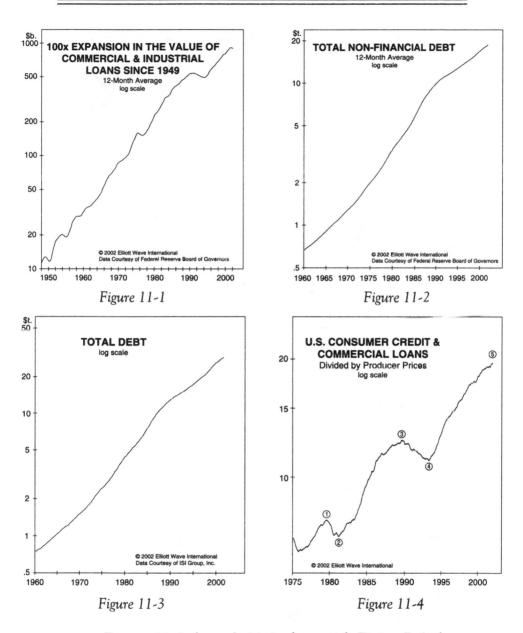

Figure 11-1

Figure 11-2

Figure 11-3

Figure 11-4

Figures 11-1 through 11-4, along with Figure 7-6, show some aspects of both the amazing *growth* in credit — as much as 100 fold since 1949 — and the astonishing *extent* of indebtedness today among corporations, governments and the public, both in terms of total dollars' worth and as a percent of GDP. There are

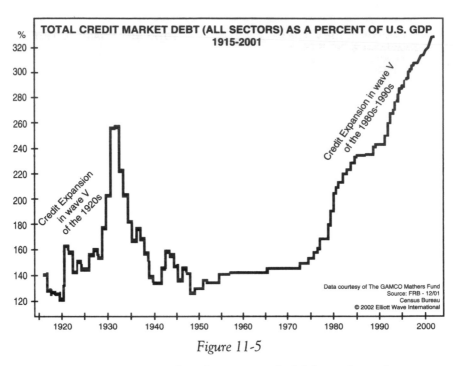

Figure 11-5

so many measures revealing how extended debtors have become that I could dedicate a whole book to that topic alone.

Runaway credit expansion is a characteristic of major fifth waves. Waxing optimism supports not only the investment boom but also a credit expansion, which in turn fuels the investment boom. Figure 11-5 is a stunning picture of the credit expansion of wave V of the 1920s (beginning the year that Congress authorized the Fed), which ended in a bust, and of wave V in the 1980s-1990s, which is even bigger.

I have heard economists understate the debt risk of the United States by focusing on the level of its net debt to foreigners, which is just above $2 trillion, as if all other debt we just "owe to ourselves." But every loan involves a creditor and a debtor, who are separate entities. No one owes a debt to himself. Creditors in other countries who have lent trillions to the U.S. and their own fellow citizens have added to the ocean of worldwide debt, not reduced it. So not only has there been an expansion of credit, but it has been the biggest credit expansion in history by a huge margin. Coextensively, not only is there a threat of deflation, but there is also the threat of the biggest deflation in history by a huge margin.

Broader Ideas of Money

It is a good thing that deflation is defined as a reduction in the relative volume of money and credit, so we are not forced to distinguish too specifically between the two things in today's world. Exactly what paper and which book entries should be designated as "money" in a fiat-enforced debt-based paper currency system with an overwhelming volume of credit is open to debate.

Many people believe that when they hold stock certificates or someone's IOUs (in the form of bills, notes and bonds), they still have money. "I have my money in the stock market" or "in municipal bonds" are common phrases. In truth, they own not money but financial assets, in the form of corporate shares or repayment contracts. As we will see in Chapter 19, even "money in the bank" in the modern system is nothing but a call on the bank's loans, which means that it is an IOU.

There is no universally accepted definition of what constitutes "the money supply," just an array of arguments over where to draw the line. The most conservative definition limits money to the value of circulating cash currency and checking accounts. As we have seen, though, even they have an origin in debt. Broader definitions of money include the short-term debt of strong issuers. They earn the description "money equivalents" and are often available in "money market funds." Today, there are several accepted definitions of the "money supply," each with its own designation, such as M1, M2 and M3.

The mental quality of modern money extends the limits of what people *think* is money. For example, a futures contract is an

IOU for goods at a certain price. Is that money? Many companies use stock options as payment for services. Is that money? Over the past fifteen years, a vast portion of the population has come to believe the oft-repeated phrase, "Owning shares of a stock fund is just like having money in the bank, only better." They have put their life's savings into stock funds under the assumption that they have the equivalent of a money account *on deposit* there. But is it money? The answer to all these questions is no, but people have come to think of such things as money. They spend their actual money and take on debt in accordance with that belief. Because the idea of money is so highly psychological today, the line between what is money and what is not has become blurred, at least in people's minds, and that is where it matters when it comes to understanding the psychology of deflation. Today the vast volume of what people consider to be money has ballooned the psychological potential for deflation far beyond even the immense monetary potential for deflation implied in Figures 11-1 through 11-5.

A Reversal in the Making

No tree grows to the sky. No shared mental state, including confidence, holds forever. The exceptional volume of credit extended throughout the world has been precarious for some time. As Bolton observed, though, such conditions can maintain for years. If the trend toward increasing confidence were to reverse, the supply of credit, and therefore the supply of money, would shrink, producing deflation. Of course, that is a big "if," because for half a century, those wary of credit growth in the U.S. have sounded warnings of collapse, and it has not happened. This is where wave analysis comes in.

Recall that two things are required to produce an expansionary trend in credit. The first is expansionary psychology, and the second is the ability to pay interest. Chapter 4 of this book makes the case that after nearly seven decades of a positive trend, *confidence* has probably reached its limit. Chapter 1 demonstrates a multi-decade deceleration in the U.S. economy that will soon stress debtors' *ability to pay*. These dual forces should serve to usher in a credit contraction very soon.

Wave analysis can also be useful when applied directly to the realm of credit growth. Figure 11-4 is a plot of consumer credit and commercial loans divided by the Producer Price Index to reflect loan values in constant dollars. It shows that the up-trend in real credit value extended to consumers and businesses has traced out five waves since the major bottom of 1974. This is nearly the same picture that we see in stock market margin debt (Figure 7-4). Plots of the credit expansion's rate of change show that the growth in credit is running out of steam at multiple degrees of trend, which is what the analysis in Chapter 1 reveals about the economy. The downturn, it appears, is imminent if not already upon us.

If borrowers begin paying back enough of their debt relative to the amount of new loans issued, or if borrowers default on enough of their loans, or if the economy cannot support the aggregate cost of interest payments and the promise to return principal, or if enough banks and investors become sufficiently reluctant to lend, the "multiplier effect" will go into reverse. Total *credit* will contract, so bank deposits will contract, so the supply of *money* will contract, *all with the same degree of leverage with which they were initially expanded*. The immense reverse credit leverage of zero-reserve (actually *negative*-reserve) banking, then, is the primary fuel for a deflationary crash.

Japan's deflation and its march into depression began in 1990. Southeast Asia's began in 1997. Argentina's has just made headlines. The U.S. and the rest of the nations that have so far escaped are next in line. When the lines in Figures 11-1 through 11-5 turn down (the first one may already have done so), the game will be up.

How Big a Deflation?

Today, under what is left of bank reserves, there are $11 billion on reserve at the Fed plus $44 billion in cash on hand in banks' vaults. This $55 billion total covers the entire stock of bank credit issued in the United States. This amount equates to 1/100 of M2, valued today at $5.5 trillion, and 1/550 of all U.S. debt outstanding, valued today at $30 trillion. If we generously designate the U.S. money supply to include all Federal Reserve notes worldwide, totaling just under $600 billion, these ratios are 1/10 and 1/55.

Of course, since the dollar itself is just a credit, there is no tangible commodity backing the debt that is outstanding today. Real collateral underlies many loans, but its total value may be as little as a few cents on the dollar, euro or yen of total credit. I say "real" collateral because although one can borrow against the value of stocks, for example, they are just paper certificates, inflated well beyond the liquidating value of the underlying company's assets. One can also borrow against the value of bonds, which is an amazing trick: using debt to finance debt. As a result of widespread loans made on such bases, the discrepancy between the value of total debt outstanding and the value of its real underlying collateral is huge. It is anyone's guess how much of that gap ultimately will have to close to satisfy the credit markets in a deflationary depression. For our purposes, it is enough to say that the gap itself, and therefore the deflationary potential, is historically large.

Although the United States is the world leader in fiat money and credit creation, a version of the story told in this and the preceding chapter has happened in every country in the world with a central bank. As a result, we risk overwhelming deflation in every corner of the globe.

Chapter 12:

Timing Deflations: The Kondratieff Cycle

I believe I have a leg to stand on with respect to forecasting monetary trends. In November 1979, right in the culminating heat of a hard-money panic following 30 years of accelerating inflation, *The Elliott Wave Theorist* reasoned, "The incredible conjunction of 'fives' in different markets [gold, silver, interest rates, bonds and commodities] all seem to point to the same conclusion: *The world is about to begin a phase of general disinflation.*" That is exactly what began the following month and has been in force ever since. For the story behind this prediction, please see Chapter 14 of *At the Crest of the Tidal Wave.*

As this example shows, Elliott waves provide an excellent tool for anticipating the nuances of inflation and deflation. However, a particular cycle of social activity has also proved useful in the effort.

Nikolai Kondratieff, a Russian economist, proposed in a 1926 paper that industrial economies followed a repeating cycle of change in prices and production. Actually, this cycle is primarily one of liquidity, not price, so rising and declining trends in prices for money, labor and goods are an effect of the cycle, not a cause. Although this cycle has averaged 54 years in duration, cyclic periodicities can expand and contract and are therefore inherently unreliable for precise timing. But the sequence of events within the Kondratieff cycle may be an immutable social process, regardless of how many decades it takes to play out. The presence of an inflating mechanism exacerbates the extremes of the cycle's manifestations.

Although the precise sequence and interplay of events can be different depending upon the position of the major Elliott waves, here is how recent Kondratieff cycles have played out: As liquidity expands in the initial phase of the cycle, commodity prices rise to reflect increasing business activity and (in most cases) inflation. As business activity and inflation accelerate, speculators begin to bid up commodity prices so as to reflect their increasing fear that inflation will *continue* to accelerate. After the *rate* of inflation peaks and begins to fall, the "acceleration premium" is removed from prices. Thus, commodity prices begin to fall despite continued but slowing inflation, a trend called disinflation. At the same time, a change in psychology away from fear and toward feelings of relief and hope induces people to channel the excess purchasing media created during disinflation into bidding up the prices of investment assets such as stocks. Because inflation continues, the wholesale prices that manufacturers charge for finished products, the retail prices that stores charge for goods and the level of wages that employers pay for labor all continue to rise but at a continuously lesser rate, following the rising but slowing trend of business activity and inflation.

Near the end of the cycle, the rates of change in business activity and inflation slip to zero. When they fall *below* zero, deflation is in force. As liquidity contracts, commodity prices fall more rapidly, and prices for stocks, wages and wholesale and retail goods join in the decline. When deflation ends and prices reach bottom, the cycle begins again.

The position of the current Kondratieff cycle supports the case for deflation directly ahead. In the previous cycle, wholesale prices of commodities generally bottomed in 1932-33. But many

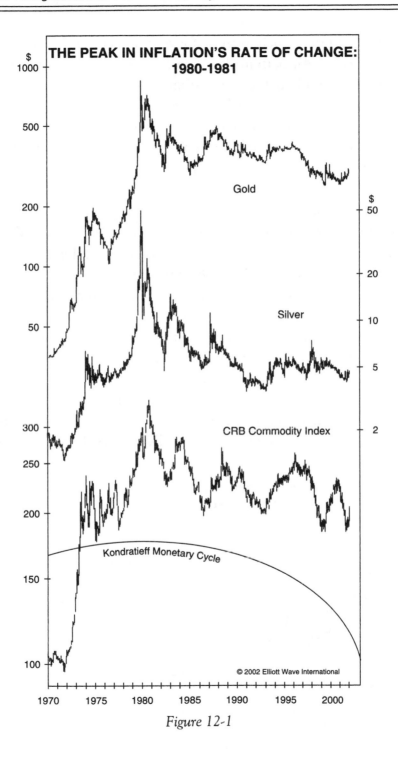

Figure 12-1

important prices, such as those for rent and corporate earnings
(see Figure 6-4), bottomed as late as 1949, 53 years after the
preceding Kondratieff cycle bottom in 1896. You can see this
influence in Figure 11-5, which shows that credit extension as a
percent of GDP also bottomed in 1949. Figure 3-1 in *At the Crest
of the Tidal Wave* shows that PPI-adjusted stock prices ended an
Elliott wave bear market pattern in 1949 as well.

The rise in liquidity after 1949 was the upside portion
of a new cycle. Figure 12-1 shows that prices for monetary and
agricultural commodities generally peaked in 1980-1981 and have
been trending lower ever since. That top marked the transition
to disinflation and the downside of the cycle.

You can also see evidence of the Kondratieff cycle in the
price of money extended to reliable borrowers. Since total borrowing contracts during deflation, prime interest rates fall. Figure
12-2 shows most of four cycles. As you can see, long-term interest
rates last bottomed in the 1940s as well. They topped again in
1981 at the peak of the current cycle and have been trending
down ever since, as it heads into its low. This cycle is not to be
taken as assurance that rates specifically on U.S. Treasury bonds

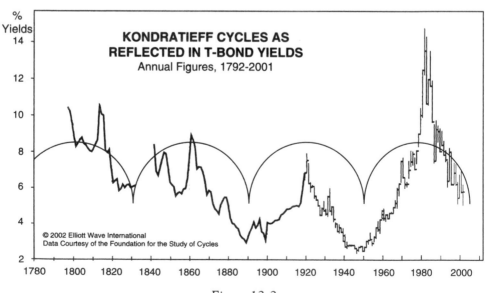

Figure 12-2

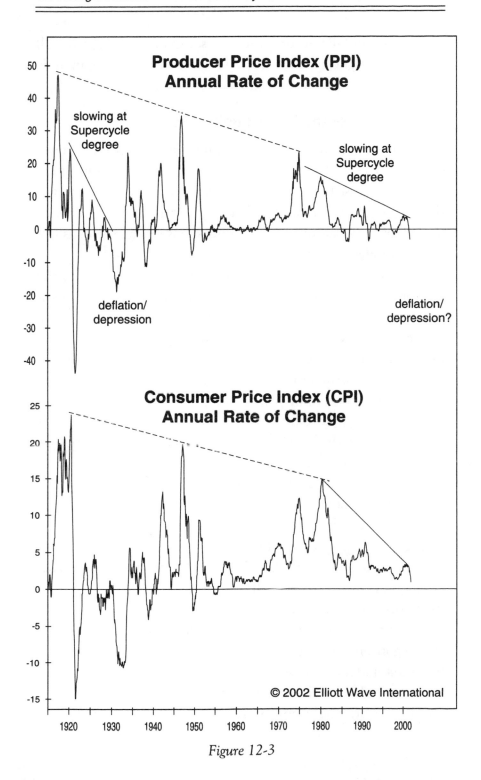

Figure 12-3

will necessarily fall further. As we will see in Chapter 15, rates fall only on the highest quality debt, which may or may not include long-term U.S. Treasuries in the current cycle.

The Position of the Kondratieff Cycle Today

Disinflation has been in force for over twenty years, since 1980-1981. During this time, wholesale and retail prices continued to rise but at a progressively lesser rate, following the slowing trend of disinflation. Today, the rate of upside change in both of these sets of prices combined has reached zero, as you can see in Figure 12-3.

In recent years, economists have been applauding the Fed for engineering a perfect world of economic growth with low inflation. We thus possess "the holy grail sought by most central bankers," as a national business magazine puts it. Are you shocked to learn that this is the same situation that economists applauded in 1929? In actuality, in both cases, the uptrend in goods prices that the Fed fostered for years through credit expansion slowed due to the drag of interest payments on the consumer's capacity to spend. As in 1930-1932, today's "perfect world" will soon be revealed as something quite different.

If the Kondratieff cycle performs normally, the combined rate of change for the PPI and CPI will soon go negative. Whatever the cycle's timing may be, its *sequence* calls for several more years of declining commodity prices, a few years of newly declining wholesale and retail prices and a sharp decline in industrial production. These trends will end when the deflation ends, at the bottom of the cycle.

If the duration of recent past cycles is to repeat, then the falling portion of the current economic cycle would last another two years, and the depression would reach bottom in 2004. If the cycle lasts as long as the longest cycle of the past three centuries, the depression would end in 2011. For our current purposes, these numbers are guides, not predictions, primarily indicating that we are talking a matter of years, not forever. As happened during the late 1700s and in 1835-1842 in the U.S., and as has been happening over the past twelve years in Japan, the economy could experience multiple contractions with intervening recoveries. In fact, since the initial stock market decline should take an A-B-C shape, I lean toward expecting two depressions with an intervening recovery. Regardless, as of today, the process of society-wide debt liquidation lies ahead. Given the long-term five-wave patterns in several debt series (see Figures 7-4 and 11-4), the near-term three-wave rallies in stock averages (see Figure 4-7), the CRB index (see Figure 21-10), gold and silver, the fall to a zero rate of change in the combined PPI and CPI (see Figure 12-3), the sharp drop in interest rates last year and the fact that house prices are scaling new heights all alone (a technical condition called a "bearish non-confirmation"), I conclude that deflation — a contraction in the total volume of money and credit — is probably due to begin just about now.

A Minority View

In the interest of full disclosure, I should warn you that most of today's economists dismiss the Kondratieff cycle as a fantasy. When markets and the economy oscillate violently, as they did for example during the 1840s-1850s, the 1930s-1940s, and the 1970s, cycles are a popular topic. Harvard professor Dr. Joseph Schumpeter wrote in the 1930s, "The Kondratieff Wave is the single-most important tool in economic forecasting." By contrast, when investment markets and the economic trend have been up for a long time, the very idea of cycles is generally dismissed out of hand. Here at the peak of a two-centuries-long uptrend, what more can cycles be other than a subject of derision? Ironically, this oscillating psychology toward the idea of cycles is exactly what allows cycles to exist.

More striking in my opinion is the fact that most of the rare believers in the Kondratieff cycle think it has already bottomed. Some say it bottomed in the early 1980s, an idea that is as contrary to Kondratieff's cycle as it could possibly be. Others were arguing that it bottomed in 1997 or 1998, which did not fit the degree of retrenchment required by the cycle at all. These interpreters have been calling for more decades of expansion, in fact an acceleration of growth.

I am convinced that the explanation for such opinions is that these analysts feel optimistic and have to rationalize why. I am aware of only two other writers who see the cycle performing in its typical way and with its normal timing. Ian Gordon, who in 1998 began publishing *The Long Wave Analyst*, is an astute historian and student of the subject. If you would like to pursue this subject further, you may request copies of his publication through the following means:

> *The Long Wave Analyst*
> Email: ian_gordon@canaccord.com
> Address: Canaccord Capital, Suite 1200, 595 Burrard St.,
> Vancouver, BC, V7X 1J1 Canada
> Phone: 604-643-0280
> Fax: 604-643-0152
> Editor: Ian Gordon

The stock market and the economy weave around the Kondratieff cycle in interesting ways. For a depiction of the Kondratieff cycle's operation over the past 300 years as reflected in stock prices, please see Appendix B of *At the Crest of the Tidal Wave*.

Chapter 13:

Can the Fed Stop Deflation?

Consensus Opinion Concerning Deflation

Seventy years of nearly continuous inflation have made most people utterly confident of its permanence. If the majority of economists have any monetary fear at all, it is fear of inflation, which is the opposite of deflation. Two of the world's most renowned economists have reiterated this fear in recent months in *The Wall Street Journal*, predicting an immediate acceleration of inflation.

As for the very idea of deflation, one economist a few years ago told a national newspaper that deflation had a "1 in 10,000" chance of occurring. The Chairman of Carnegie Mellon's business school calls the notion of deflation "utter nonsense." A professor of economics at Pepperdine University states flatly, "Rising stock prices will inevitably lead to rising prices in the rest of the economy." The publication of an economic think-tank insists, "Anyone who asserts that deflation is imminent or already underway ignores the rationale for fiat currency — that is, to facilitate the manipulation of economic activity." A financial writer explains, "Deflation…is totally a function of the Federal Reserve's management of monetary policy. It has nothing to do with the business cycle, productivity, taxes, booms and busts or anything else." Concurring, an adviser writes in a national magazine, "U.S. deflation would be simple to stop today. The Federal Reserve

could just print more money, ending the price slide in its tracks."
Yet another sneers, "Get real," and likens anyone concerned
about deflation to "small children." One maverick economist
whose model accommodates deflation and who actually expects
a period of deflation is nevertheless convinced that it will be a
"good deflation" and "nothing to fear." On financial television,
another analyst (who apparently defines deflation as falling prices)
quips, "Don't worry about deflation. All it does is pad profits." A
banker calls any episode of falling oil prices "a positive catalyst
[that] will put more money in consumers' pockets. It will benefit
companies that are powered by energy and oil, and it will benefit the overall economy." Others excitedly welcome recently
falling commodity prices as an economic stimulus "equivalent
to a massive tax cut." A national business magazine guarantees,
"That's not deflation ahead, just slower inflation. Put your deflation worries away." The senior economist with Deutsche Bank
in New York estimates, "The chance of deflation is at most one
in 50" (apparently up from the 1 in 10,000 of a couple of years
ago). The President of the San Francisco Fed says, "The idea
that we are launching into a prolonged period of declining prices
I don't think has substance." A former government economist
jokes that deflation is "57th on my list of worries, right after the
56th — fear of being eaten by piranhas." These comments about
deflation represent entrenched professional opinion.

As you can see, anyone challenging virtually the entire
army of financial and economic thinkers, from academic to professional, from liberal to conservative, from Keynesian socialist
to Objectivist free-market, from Monetarist technocratic even
to many vocal proponents of the Austrian school, must respond
to their belief that inflation is virtually inevitable and deflation
impossible.

"Potent Directors"

The primary basis for today's belief in perpetual prosperity and inflation with *perhaps* an occasional recession is what I call the "potent directors" fallacy. It is nearly impossible to find a treatise on macroeconomics today that does not assert or assume that the Federal Reserve Board has learned to control both our money and our economy. Many believe that it also possesses immense power to manipulate the stock market.

The very idea that it *can* do these things is false. Last October, before the House and Senate Joint Economic committee, Chairman Alan Greenspan himself called the idea that the Fed could prevent recessions a "puzzling" notion, chalking up such events to exactly what causes them: "human psychology." In August 1999, he even more specifically described the stock market as being driven by "waves of optimism and pessimism." He's right on this point, but no one is listening.

The Chairman also expresses the view that the Fed has the power to temper economic swings for the better. Is that what it does? Politicians and most economists assert that a central bank is necessary for maximum growth. Is that the case?

This is not the place for a treatise on the subject, but a brief dose of reality should serve. Real economic growth in the U.S. was greater in the nineteenth century without a central bank than it has been in the twentieth century with one. Real economic growth in Hong Kong during the latter half of the twentieth century outstripped that of every other country in the entire world, and it had no central bank. Anyone who advocates a causal connection between central banking and economic performance must conclude that a central bank is harmful to economic growth. For recent examples of the failure of the idea of efficacious economic directors, just look around. Since Japan's boom ended in 1990, its regulators have been using every presumed macroeconomic "tool" to get the Land of the Sinking Sun rising again, as yet to no avail. The World Bank, the IMF, local central banks and government officials were "wisely managing" Southeast Asia's boom until it collapsed spectacularly in 1997. Prevent the bust? They expressed profound dismay that it even happened. As I write this paragraph, Argentina's economy has just crashed despite the machinations of its own presumed "potent directors." I say "despite," but the truth is that directors, whether they are Argentina's, Japan's or America's, *cannot* make things better and have *always* made things worse. It is a principle that meddling in the free market can only disable it. People think that the Fed has "managed" the economy brilliantly in the 1980s and 1990s. Most financial professionals believe that the only potential culprit of a deviation from the path to ever greater prosperity would be current-time central bank actions so flagrantly stupid as to be beyond the realm of possibility. But the deep flaws in the Fed's manipulation of the banking system to induce and facilitate the extension of credit will bear bitter fruit in the next depression. Economists who do not believe that a prolonged expansionary credit policy has consequences will soon be blasting the Fed for "mistakes" in the present, whereas the errors that matter most reside in the past. Regardless of whether this truth comes to light, the populace will disrespect the Fed and other central banks mightily by the time the depression is over. For many people, the single biggest financial shock and surprise over the next decade will be the revelation that the Fed has never really known what on earth it was doing. The spectacle of U.S. officials in recent weeks lecturing Japan on how to contain deflation will be revealed as the grossest hubris. Make sure that you avoid the disillusion and financial devastation that will afflict those who harbor a misguided faith in the world's central bankers and the idea that they can manage our money, our credit or our economy.

The Fed's Final Card

The Fed used to have two sources of power to expand the total amount of bank credit: It could lower reserve requirements or lower the discount rate, the rate at which it lends money to banks. In shepherding reserve requirements down to zero, it has expended all the power of the first source. In 2001, the Fed lowered its discount rate from 6 percent to 1.25 percent, an unprecedented amount in such a short time. By doing so, it has expended much of the power residing in the second source. What will it do if the economy resumes its contraction, lower interest rates to zero? *Then what?*

Why the Fed Cannot Stop Deflation

Countless people say that deflation is impossible because the Federal Reserve Bank can just *print money* to stave off deflation. If the Fed's main jobs were simply establishing new checking accounts and grinding out banknotes, that's what it might do. But in terms of *volume*, that has not been the Fed's primary function, which for 89 years has been in fact to foster the *expansion of credit*. Printed fiat currency depends almost entirely upon the whims of the issuer, but credit is another matter entirely.

What the Fed does is to set or influence certain very short-term interbank loan rates. It sets the discount rate, which is the Fed's nominal near-term lending rate to banks. This action is primarily a "signal" of the Fed's posture because banks almost never borrow from the Fed, as doing so implies desperation. (Whether they will do so more in coming years under duress is another question.) More actively, the Fed buys and sells overnight "repurchase agreements," which are collateralized loans among banks and dealers, to defend its chosen rate, called the "federal funds" rate. In stable times, the lower the rate at which banks can borrow short-term funds, the lower the rate at which they can offer long-term loans to the public. Thus, though the Fed undertakes its operations to influence bank borrowing, its ultimate goal is to influence public borrowing from banks. Observe that the Fed makes bank credit more available or less available to two sets of *willing borrowers.*

During social-mood uptrends, this strategy appears to work, because the borrowers — i.e., banks and their customers — are confident, eager participants in the process. During monetary crises, the Fed's attempts to target interest rates don't appear to work because in such environments, the demands of creditors overwhelm the Fed's desires. In the inflationary 1970s to early 1980s, rates of interest soared to 16 percent, and the Fed was forced to follow, not because it wanted that interest rate but because debt investors demanded it.

Regardless of the federal funds rate, banks set their own lending rates to customers. During economic contractions, banks can become fearful to make long-term loans even with cheap short-term money. In that case, they raise their loan rates to make up for the perceived risk of loss. In particularly scary times, banks have been known virtually to cease new commercial and consumer lending altogether. Thus, the ultimate success of the Fed's attempts to influence the total amount of credit outstanding depends not only upon willing borrowers but also upon the banks as *willing creditors.*

Economists hint at the Fed's occasional impotence in fostering credit expansion when they describe an ineffective monetary strategy, i.e., a drop in the Fed's target rates that does not stimulate borrowing, as "pushing on a string." At such times, low Fed-influenced rates cannot overcome creditors' disinclination to lend and/or customers' unwillingness or inability to borrow. That's what has been happening in Japan for over a decade, where rates have fallen effectively to zero but the volume of credit is still contracting. Unfortunately for would-be credit manipulators, the leeway in interest-rate manipulation stops at zero percent.

When prices for goods fall rapidly during deflation, the value of money rises, so even a zero interest rate imposes a heavy real cost on borrowers, who are obligated to return more valuable dollars at a later date. No one with money wants to pay someone else to borrow it, so interest rates cannot go negative. (Some people have proposed various pay-to-borrow schemes for central banks to employ in combating deflation, but it is doubtful that the real world would accommodate any of them.)

When banks and investors are reluctant to lend, then only *higher* interest rates can induce them to do so. In deflationary times, the market accommodates this pressure with falling bond prices and higher lending rates for all but the most pristine debtors. But wait; it's not that simple, because higher interest rates do not serve only to *attract* capital; they can also make it flee. Once again, the determinant of the difference is market psychology: Creditors in a defensive frame of mind can perceive a borrower's willingness to pay high rates as desperation, in which case, the higher the offer, the more repelled is the creditor. In a deflationary crash, rising interest rates on bonds mean that creditors fear default.

A defensive credit market can scuttle the Fed's efforts to get lenders and borrowers to agree to transact at all, much less at some desired target rate. If people and corporations are unwilling to borrow or unable to finance debt, and if banks and investors are disinclined to lend, central banks cannot force them to do so. During deflation, they cannot even induce them to do so with a zero interest rate.

Thus, regardless of assertions to the contrary, the Fed's purported "control" of borrowing, lending and interest rates ultimately depends upon an accommodating market psychology and cannot be set by decree. So ultimately, the Fed does not control either interest rates or the total supply of credit; the market does.

There is an invisible group of lenders in the money game: *complacent depositors*, who — thanks to the FDIC (see Chapter 19) and general obliviousness — have been letting banks engage in whatever lending activities they like. Under pressure, bankers have occasionally testified that depositors might become highly skittish (if not horrified) if they knew how their money is being handled. During emotional times, the Fed will also have to try to maintain bank depositors' confidence by refraining from actions that appear to indicate panic. This balancing act will temper the Fed's potency and put it on the defensive yet further.

In contrast to the assumptions of conventional macro-economic models, people are not machines. They get emotional. People become depressed, fearful, cautious and angry during depressions; that's essentially what causes them. A change in the population's mental state from a desire to expand to a desire to conserve is key to understanding why central bank machinations cannot avert deflation.

When ebullience makes people expansive, they often act on impulse, without full regard to reason. That's why, for example, consumers, corporations and governments can allow themselves to take on huge masses of debt, which they later regret. It is why creditors can be comfortable lending to weak borrowers, which they later regret. It is also why stocks can reach unprecedented valuations.

Conversely, when fear makes people defensive, they again often act on impulse, without full regard to reason. One example of action impelled by defensive psychology is govern-ments' recurring drive toward protectionism during deflationary periods. Protectionism is correctly recognized among economists of all stripes as destructive, yet there is always a call for it when people's mental state changes to a defensive psychology. Voting blocs, whether corporate, union or regional, demand import tariffs and bans, and politicians provide them in order to get re-elected.

If one country does not adopt protectionism, its trading partners will. Either way, the inevitable dampening effect on trade is inescapable. You will be reading about tariff wars in the newspapers before this cycle is over. Another example of defensive psychology is the increasing conservatism of bankers during a credit contraction. When lending officers become afraid, they call in loans and slow or stop their lending no matter how good their clients' credit may be in actuality. Instead of seeing opportunity, they see only danger. Ironically, much of the actual danger appears as a consequence of the reckless, impulsive decisions that they made in the preceding uptrend. In an environment of pessimism, corporations likewise reduce borrowing for expansion and acquisition, fearing the burden more than they believe in the opportunity. Consumers adopt a defensive strategy at such times by opting to save and conserve rather than to borrow, invest and spend. Anything the Fed does in such a climate will be seen through the lens of cynicism and fear. In such a mental state, people will interpret Fed actions differently from the way that they did when they were inclined toward confidence and hope.

With these thoughts in mind, let's return to the idea that the Fed could just print banknotes to stave off bank failures. One can imagine a scenario in which the Fed, beginning soon after the onset of deflation, trades banknotes for portfolios of bad loans, replacing a sea of bad debt with an equal ocean of banknotes, thus smoothly monetizing all defaults in the system without a ripple of protest, reaction or deflation. There are two problems with this scenario. One is that the Fed is a bank, and it would have no desire to go broke buying up worthless portfolios, debasing its own reserves to nothing. Only a government mandate triggered by crisis could compel such an action, which would come only after deflation had ravaged the system. Even in 1933, when the Fed agreed to monetize some banks' loans, it offered cash in exchange for only the very best loans in the banks'

portfolios, not the precarious ones. Second, the smooth reflation scenario is an ivory-tower concoction that sounds plausible
only by omitting human beings from it. While the Fed could
embark on an aggressive plan to liquefy the banking system with
cash in response to a developing credit crisis, that action itself
ironically could serve to aggravate deflation, not relieve it. In a
defensive emotional environment, evidence that the Fed or the
government had decided to adopt a deliberate policy of inflating
the currency could give bondholders an excuse, justified or not,
to panic. It could be taken as evidence that the crisis is worse
than they thought, which would make them fear defaults among
weak borrowers, or that hyperinflation lay ahead, which could
make them fear the depreciation of all dollar-denominated debt.
Nervous holders of suspect debt that was near expiration could
simply decline to exercise their option to repurchase it once the
current holding term ran out. Fearful holders of suspect long-
term debt far from expiration could dump their notes and bonds
on the market, making prices collapse. If this were to happen,
the net result of an attempt at inflating would be a system-wide
reduction in the purchasing power of dollar-denominated debt,
in other words, a drop in the dollar value of total credit extended,
which is deflation.

The myth of Fed omnipotence has three main counter-
vailing forces: the bond market, the gold market and the currency
market. With today's full disclosure of central banks' activities,
governments and central banks cannot hide their monetary decisions. Indications that the Fed had adopted an unwelcome policy
would spread immediately around the world, and markets would
adjust accordingly. Downward adjustments in bond prices could
not only negate but also *outrun* the Fed's attempts at undesired
money or credit expansion.

The problems that the Fed faces are due to the fact that
the world is not so much awash in money as it is awash in credit.

Because today the amount of outstanding credit dwarfs the quantity of money, debt investors, who always have the option to sell bonds in large quantities, are in the driver's seat with respect to interest rates, currency values and the total quantity of credit, which means that they, not the Fed, are now in charge of the prospects for inflation and deflation. The Fed has become a slave to trends that it has already fostered for seventy years, to events that have already transpired. For the Fed, the mass of credit that it has nursed into the world is like having raised King Kong from babyhood as a pet. He might behave, but only if you can figure out what he wants and keep him satisfied.

In the context of our discussion, the Fed has four relevant tasks: to keep the banking system liquid, to maintain the public's confidence in banks, to maintain the market's faith in the value of Treasury securities, which constitute its own reserves, and to maintain the integrity of the dollar relative to other currencies, since dollars are the basis of the Fed's power. In a system-wide financial crisis, these goals will conflict. If the Fed chooses to favor any one of these goals, the others will be at least compromised, possibly doomed.

The Fed may have taken its steps to eliminate reserve requirements with these conflicts in mind, because whether by unintended consequence or design, that regulatory change transferred the full moral responsibility for depositors' money onto the banks. The Fed has thus excused itself from responsibility in a system-wide banking crisis, giving itself the option of defending the dollar or the Treasury's debt rather than your bank deposits. Indeed, from 1928 to 1933, the Fed raised its holdings of Treasury securities from 10.8 percent of its credit portfolio to 91.5 percent, effectively fleeing to "quality" right along with the rest of the market. What actual path the Fed will take under pressure is unknown, but it is important to know that it is under no *obligation* to save the banks, print money or pursue any other rescue. Its primary legal obligation is to provide backing for the nation's currency, which it could quite merrily fulfill no matter what happens to the banking system.

Local Inflation by Repatriation?

Other countries hold Treasury securities in their central banks as reserves, and their citizens keep dollar bills as a store of value and medium of exchange. In fact, foreigners hold 45 percent of Treasury securities in the marketplace and 75 percent of all $100 bills. Repatriation of those instruments, it has been proposed, could cause a dramatic local inflation. If in fact investors around the world were to panic over the quality of the Treasury's debt, it would cause a price collapse in Treasury securities, which would be deflationary. As for currency repatriation, if overall money and credit were deflating in dollar terms, dollar bills would be rising in value. Foreigners would want to hold onto those remaining dollar bills with both hands. Even if foreigners did return their dollars, the Fed, as required by law, would offset returned dollar currency with sales of Treasury bonds, thus neutralizing the monetary effect.

Can Fiscal Policy Halt Deflation?

Can the government spend our way out of deflation and depression? Governments sometimes employ aspects of "fiscal policy," i.e., altering spending or taxing policies, to "pump up" demand for goods and services. Raising taxes for any reason would be harmful. Increasing government spending (with or without raising taxes) simply transfers wealth from savers to spenders, substituting a short-run stimulus for long-run financial deterioration. Japan has used this approach for twelve years, and it hasn't worked. Slashing taxes absent government spending cuts would be useless because the government would have to borrow the difference. Cutting government spending is a good thing, but politics will prevent its happening prior to a crisis.

Understand further that even the government's "tools" of macroeconomic manipulation are hardly mechanical levers on a machine; they are subject to psychology. Have you noticed the government's increasing fiscal conservatism over the past decade? Even Democrats have been voicing the virtues of a balanced budget! This is a sea change in *thinking*, and that is what ultimately causes trends such as inflation and deflation.

Endgame

The lack of solutions to the deflation problem is due to the fact that the problem results from prior excesses. Like the discomfort of drug addiction withdrawal, the discomfort of credit addiction withdrawal cannot be avoided. The time to have thought about avoiding a system-wide deflation was years ago. Now it's too late.

It does not matter how it happens; in the right psychological environment, *deflation will win*, at least initially. People today, raised in the benign, expansive environment of Supercycle wave (V), love to quote the conventional wisdom, "Don't fight the Fed." Now that the environment is about to change, I think that the cry of the truly wise should be, *"Don't fight the waves."*

Currency Hyperinflation

While I can discern no obvious forces that would counteract deflation, *after* deflation is another matter. At the bottom, when there is little credit left to destroy, currency inflation, perhaps even hyperinflation, could well come into play. In fact, I think this outcome has a fairly high probability in the next Kondratieff cycle.

When a government embarks on a policy of currency hyperinflation, such as the Confederate States did in the 1860s, Germany did in the early 1920s or France did after World War II, the monetary path is utterly different from that of deflation, but ironically, the end result is about the same as that of a deflationary crash. At the end of hyperinflation, total bank accounts denominated in the hyperinflated currency are worth far less than they were, sometimes nothing at all. Total debts have shrunk or disappeared because the notes were denominated in depreciated money. In the severest cases, even the money disappears. In this sense, even with hyperinflation, the end result is the destruction of money and credit, which is deflation.

The Markets Will Signal Inflation

Despite my thoughts on the matter, I recognize that international money flows are massive, central bankers can be ingenious, and politics can be volatile. Perhaps there is some way that inflation, whether globally or locally, could accelerate in the immediate future. How can you tell if my conclusion about deflation is wrong and that inflation or hyperinflation is taking place *instead* of deflation?

There are two sensitive barometers of major monetary trends. One is the currency market. If the price of the dollar against other currencies begins to plummet, it *might* mean that the market fears dollar inflation, but it might simply mean that credit denominated in other currencies is deflating faster than that denominated in dollars. The other monetary barometer, which is more important, is the gold market. If gold begins to soar in dollar terms, then the market almost surely fears inflation. The bond market will not make the best barometer of inflation because much of it will fall under either scenario. I hope to recommend gold at lower prices near the bottom of the deflationary trend, but if gold were to move above $400 per ounce, I would probably be convinced that a major low had passed. The ideas in Chapters 18 and 22 will show you how to protect yourself simultaneously against deflation and a collapse in dollar value.

A High Degree of Complexity

Stocks are not registering a Supercycle top like that of 1929 but a Grand Supercycle top, per Figure 4-1. This means that the ultimate — if not the immediate — consequences will be more severe and more confounding than the consequences of the 1929-1932 crash. As Chapter 5 of *At the Crest of the Tidal Wave* explains, the entirety of Grand Supercycle wave (IV) should last a century and comprise two or three major bear markets with one or two intervening bull markets. This book addresses primarily the first bear market, although the two preceding sections attempt to outline some of the longer-term risks. Because in some ways the financial world is in uncharted waters, this book may not have all the answers.

BOOK TWO

HOW TO PROTECT YOURSELF AND PROFIT FROM DEFLATION AND DEPRESSION

"...but Philamis...followed his ould course...thinking that the tide would have no ebb, the tune would have no ende."
— Thomas Lodge, *Euphues' Shadowe* (1592)

For Your Safety

If present or future laws pertaining to the reader prohibit any financial or other activity suggested in this book, the reader is advised to consider any contrary suggestion null and void and proceed according to applicable law. Neither the author nor the publisher acts as portfolio manager, securities advisor, commodity trading advisor, attorney, underwriter, solicitor or broker. At no time does the author or publisher advocate the reader's acquisition of any specific financial product or service. If you require personalized advice, you should seek the services of a competent professional.

Chapter 14:

Making Preparations and Taking Action

The ultimate effect of deflation is to reduce the supply of money and credit. Your goal is to make sure that it doesn't reduce the supply of *your* money and credit. The ultimate effect of depression is financial ruin. Your goal is to make sure that it doesn't ruin you.

Many investment advisors speak as if making money by investing is easy. It's not. What's easy is *losing* money, which is exactly what most investors do. They might make money for a while, but they lose eventually. Just keeping what you have over a lifetime of investing can be an achievement. That's what this book is designed to help you do, in perhaps the single most difficult financial environment that exists.

Protecting your liquid wealth against a deflationary crash and depression is pretty easy once you know what to do. Protecting your other assets and ensuring your livelihood can be serious challenges. Knowing how to proceed used to be the most difficult part of your task because almost no one writes about the issue. This book remedies that situation.

Preparing To Take the Right Actions

In a crash and depression, we will see stocks going down 90 percent and more, mutual funds collapsing, massive layoffs, high unemployment, corporate and municipal bankruptcies, bank and insurance company failures and ultimately financial and political crises. The average person, who has no inkling of the risks in the financial system, will be shocked that such things could happen, despite the fact that they have happened repeat-edly throughout history.

Being unprepared will leave you vulnerable to a major disruption in your life. Being prepared will allow you to make exceptional profits both in the crash and in the ensuing recovery. For now, you should focus on making sure that you do not become a zombie-eyed victim of the depression.

The best news of all is that this depression should be relatively brief, though it will seem like an eternity while it is in force. The longest depression on record in the U.S. lasted three years and five months, from September 1929 to February 1933. The longest sustained stock market decline in U.S. history lasted seven years, from 1835 to 1842, and featured two depressions in close proximity. As the expected trend change is of one larger degree than those, it should be a commensurately large setback, but it should still be brief relative to the duration of the preced-ing advance.

Taking the Right Actions

Countless advisors have touted "stocks only," "gold only," "diversification," a "balanced portfolio" and other end-all solu-tions to the problem of attending to your investments. These approaches are usually delusions. As I try to make clear in the following pages, no investment strategy will provide stability *forever*. You will have to be nimble enough to see major trends coming and make changes accordingly. What follows is a good guide, I think, but it is only a guide.

The main goal of investing in a crash environment is *safety*. When deflation looms, almost every investment category becomes associated with immense risks. Most investors have no idea of these risks and will think you are a fool for taking precautions.

What's *that* for?

Many readers will object to taking certain prudent actions because of the presumed cost. For example: "I can't take a profit; I'll have to pay taxes!" My reply is, if you don't want to pay taxes, well, you'll get your wish; your profit will turn into a loss, and you won't have to pay any taxes. Or they say, "I can't sell my stocks for cash; interest rates are only 2 percent!" My reply is, if you can't abide a 2 percent annual gain, well, you'll get your wish there, too; you'll have a 30 percent annual loss instead. Others say, "I can't cash out my retirement plan; there's a penalty!" I reply, take your money out before there is none to

get. Then there is the venerable, "I can't sell now; I'd be taking
a loss!" I say no, you are recovering some capital that you can
put to better use. My advice always is, make the right move, and
the costs will take care of themselves.

If you are preoccupied with pedestrian concerns or
blithely going along with mainstream opinions, you need to wake
up now, while there is still time, and actively take charge of your
personal finances. First you must make your capital, your person
and your family safe. Then you can explore options for making
money during the crash and especially after it's over.

As the subtitle implies, this book is designed as a guide for
arranging your finances prior to any future deflationary depression, whether one occurs now, as I expect, or not. Although I
want this book to have value beyond the present situation, some
of the specifics of my suggestions are time-sensitive by nature. If
you need to know today where you can find the few exceptionally sound banks, insurers and other essential service providers,
if you want to locate the safest structures in the world for storing
your wealth, whether in paper monetary instruments or physical
assets such as precious metals, you will find the answers in these
chapters. Yet over time, the best institutions and services today
might be long gone, and others may have taken their place. For
a few years at least, we will post free updates to this information
at www.conquerthecrash.com/readerspage. But if you read this
book 50 years from now, you may have to do your own research
to fit the investment options and service providers available at
the time. Nevertheless, the general nature of your goals should
be much as outlined herein.

Most people do not have the foggiest idea how to prepare
their investments for a deflationary crash and depression, so the
techniques are almost like secrets today. The following chapters
show you a few steps that will make your finances secure despite
almost anything that such an environment can throw at them.

Chapter 15:

Should You Invest in Bonds?

If there is one bit of conventional wisdom that we hear repeatedly with respect to investing for a deflationary depression, it is that long-term bonds are the best possible investment. This assertion is wrong. Any bond issued by a borrower who cannot pay goes to *zero* in a depression. In the Great Depression, bonds of many companies, municipalities and foreign governments were crushed. They became wallpaper as their issuers went bankrupt and defaulted. Bonds of *suspect* issuers also went way down, at least for a time. Understand that in a crash, no one knows its depth, and almost everyone becomes afraid. That makes investors sell bonds of any issuers that they fear could default. Even when people trust the bonds they own, they are sometimes forced to sell them to raise cash to live on. For this reason, even the safest bonds can go down, at least temporarily, as AAA bonds did in 1931 and 1932.

Figure 15-1 shows what happened to bonds of various grades in the last deflationary crash. Figure 15-2 shows what happened to the Dow Jones 40-bond average, which lost 30 percent of its value in four years. Observe that the collapse of the early 1930s brought these bonds' prices *below* — and their interest rates above — where they were in 1920 near the peak in the intense inflation of the 'Teens. Figure 15-3 shows a comparable data series (the Bond Buyer 20-Bond average) in recent decades.

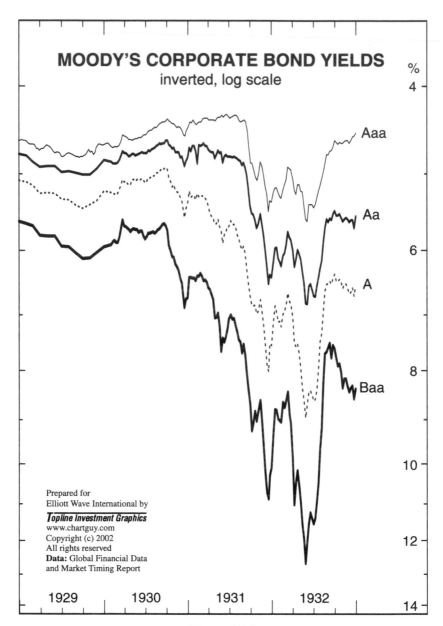

Figure 15-1

Notice how similar the pattern is to that of 1915-1928. If bonds follow the path that they did in the 1930s, their prices will fall *below the 1981 low, and their interest rates will exceed that year's peak of 13+ percent.*

Conventional analysts who have not studied the Great Depression or who expect bonds to move "contra-cyclically" to stocks are going to be shocked to see their bonds plummeting in value right along with the stock market. Ironically, economists will see the first wave down in bonds as a sign of inflation and recovery, when in fact, it will be the opposite.

The Specter of Downgrading

The main problem with even these cautionary graphs is that they do not show the full impact of *downgrades.* They show what bonds *of a certain quality* sold for at each data point. Bonds rated AAA or BBB at the start of a depression generally do not keep those ratings throughout it. Many go straight to D and then become de-listed because of default. Figure 15-1 does not take the price devastation of these issues into account. Like keepers of stock market averages who replace the companies that fail along the way, keepers of the bond averages of Figures 15-2 and 15-3 stand ready to replace component bonds whose ratings fall too far. As scary as they look, these graphs fail to depict the real misery that a depression inflicts upon bond investors.

High-Yield Bonds

When rating services rate bonds between BBB and AAA, they imply that they are considered safe investments. Anything rated BB or lower is considered speculative, implying that there is a risk that the borrower someday could default. The lower the rating, the greater that risk. Because of this risk, Wall Street, in a rare display of honesty, calls bonds rated BB or lower "junk." They appear to have "high yields," so people still buy them.

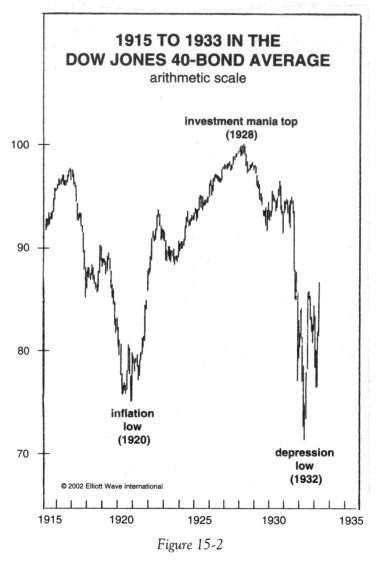

Figure 15-2

That very yield, though, compounds the risk to principal. In a bad economy, companies and municipalities that have issued bonds at high yields find it increasingly difficult to meet their interest payments. The prices of those bonds fall as investors perceive increased risk and sell them. The real result in such cases is a *low* yield or a *negative* yield, particularly if the issuer defaults and your principal is gone.

Figure 15-3

The converse is not necessarily true. We are *told* that in a good economy, high-yield bonds are safe because the economic expansion means good business conditions, which should support the company that issued the bond. Can you rely on this reasoning? Figure 15-4 shows what has been happening to junk bonds over the past 14 years. As you can see, they have been crashing in value *even though the economy was mostly expanding during that*

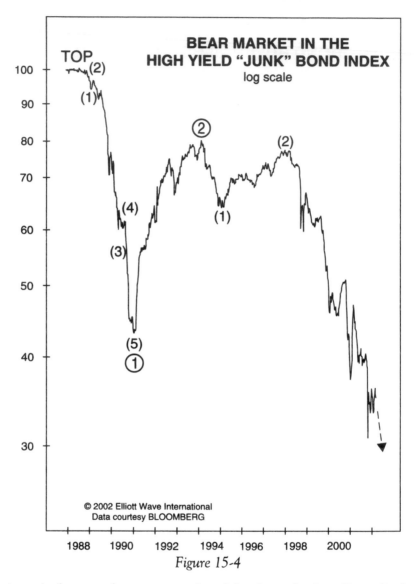

Figure 15-4

time. At least with respect to this debt class, the late Franz Pick, who used to call bonds "certificates of guaranteed confiscation," seems not to have been overly strident.

In recent weeks, advisors have been assuring readers that the recession is ending, so it is the "perfect time" to buy "depressed" junk bonds. The main entities that will be further greatly depressed in coming years besides these junk bonds are the suckers who buy them. Way back in 1988, I published a special analysis urging readers to avoid junk bonds entirely. I added, "If you can figure out a way to short junk bonds, do it." That's when they started down. Their "high yields" have been a chimera, as the bonds' prices have fallen 70 percent on average since then. Most of these issues are headed straight for default.

Today's "High-Grade" Bonds

Don't think that you will be safe buying bonds rated BBB or above. The unprecedented mass of vulnerable bonds extant today is on the verge of a waterfall of downgrading. Many bonds that are currently rated investment grade will be downgraded to junk status and then go into default. The downgrades will go hand-in-hand with falling prices, so you will not be afforded advance warning of loss. When the big slide begins, I doubt that the rating services will even be able to keep up with the downgrades at the rate that they will be required.

An added problem with owning government bonds is the political risk. Governments have a long record of stiffing their creditors in a crisis, and no government is immune from adopting that solution to its financial problems. A new regime especially may have little regard for previously squandered credit.

Today, millions of individuals and institutions own tax-exempt municipal bonds. While there are assuredly many exceptions, this class of bonds is the riskiest among popular government issues. In the United States, default could happen to municipal bonds at any time after times get difficult. Politicians in many jurisdictions have borrowed and spent way more money than is likely ever to be paid back. Merely paying the interest on that debt in tough economic times will become an acute problem for many issuers. In such cases, default for many cities and counties will be inevitable. Even the debt of some higher-level government agencies is at serious risk of default in a worst-case scenario.

The Answer To Bond Selection

So if conventional wisdom is wrong, what is the correct way to frame the problem of investment opportunity and risk with respect to bonds in a deflationary depression? It is this: Any bond that is AAA at the start of the depression *and remains AAA throughout it* will be a satisfactory investment. The problem is, who can figure out which bonds those are? As we will see in Chapter 25, you cannot rely on bond rating services to guide you in a crunch.

If a crash and depression take place, some corporations whose products or services are important in that environment will become special situations, and their bonds will shine as viable investments. Unfortunately, I don't have the expertise to pick out the handful of long-term corporate bonds that will hold their value in a deflationary crash; I can only speculate on what will obviously be some of the worst. Since you can't short individual bonds, there's no point in making a list.

As debt prices fall, yields rise. If you're in long-term bonds, you're stuck with only the "falling prices" part of the equation. It's better to own short-term debt instruments, which can keep rolling over at ever-higher yields to compensate substantially for price losses. So, generally speaking, for safety, it is better to own high-quality *short-term* debt than long-term debt. We will explore that option in Chapter 18.

Chapter 16:

Should You Invest in Real Estate?

So bonds are risky. But we all know that property values never go down. Right?

After the stock experience of 2000-2001, people are saying, "Maybe stocks *can* come down for a few months from time to time, but real estate won't; real estate never has." They are saying it because real estate is the last thing still soaring at the top of the Great Asset Mania, but it, too, will fall in conjunction with a deflationary depression. Property values collapsed along with the depression of the 1930s. Few know that many values associated with property — such as rents — continued to fall through most of the 1940s, even after stocks had recovered substantially.

The worst thing about real estate is its *lack of liquidity* during a bear market. At least in the stock market, when your stock is down 60 percent and you realize you've made a horrendous mistake, you can call your broker and *get out* (unless you're a mutual fund, insurance company or other institution with millions of shares, in which case, you're stuck). With real estate, you can't pick up the phone and sell. You need to find a *buyer* for your house in order to sell it. In a depression, buyers just go away. Mom and Pop move in with the kids, or the kids move in with Mom and Pop. People start living in their offices or moving their offices into their living quarters. Businesses close down. In time, there is a massive glut of real estate.

In the initial stages of a depression, sellers remain under an illusion about what their property is really worth. They keep a high list price on their house, reflecting what it was worth last year. I know people who are doing that now. This stubbornness leads to a drop in sales volume. At some point, a few owners cave in and sell at much lower prices. Then others are forced to drop their prices, too. What is the potential *buyer's* psychology at that point? "Well, gee, property prices have been coming down. Why should I rush? I'll wait till they come down further." The further they come down, the more the buyer wants to wait. It's a downward spiral.

When Real Estate Falls

Real estate prices have always fallen hard when stock prices have fallen hard. Figure 16-1 displays this reliable relationship.

The overwhelming evidence for a major stock market decline presented in Chapters 4 through 7 is enough by itself to portend a tumble in real estate prices. Usually the culprit behind these joint declines is a credit deflation. If there were ever a time we were poised for such a decline, it is now.

The Extension of Credit

What screams "bubble" — giant, historic bubble — in real estate today is the system-wide extension of *massive* amounts of credit to finance property purchases. As a result, a record percentage of Americans today are nominal "homeowners" via $7.6 trillion in mortgage debt. Two-thirds of them owe an average of two-thirds of the value of their homes, plus interest, and both ratios have been increasing at a blistering pace.

People can buy a house with little or no down payment in many cases. They can refinance a house for its entire value. "How can this be?" you ask. "Isn't at least 20 percent homeowner

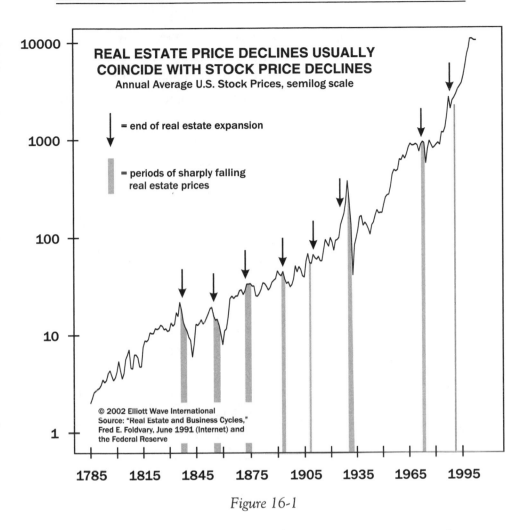

REAL ESTATE PRICE DECLINES USUALLY
COINCIDE WITH STOCK PRICE DECLINES
Annual Average U.S. Stock Prices, semilog scale

↓ = end of real estate expansion

▮ = periods of sharply falling
real estate prices

© 2002 Elliott Wave International
Source: "Real Estate and Business Cycles,"
Fred E. Foldvary, June 1991 (Internet) and
the Federal Reserve

Figure 16-1

equity required?" Well, sort of. Credit institutions are supposed to be penalized for lending more than 80 percent on an uninsured mortgage. But if they get it insured, which is generally not difficult, the limit can go up to 90 percent. With VA or FHA approval, it can go up to 95 percent. "Prime borrowers" can refinance for up to 125 percent of a home's appraised value.

What if none of these exceptions apply? Real estate insiders on a quiet Saturday afternoon will tell you that many banks skirt the intent of laws aimed to ensure some homeowner equity in refinancing deals. For example, suppose the owner of a $500,000 home wants to refinance it at the full amount, but the bank is restricted to lending him only 80 percent of the value of the property, which is $400,000. If the homeowner wants the whole half-million anyway, the bank will send in an appraiser who magically discerns that the property is actually worth $625,000. Get it? 80 percent of $625,000 is $500,000. The homeowner has his 100 percent loan, the bank earns more interest, and the rules are satisfied. If you are creative, you can wangle even more than 100 percent out of a deal. The principle (and maybe later the principal) is out the window, and no one's the wiser, at least until a bear market imparts wisdom.

The problem with these schemes is that their success and continuation depend upon continuously rising property prices. Once the bank extends a loan of that size, it owns the house at full value. *Then, any drop in that value directly causes a drop in the value of the bank's capital.* By contrast, when the bank lends only half of the value of a home, its value can drop as much as half, and the bank can still get all of its depositors' money out of the deal by selling the house. With these latest methods of "creative financing," depositors' money is utterly unprotected from market risk.

Bank loans to home buyers are bad enough, but government-sponsored mortgage lenders — the Federal National Mortgage Corp. (Fannie Mae), the Federal Home Loan Mortgage Corp. (Freddie Mac) and the Federal Home Loan Bank — have extended $3 *trillion* worth of mortgage credit. Major financial institutions actually *invest* in huge packages of these mortgages, an investment that they and their clients (which may include you) will surely regret. *Money* magazine (December 2001) reports that the CEO of Fannie Mae "may be the most confident CEO in America." Certainly his stockholders, clients and mortgage-package investors had better share that feeling, because confidence is the only thing holding up this giant house of cards. When real estate prices begin to fall in a deflationary crash, lenders will experience a rising number of defaults on the mortgages they hold. My guess is that the Treasury will lose the $7 billion line of credit that it is required by law to extend to these quasi-government companies and even more if it attempts a bailout.

Another remarkable trend of recent years adds to the precarious nature of mortgage debt. Many people have been rushing to borrow the last pennies possible on their homes. They have been taking out home equity loans so they can buy stocks and TVs and cars and whatever else their hearts desire at the moment. This widespread practice is brewing a *terrible* disaster. Taking out a home equity loan is nothing but turning ownership of your home over to your bank in exchange for whatever other items you would like to own or consume. It's a reckless course, and it stems from the extreme confidence that accompanies a major top in social mood.

At the bottom of the depression, banks are going to own many, many homes, and their previous owners will be out in the street. That's not so bad; at least they got their money's worth from the TVs and cars. It will be a disaster for the banks' depositors, though, because there will be no one to buy the homes at mortgage-value prices. Depositors' money will be stuck in lifeless property deals, marked down 50 percent, 90 percent or (as happened in the Great Depression) even more.

Credit expansion has supported real estate prices, but it is late in the game. The dramatic tumble in interest rates in 2001 has spurred a record number of home sales because financing rates appear low. Marginal buyers, who had waited on the sidelines, are finally taking the plunge. People around the country are nearly unanimous in thinking that this is their last great opportunity to buy a house. Naturally, it is the opposite: It's your last chance to sell. The market is becoming as bought up as it can get, and there is little interest-rate ammunition left to win the battle for even more borrowers.

Some Things To Do

For more on the prospects for property values, please see Chapter 20 of *At the Crest of the Tidal Wave*. In the meantime, you can take the following steps:

• Make sure you avoid real estate investment trusts, which are perhaps the worst property-related investments during a bear market. Some REITs valued at $100 a share in the early 1970s fell to ¼ by late 1974, and most of them never recovered. REITs are sold to the public because the people who do the deals don't want to stick with them. The public falls for REITs cycle after cycle. These "investments" hold up in the best part of bull markets, but they are disasters in bear markets.

• If you are in the real estate business, wrap up any sales deals you are working and get out of all investment real estate holdings that are not special situations about which you know much more than the market. In general, wait for lower prices to re-invest.

• If you hold a big mortgage on expensive property that depends upon massive public patronage, such as an arena, playhouse, amusement park, arts center or other such facility, consider selling it or subleasing it insured.

• If you are a banker, sell off your largest-percentage mortgages and get into safer investments.

• If you rent your living or office space, make sure that your lease either allows you to leave on short notice or has a clause lowering your rent if like units are reduced in price to new renters.

• If you have a huge mortgage on a McMansion or condo that you cannot afford unless your current income maintains, sell it and move into something more reasonable. If at all possible, join the 1/3 of title-holding Americans who own their homes outright. Be willing to trade down to make it happen. See Chapter 29 for more on this topic.

• If you consider your home a consumption item, and you wish to keep it on that basis, fine. If you are just as happy renting your residence as owning, do so.

• At the bottom, buy the home, office building or business facility of your dreams for ten cents or less per dollar of its peak value.

Chapter 17:

Should You Invest in Collectibles?

Collecting for Investment

Collecting for investment purposes is almost always foolish. Never buy anything *marketed* as a collectible. The chances of losing money when collectibility is priced into an item are huge. Usually, collecting trends are fads. They might be short-run or long-run fads, but they eventually dissolve. The inflation of the 1970s pushed gold and silver higher, so rare coins got a free ride of new interest. What did coin rarity have to do with inflation? Nothing.

Except perhaps for certain enduring masters' works, the focus of art appreciation goes through cycles. So do prices, even for the best art. The Japanese investors who bought paintings at record prices a decade ago have lost much of the value of their "investments."

There are times when collecting makes sense, but you have to be in on the ground floor. When I was a kid, I collected coins. You could find rare coins in everyday pocket change. In the 1950s, my grandmother persuaded the local parking meter collector to let her sort through the town's weekly take of coins and exchange them one for one. There was *no downside* to the hobby because the coins were always worth at least face value.

If you have speculated in rare coins or other collectibles that you do not want for their aesthetic or nostalgic value, sell them at today's prices, before they fall further in the crash. In depressions, people care about gold or silver content in coins, not rarity. One company that specializes in liquidating U.S. coin collections is American Federal, which can broker your coins or buy them outright. Be sure to compare prices with other dealers, some of which are listed in Chapter 22. Here is the contact information:

American Federal Rare Coin & Bullion
Website: americanfederal.com
Email: info@americanfederal.com
Address: 14602 North Cave Creek Rd., Ste. C,
            Phoenix, AZ 85022
Phone: 1-800-221-7694 or 602-992-6857
Fax: 602-493-8158
CEO: Nick Grovich

See Appendix A for updated contact information

Also taking a hard-nosed, consumer-advocacy stance is the *Rosen Numismatic Advisory*, which has won many awards over its 27 years of publication. If you prefer handling your own financial dealings, this is a good source of buy-and-sell coin strategies, information and advice. Here's how to get in touch:

Rosen Numismatic Advisory
Numismatic Counseling, Inc.
Email: mauricerosen@aol.com
Address: PO Box 38, Plainview, NY 11803
Phone: 516-433-5800
Fax: 516-433-5801
CEO: Maurice Rosen

See Appendix A for updated contact information

Rock 'n' roll memorabilia and other baby-boomer collectibles are probably at an all-time top. Baby boomers who covet reminders of their youth will die off in the next 30 years, and most of their collectibles will be considered little more than curios.

For many supposed collectibles, such as Beanie Babies and such, it's already too late. Others, such as baseball cards, comic books and Barbie dolls, still have some value. If you want to sell your pedestrian collectibles, few venues are better than Ebay on the web, at www.ebay.com. For fine art sales, contact:

Christie's
Website: christies.com
Address: 20 Rockefeller Place, New York, NY 10020
Phone: 212-646-2000
Fax: 212-636-2399

Sotheby's
Website: sothebys.com
Address: 1334 York Ave, New York, NY 10021
Phone: 212-606-7000/541-312-5682
Fax: 212-606-7107/541-312-5684

See Appendix A for updated contact information

For more on collectibles in a bear market, see Chapter 19 of *At the Crest of the Tidal Wave.*

Collecting for Pleasure

If you collect certain items for the love of them, you are about to be made very happy. Prices for art and collectibles, so outrageous today, will fall to joyously affordable levels in a depression. If you want to enhance your collection, keep your capital safe, wait until the bottom, and buy up all the items you want at pennies on today's dollar value.

Chapter 18:

Should You Invest in "Cash"?

The Wonder of Cash

For those among the public who have recently become concerned that being fully invested in one stock or stock fund is not risk-free, the analysts' battle cry is "diversification." They recommend having your assets spread out in numerous different *stocks*, numerous different stock *funds* and/or numerous different (foreign) stock *markets*. Advocates of junk bonds likewise counsel prospective investors that having lots of different issues will reduce risk.

This "strategy" is bogus. Why invest in anything unless you have a strong opinion about where it's going and a game plan for when to get out? Diversification is gospel today because investment assets of so many kinds have gone up for so long, but the future is another matter. Owning an array of investments is financial *suicide* during deflation. They all go down, and the logistics of getting out of them can be a nightmare. There can be weird exceptions to this rule, such as gold in the early 1930s when the government fixed the price, or perhaps some commodity that is crucial in a war, but otherwise, *all assets go down in price during deflation except one: cash.*

Today, few people give cash a thought. They sneer at the mere suggestion. "Cash is trash," goes the popular saying. Because interest rates are "too low," investors claim that they have "no

choice" but to invest in something with more "upside potential."
Ironically but obviously necessarily, the last major interest-rate
cycle was perfectly aligned to convince people to do the wrong
thing. Two decades ago, when rates were high, people insisted
that stocks were not worth buying. Now that rates are low, they
insist that cash is not worth holding. It's a psychological trap
keeping investors from doing the right thing: buying stocks at
the bottom (when rates were high) and selling them at the top
(when rates are low).

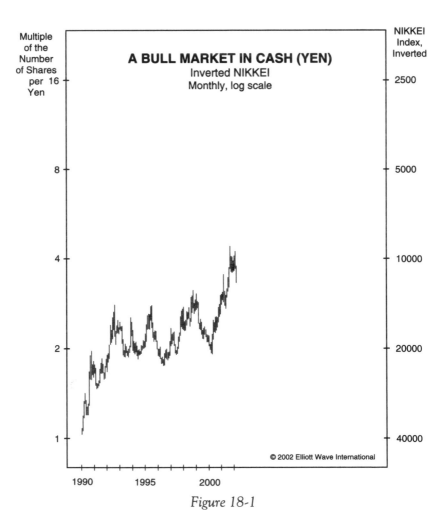

Figure 18-1

Now let's dispose of the idea that the return on cash is "low." How would you like to own an asset that goes up *four times in value* in eleven years? Figure 18-1 is a picture of the soaring value of cash in Japan from 1990 through 2001. Cash has appreciated 300 percent in eleven years in terms of how many shares of Japanese stocks it can buy. Figure 18-2 is one picture of the rising value of cash in the United States, which appreciated nearly 250 percent from March 2000 to the present in terms of how many shares of the NASDAQ index it can buy. Wouldn't

Figure 18-2

you like to enjoy this kind of performance, too? You can, if you move into cash before a major deflation. Then when the stock markets reach bottom, you can buy incredibly cheap shares that almost no one else can afford because they lost it all when their stocks collapsed.

"*If I hadn't lost everything I'd definitely be buying right now.*"

reproduced by permission of Leo Cullum

Cash is the only asset that assuredly rises in value during deflation. One safe "parking place" for capital during a deflationary crash is cash notes — for example, $100 bills, £50 notes or the equivalent in your home currency — in a safe depository to which you will always have access. That way, you will have money if the bank fails, you will have money if credit collapses, and you will have money if the government defaults on its debt. I suggest that you have at least *some* currency on hand if you expect a deflationary crash.

Unfortunately, currency has no yield, it is destructible, and it cannot be transferred with a phone call. Carefully selected "cash equivalents" can solve those problems.

The Risk in Many "Cash Equivalents"

Cash equivalents are high-quality short-term debt. They are extremely attractive investments in a deflationary crash. Choosing them, however, can be tricky. You must own *safe* instruments stored in a *safe* facility.

Most cautious investors think that their funds are utterly safe, even guaranteed, in any money market fund. Do not fall for this illusion. Money market funds are *relatively* safe, but they are still nothing but portfolios of debt, short-term debt to be sure, but debt nonetheless. When a company or government goes bankrupt, it stops paying interest on its debts, short-term or long, *right then*. If you own any of it at the time, your investment is compromised, if not gone.

In a strong economy, few give this risk any thought. They do not imagine that companies, governments and their agencies will ever cease paying interest due. Many people also erroneously believe that the debt issued by government-sponsored enterprises, such as U.S. mortgage insurers Fannie Mae and Freddie Mac, are government-guaranteed, but they're not. *You* take the risk when you buy their debt or their investment products.

Some money market funds realized early on that they could buy slightly riskier debt issues in order to squeeze out an extra 0.1 percent annual yield above that of their competitors, which they could then advertise to attract deposits. Others began to try to top *them* using the same tactics. Some funds have ended up owning a lot of weak debt. To the extent that a money-market fund's holdings are downgraded, the fund is that much riskier. Funds do not report downgrades to you or warn you if they think any of their holdings may be at risk. You hear about it only when it has to explain to you the loss statement that you receive in the mail.

In a depression, many money market funds will shock their depositors when they report losses. Once the process of debt defaults begins, to whom — and at what price — will the funds sell their portfolios if they wish to replace their risky assets with safer ones? They are all on the same ship, and there are few lifeboats.

The Safest Cash Equivalents Inside the U.S.

The safest cash equivalents in a depression are the very best near-term debt instruments, issued by a strong enterprise or government. The strongest such issues today lie *outside* the United States. In the U.S., the primary option is short-term Treasury securities, which includes not only Treasury bills but also longer-term notes and bonds that are within months of maturity, which can be purchased on the secondary market. For the time being, and for the investor who must or prefers to keep all assets inside the United States, Treasury bills or money market funds that hold only short-term U.S. Treasury debt appear to be the best financial haven available next to bullion-type gold and silver coins. These investments might also be attractive for some investors outside the U.S., although there is always currency risk to take into account, because if the dollar falls against your home currency, you will lose money.

The beauty of safe near-term debt is that instead of getting killed by rising interest rates, you can benefit from them. In 1931, the Fed was forced to raise its discount rate in the face of deflation in order to prop up the value of a falling dollar. Other investments fell harder as a result, but holders of very short-term T-bills who kept purchasing new ones at expiration watched their returns increase. This is a good way to defend your portfolio against rising interest rates.

Treasury bills and "Treasury only" money market funds have the added advantage of incurring no state income tax obligation on the interest they pay, which saves you some money if you live in a state with an income tax. Most of these funds also allow you to write checks on the account, so you will be getting a fairly safe yield on what amounts to your checking account. Usually they limit check amounts to $100 or more each, so you will still need a bank checking account for smaller checks, but that shouldn't put much of your total wealth at risk.

You could choose to buy Treasury bills directly from a broker or the U.S. Treasury Department from instructions available at its websites www.publicdebt.treas.gov. and www.treasurydirect. gov. For the record, you no longer get actual Treasury bills for your money. You get a bookkeeping entry that *says* you own Treasury bills. The Treasury department makes it easy to roll over your position automatically upon expiration, but on the other hand, you get none of the amenities of a money-market fund. You do get a modicum of additional safety from more direct ownership. Like many money-market funds, Treasury-only funds are bonded by insurance companies against fraud or theft. However, in a depression environment, such a bond is only as good as its insurer (see Chapter 24). Also, if the fund's custodial bank fails, your T-bills could be under wraps until things are sorted out. So buying T-bills directly from the government has the same advantage as holding actual gold in your hand as opposed to stock shares or warehouse receipts: There is no middleman. If top domestic safety and uninterrupted liquidity are crucial to your investment plan, go ahead and buy T-bills directly. Otherwise, the funds should serve. Personally, I prefer to err on the side of being as safe as possible.

Despite the assumptions of virtually everyone, there are some risks in owning T-bills, directly or indirectly. For example, you could lose some of the value of your certificates or fund shares if there were a rush to sell debt assets in general or merely a panic over possible U.S. government insolvency, either of which could drive the prices of short-term Treasury debt down (and their interest rates up) until the market recovered its equilibrium or confidence. Aside from the above-mentioned risks associated with funds, the only way for holders of Treasury bills to lose all their money would be for the U.S. government to default on its debt.

A federal government default is not impossible. The U.S. Treasury's $3.4 trillion debt and extensive unfunded government liabilities will present significant financial burdens in a depression. The deepest depression in three centuries could force Treasury issues down to junk status, like so many South American IOUs. Despite this risk, the U.S. government still has immense taxing power, and its world-class reputation should attract a share of capital if there is a "flight to quality" during a worldwide monetary crisis. As many stocks and bonds collapse during the crash, those who thought they were pretty smart investing in historically overpriced stocks, Russian and Argentinean bonds, retail consumer debt, junk bonds and worse will come to realize, "We need to sell these losers for what we can get and buy something else with the money we have left." In such a situation, money is likely to flow into what investors perceive as stronger issues. These could well include Treasury bills, making their issuer, the U.S. Treasury, even more liquid. Of course, politics could scuttle this potential. Foreign governments could outlaw money exports, or the U.S. could become politically unstable, reducing its status as an investment haven. The truth is that no one can know exactly how Treasury securities will fare in a major depression. What I *can* say is that, apart from special situations in the corporate realm that I dare not attempt to anticipate, T-bills are probably the safest U.S.-based interest-bearing investment. The next section will present attractive alternatives to holding short-term U.S. Treasury securities.

5 LARGEST TREASURY-ONLY MONEY MARKET FUNDS WITH NO CHARGES OR TRANSACTION LIMITS Source: Weiss Ratings, Inc.		
Fund Name	**Toll-Free No.**	**Web Address**
Alliance Treasury Reserves	(800) 247-4154	www.alliancecapital.com
American Century Capital Presv Fund I	(800) 345-2021	www.americancentury.com
Dreyfus 100% US Treasury MMF	(800) 242-8671	www.dreyfus.com
Evergreen Treasury MMF/CI A	(800) 343-2898	www.evergreen-funds.com
One Group US Treas Secs MMF/CI A	(800) 480-4111	www.onegroup.com

Table 18-1   (*see updated list in Appendix B*)

Of the many hundreds of money market funds in the United States, surprisingly few hold exclusively short-term U.S. Treasury obligations. Among the largest fifteen of these funds, only five have all these features: no other required accounts, no transaction limits, and no separate charges for printing checks, bounced checks or wire transfers into or out of your account. Table 18-1 provides a list. All of these funds' costs are covered by their "expense ratios," i.e., the percentage of your account that they charge as a management fee. They do vary, so do some comparative shopping. If you would like to examine the full list of Treasury-only money-market funds, contact the following:

Weiss Ratings, Inc.
Website: www.weissratings.com
Email: wr@weissinc.com
Address: P.O. Box 109665, Palm Beach Gardens, FL
    33410
Phone: 800-289-9222 and 561-627-3300
Fax: 561-625-6685

See Appendix A for updated contact information

While I am comfortable saying that T-bills are the safest asset to hold inside the United States this side of gold and silver, *At the Crest of the Tidal Wave* warned that some day, even Treasury bills would probably become risky. If the dollar ever re-enters its long-term bear market, and particularly if it goes into free-fall, then even soaring short-term Treasury yields might not be able to overcome investors' imperative to get out. Each uptick in yield would be a yet greater burden to the government in the form of debt service, a fact that might frighten T-bill investors as much as entice them. If the federal government defaults, it might resort to a desperate action such as declaring that Treasury bills are now long-term bonds, to be paid off in ten years instead of ten weeks. You don't want to be stuck with any such deal.

If you come to believe that T-bills will get into trouble, you should buy safe foreign short-term debt or gold and silver to protect your capital. For details, see the next section and Chapter 22. Always be vigilant; always be practical; always try to get out of a potentially risky investment *before* others perceive that risk. If you need help, Elliott Wave International continuously monitors risks and opportunities in these markets from the standpoint of price trends and investor psychology.

Finding the Safest Cash Equivalents Outside the U.S.

For the globally sophisticated investor, there are excellent alternatives to U.S.-based debt. Most people hesitate to look outside their own areas, but if you have substantial capital to protect, you should expand your geographical horizons. The first reason is for the sake of diversity (*targeted* diversity, not the willy-nilly type), but there is a better reason: The safest investment debt resides within the safest financial systems.

Even if a debt-issuing *entity* is financially secure, events that are barely its fault might compromise it. For example, a manufacturer or municipality might be fully sound, except that it unwarily entrusts all its reserves to a single bank, and the bank fails. Suddenly, the issuing entity is in financial trouble, and its debt is much riskier.

So ideally, you should begin by identifying a country whose financial system is among the soundest available. According to SafeWealth Group, a firm of wealth preservation experts, *Switzerland* is the standout in this respect in Europe, and *Singapore* is the standout in Asia, currently and for the immediately foreseeable future.

Swiss voters are financially conservative. Under the Swiss Constitution, citizen-led referendums and initiatives can, and often do, challenge or revoke government policies or legislation, keeping excesses in check. Swiss citizens also have the highest savings rate in Europe, which helps liquefy the local banking system. Singapore issues little short-term debt because the government, with its conservative spending policy, doesn't need much short-term money. The country's bank reserves are strong because its citizens have a 25 percent savings rate mandated by law, which they routinely exceed. For comparison, the savings rate in the U.S. has fallen in the past 18 years from an average rate of 10 percent all the way down to zero. (Figures actually dropped to a 4 percent *negative* savings rate — i.e., spending exceeding income — but U.S. statisticians adjusted the definition of savings, so the lowest rate officially recognized to date is 0.2 percent of disposable income.) Moreover, each of these countries has a small total government debt relative to its financial base. Switzerland's national debt load is only about 170 billion Swiss francs, a fraction of the 3 trillion Sfr deposited in that country's banks, much of which would surely be freely available to refinance Swiss government debt given difficult times, when capital seeks conservative investments. Thus, while keeping in mind that politics can change, it appears at this time far less likely that a Swiss or Singaporean government entity will renege on its jurisdiction's obligations than perhaps any other government entities in the world.

The next step is to find the safest debt issues within one or both of the safest countries. In Switzerland, Swiss Money Market Claims (the equivalent of T-bills), near-term Swiss Confederation bonds and carefully selected cantonal (a canton is a state) bonds are probably as close to safe debt as you can get. Singapore's safest offerings are long-term government bonds with nearby maturities.

To be even safer, you will want to get more specific. While most Swiss cantons' paper has a top safety rating, the standard rating services, as we will see in Chapter 25, do not take the possibility of severe system-wide financial pressures into account. It is advisable, then, to invest in cantons that have little debt and whose bonds have a modicum of liquidity.

As you can probably tell by now, this is a field for specialists. I am not one of them. If you are a major institution or Arab oil magnate, you may already get good advice. But as far as I know, the SafeWealth Group is the best option. It has researched banks, insurance companies and debt issuers and isolated those that it believes have the highest level of safety on the planet. It has also identified wealth managers who focus primarily on protecting and preserving capital as opposed to aggressive growth with risk. Wherever you reside, if you would like to own a portfolio of the safest short-term foreign debt or even a fund of U.S. Treasury bills through a safe Swiss institution, this is a good place to start. Be aware that the available custodial institutions typically require minimum investments beginning at 100,000 Sfr or more. You may contact the firm as follows:

SafeWealth Group Service Center
Cari Lima, Senior Vice President
Email: clientservices@safewealthgroup.ch
Address: CP 476, 1000 Lausanne, 30 Grey, Switzerland
Phone: (from U.S. 011) 41-21-641-1640
Fax: (from U.S. 011) 41-21-641-1640-1390

See Appendix A for updated contact information

Equally comforting, SafeWealth traditionally counsels people as if a global financial disaster lay immediately around the corner, so you don't have to explain concerns that most investment counselors view as little different from paranoia. As the old saying goes, I may be paranoid, but that doesn't mean there isn't someone following me. In the final analysis, it is better to be safe and wrong than exposed and wrong.

Protecting Against Hyperinflation

When a state follows the course of printing banknotes rapidly to fund its spending, the result is hyperinflation. I expect deflation in the U.S., not inflation. Nevertheless, I conceded in Chapter 13 that monetary foresight cannot be 20/20. Also, you may live in a country that is in a position to hyperinflate.

If you face a currency-based hyperinflation, some aspects of your financial defense are substantially different from those that you will use to protect against deflation. For example, you do not want to hold *anything* denominated in the hyperinflating currency, and you do not want to sell local stocks short. You can protect yourself best with a portfolio of notes and bills denominated in stable foreign currencies, along with gold and silver (see Chapter 22).

Small investors in qualified countries outside Europe who are afraid of home currency hyperinflation have an option, too. The Prudent Safe Harbor Fund issues from the same fund family that offers the Prudent Bear Fund (see contact information in Chapter 20). This fund invests primarily in sovereign foreign notes and bonds of major European nations, but part of the fund (typically around 15 percent) is invested in gold stocks and gold bullion. The fund is also appropriate for Europeans who anticipate deflation. The minimum is an affordable $2000. Keep in mind that European currencies can fall in value, too, and interest rates for European bonds can fluctuate as much as those in other areas.

This fund is fine for some of your holdings, but you must be sure of your market analysis to use it for the bulk of your assets.

A Combination Strategy

Observe that one defense works for both a deflationary crash *and* a local hyperinflation: *holding notes and bills of strong issuers, denominated in a stable currency*. If you are worried about either deflation or hyperinflation in your country and want to protect against it, you should explore a mechanism through which you can hold a portfolio of the highest-grade near-term debt with the option of switching its denomination easily from one currency to another so that you can keep your money continuously lodged with the most conservative and stable governments. If you want to have a handle on the most likely future trends among the world's currencies, Elliott Wave International's services can help you. Of course, if a worldwide hyperinflation were to spare no currency at all, then precious metals would be your primary recourse. To prepare even for that remote possibility, you should also have a mechanism already in place to convert your holdings quickly to precious metals. If you can meet the minimums associated with their recommended institutions, SafeWealth Group can help you make all these arrangements under one roof. If you are a small investor, you can still achieve close to the desired result by choosing the most liquid banks, money market funds and precious metals available to you, using the lists and leads in this chapter and Chapters 19 and 22 as a guide.

Chapter 19:

How To Find a Safe Bank

Risks in Banking

Between 1929 and 1933, 9000 banks in the United States closed their doors. President Roosevelt shut down *all* banks for a short time after his inauguration. In December 2001, the government of Argentina froze virtually all bank deposits, barring customers from withdrawing the money they thought they had. Sometimes such restrictions happen naturally, when banks fail; sometimes they are imposed. Sometimes the restrictions are temporary; sometimes they remain for a long time.

Why do banks fail? For nearly 200 years, the courts have sanctioned an interpretation of the term "deposits" to mean *not* funds that you deliver for safekeeping but a *loan* to your bank. Your bank balance, then, is an IOU from the bank to you, even though there is no loan contract and no required interest payment. Thus, legally speaking, you have a claim on your money deposited in a bank, but practically speaking, you have a claim only on the loans that the bank makes with your money. If a large portion of those loans is tied up or becomes worthless, your money claim is compromised. A bank failure simply means that the bank has reneged on its promise to pay you back. The bottom line is that your money is only as safe as the bank's loans. In boom times, banks become imprudent and lend to almost anyone. In busts, they can't get much of that money back due to widespread defaults. If the bank's portfolio collapses in value, say, like those of the Savings & Loan institutions in the U.S. in the late 1980s and early 1990s, the bank is broke, and its depositors' savings are gone.

Because U.S. banks are no longer required to hold any of their deposits in reserve (see Chapter 10), many banks keep on hand just the bare minimum amount of cash needed for everyday transactions. Others keep a bit more. According to the latest Fed figures, the net loan-to-deposit ratio at U.S. commercial banks is 90 percent. This figure omits loans considered "securities" such as corporate, municipal and mortgage-backed bonds, which from my point of view are just as dangerous as everyday bank loans. The true loan-to-deposit ratio, then, is 125 percent and rising. Banks are not just lent to the hilt; they're past it. Some bank loans, at least in the current benign environment, could be liquidated quickly, but in a fearful market, liquidity even on these so-called "securities" will dry up. If just a few more depositors than normal were to withdraw money, banks would have to sell some of these assets, depressing prices and depleting the value of the securities remaining in their portfolios. If enough depositors were to attempt simultaneous withdrawals, banks would have to refuse. Banks with the lowest liquidity ratios will be particularly susceptible to runs in a depression. They may not be technically broke, but you still couldn't get your money, at least until the banks' loans were paid off.

You would think that banks would learn to behave differently with centuries of history to guide them, but for the most part, they don't. The pressure to show good earnings to stockholders and to offer competitive interest rates to depositors induces them to make risky loans. The Federal Reserve's monopoly powers have allowed U.S. banks to lend aggressively, so far without repercussion. For bankers to educate depositors about safety would be to disturb their main source of profits. The U.S. government's

Federal Deposit Insurance Corporation guarantees to refund depositors' losses up to $100,000, which *seems* to make safety a moot point. Actually, this guarantee just makes things far worse, for two reasons. First, it removes a major motivation for banks to be conservative with your money. Depositors feel safe, so who cares what's going on behind closed doors? Second, did you know that most of the FDIC's money comes from other banks? This funding scheme makes prudent banks pay to save the imprudent ones, imparting weak banks' frailty to the strong ones. When the FDIC rescues weak banks by charging healthier ones higher "premiums," overall bank deposits are depleted, causing the net loan-to-deposit ratio to rise. This result, in turn, means that in times of bank stress, *it will take a progressively smaller percentage of depositors to cause unmanageable bank runs.* If banks collapse in great enough quantity, the FDIC will be unable to rescue them all, and the more it charges surviving banks in "premiums," the more banks it will endanger. Thus, this form of insurance compromises the entire system. Ultimately, the federal government guarantees the FDIC's deposit insurance, which sounds like a sure thing. But if tax receipts fall, the government will be hard pressed to save a large number of banks with its own diminishing supply of capital. The FDIC calls its sticker "a symbol of confidence," and that's exactly what it is.

Some states in the U.S., in a fit of deadly "compassion," have made it illegal for a bank to seize the home of someone who has declared bankruptcy. In such situations, the bank and its depositors are on the hook indefinitely for a borrower's unthrift. Other states have made it illegal for a bank attempting to recover the value of a loan to seize any of a defaulting mortgage holder's assets other than the mortgaged property. In such situations, the bank assumes the price risk in the real estate market. These states' banks are vulnerable to severe losses in their mortgage portfolios and are at far greater risk of failure.

Many major national and international banks around the world have huge portfolios of "emerging market" debt, mortgage debt, consumer debt and weak corporate debt. I cannot understand how a bank trusted with the custody of your money could ever even *think* of buying bonds issued by Russia or Argentina or any other unstable or spendthrift government. As *At the Crest of the Tidal Wave* put it in 1995, "Today's emerging markets will soon be *sub*merging markets." That metamorphosis began two years later. The fact that banks and other investment companies can repeatedly ride such "investments" all the way down to *write-offs* is outrageous.

Many banks today also have a shockingly large exposure to leveraged derivatives such as futures, options and even more exotic instruments. The underlying value of assets represented by such financial derivatives at quite a few big banks is greater than the total value of all their deposits. The estimated representative value of all derivatives in the world today is $90 trillion, over half of which is held by U.S. banks. Many banks use derivatives to hedge against investment exposure, but that strategy works only if the speculator on the other side of the trade can pay off if he's wrong.

Relying upon, or worse, speculating in, leveraged derivatives poses one of the greatest risks to banks that have succumbed to the lure. Leverage almost *always* causes massive losses eventually because of the psychological stress that owning them induces. You have already read of the tremendous debacles at Barings Bank, Long-Term [sic] Capital Management, Enron and other institutions due to speculating in leveraged derivatives. It is traditional to discount the representative value of derivatives because traders will presumably get out of losing positions well before they cost as much as what they represent. Well, maybe. It is at least as common a human reaction for speculators to double their bets when the market goes against a big position. At least, that's what bankers might do with your money.

Today's bank analysts assure us, as a headline from *The Atlanta Journal-Constitution* put it on December 29, 2001, that "Banks [Are] Well-Capitalized." Banks today are indeed generally considered well capitalized compared to their situation in the 1980s. Unfortunately, that condition is mostly thanks to the great asset mania of the 1990s, which, as explained in Book One, is probably over. Much of the record amount of credit that banks have extended, such as that lent for productive enterprise or directly to strong governments, is relatively safe. Much of what has been lent to weak governments, real estate developers, government-sponsored enterprises, stock market speculators, venture capitalists, consumers (via credit cards and consumer-debt "investment" packages), and so on, is not. One expert advises, "The larger, more diversified banks at this point are the safer place to be." That assertion will surely be severely tested in the coming depression.

There are five major conditions in place at many banks that pose a danger: (1) low liquidity levels, (2) dangerous exposure to leveraged derivatives, (3) the optimistic safety ratings of banks' debt investments, (4) the inflated values of the property that borrowers have put up as collateral on loans and (5) the substantial size of the mortgages that their clients hold compared both to those property values and to the clients' potential inability to pay under adverse circumstances. All of these conditions compound the risk to the banking system of deflation and depression.

Financial companies are enjoying big advances in the current stock market rally. Depositors today trust their banks more than they trust government or business in general. For example, a recent poll asked web surfers which among a list of seven types of institutions they would most trust to operate a secure identity service. Banks got nearly 50 percent of the vote. General bank trustworthiness is yet another faith that will be shattered in a depression.

Well before a worldwide depression dominates our daily lives, you will need to deposit your capital into safe institutions. I suggest using two or more to spread the risk even further. They must be far better than the ones that today are too optimistically deemed "liquid" and "safe" by rating services and banking officials.

Safe Banking in the United States

If you must bank in the U.S., or if you prefer it, choose the best bank(s) available. I believe that even in a deflationary crash, many of the safest U.S. banks have a good shot at survival and even prosperity. The reason is that relatively safe banks, if they have the sense to inform the public of their safety advantage, are likely to become *even safer* during difficult times. Why? Because depositors in a developing financial crisis will move funds out of the weakest banks into the strongest ones, making the weak ones weaker and the strong ones stronger. One of the great ironies of banking is that the more liquid a bank, the less likely it is that depositors will conduct a run on it in the first place.

Weiss Ratings, Inc. provides one of the most reliable bank-rating services in America. (See Chapter 18 or the last section of this book for contact information.) CEO Martin Weiss has graciously consented to provide a practical guide for this book. Table 19-1 lists what his researchers consider the two strongest banks in each state in the union. Table 19-2 lists what they consider the 24 strongest *large* banks in the U.S. For our purposes, I see little point in listing the weakest banks, but if you want to know which ones they are, you can find them listed in the brand-new *Ultimate Safe Money Guide*, by Martin Weiss (John Wiley & Sons, 2002). Weiss' book is a good complement to this one for many reasons. Aside from banks and insurance companies (see Chapter 24), his firm also rates mutual funds, brokerage firms, HMOs and corporations with common stock.

THE TWO HIGHEST-RATED BANKS IN EACH STATE
Source: TheStreet.com Ratings, Inc. (based on 9/30/01 data)

Name	City	State	Total Assets in millions	TheStreet Safety Rating
Alabama				
FIRST NB OF SCOTTSBORO	SCOTTSBORO	AL	284.74	A-
FIRST UNITED SECURITY BANK	THOMASVILLE	AL	513.4	B+
Alaska				
FIRST NB ALASKA	ANCHORAGE	AK	1779.6	A+
MOUNT MCKINLEY MSB	FAIRBANKS	AK	174.1	A
Arizona				
SEARS NB	TEMPE	AZ	178.4	A-
MOHAVE ST BK	LAKE HAVASU CITY	AZ	160.7	A-
Arkansas				
FIRST NB OF FT SMITH	FORT SMITH	AR	633.8	A-
FIRST FEDERAL BANK OF AR	HARRISON	AR	697.7	B+
California				
FARMERS & MERCHANTS BK	LONG BEACH	CA	2094.0	A+
SAVINGS BK OF MENDOCINO CTY	UKIAH	CA	519.8	A+
Colorado				
AMERICAN BUSINESS BK NA	DENVER	CO	878.0	A-
ALPINE BANK	GLENWOOD SPRINGS	CO	883.5	B+
Connecticut				
NEW HAVEN SVGS BK	NEW HAVEN	CT	2223.9	A+
AMERICAN SVGS BK	NEW BRITAIN	CT	1907.9	A+
Delaware				
PNC BANK	WILMINGTON	DE	2417.4	A-
CITIBANK-DELAWARE	NEW CASTLE	DE	6290.9	B+
District of Columbia				
NATIONAL CAPITAL BK OF WA	WASHINGTON	DC	153.2	A+
ADAMS NB	WASHINGTON	DC	168.2	A-
Florida				
HARBOR FEDERAL SVGS BK	FORT PIERCE	FL	1747.6	A+
MELLON UNITED NB	MIAMI	FL	1555.4	A-
Georgia				
COLUMBUS B&TC	COLUMBUS	GA	3747.5	A-
MAIN STREET BK	COVINGTON	GA	1075.9	A-
Hawaii				
BANK OF HAWAII	HONOLULU	HI	10,085.2	B+
CENTRAL PACIFIC BANK	HONOLULU	HI	1860.7	B+
Idaho				
BANK OF COMMERCE	IDAHO FALLS	ID	431.5	A+
IDAHO INDEPENDENT BK	COEUR D'ALENE	ID	278.4	B+
Illinois				
CORUS BK NA	CHICAGO	IL	2568.6	A
COMMERCE BK NA	PEORIA	IL	917.9	B+
Indiana				
FIRST SOURCE BK	SOUTH BEND	IN	3362.1	A-
TERRE HAUTE FIRST NB	TERRE HAUTE	IN	1299.3	B+
Iowa				
WEST DES MOINES ST BK	W DES MOINES	IA	807.5	A-
HILLS B&TC	HILLS	IA	885.8	B+

Table 19-1   (*see updated list in Appendix B*)

Kansas				
VALLEY VIEW ST BK	CLEVELAND PARK	KS	557.2	A+
CAPITOL FEDERAL SAVINGS BK	TOPEKA	KS	8666.0	A-
Kentucky				
AREA BK	OWENSBORO	KY	2625.7	A-
BANK OF LOUISVILLE	LOUISVILLE	KY	1679.1	B+
Louisana				
WHITNEW NB OF NEW ORLEANS	NEW ORLEANS	LA	6874.3	B+
HANCOCK BK OF LOUISIANA	BATON ROUGE	LA	1348.8	B+
Maine				
KENNEBECK SVGS BK	AUGUSTA	ME	404.0	B+
OCEAN NB	KENNEBUNK	ME	276.2	B+
Maryland				
PENINSULA BK	PRINCESS ANNE	MD	702.7	A+
WESTMINSTER UNION BK	WESTMINSTER	MD	544.1	A+
Massachusetts				
BRISTOL COUNTY SVGS BK	TAUNTON	MA	679.1	A+
COUNTRY BK FOR SVGS	WARE	MA	772.6	A
Michigan				
CHEMICAL B&TC	MIDLAND	MI	1479.7	A
CHEMICAL BK WET	CADILLAC	MI	762.3	A
Minnesota				
FIRST NB OF BEMIDJI	BEMIDJI	MN	305.0	A+
MIDWAY NB OF ST PAUL	ST PAUL	MN	437.3	B+
Mississippi				
TRUSTMARK NB	JACKSON	MS	6834.8	A-
NATIONAL BK OF COMMERCE	STARKVILLE	MS	1027.8	A-
Missouri				
BANK MIDWEST NA	KANSAS CITY	MO	2696.9	A-
COMMERCE BK NA	KANSAS CITY	MO	10363.6	B+
Montana				
YELLOWSTONE BK	LAUREL	MT	242.5	A+
FIRST SECURITY BK	BOZEMAN	MT	295.6	A-
Nebraska				
PINNACLE BK	PAPILLION	NE	1386.9	B+
FIVE POINTS BK	GRAND ISLAND	NE	323.8	B+
Nevada				
HOUSEHOLD BK NEVADA NA	LAS VEGAS	NV	1591.3	A-
FIRST NB OF ELY	ELY	NV	38.5	B+
New Hampshire				
MEREDITH VILLAGE SVGS BK	MEREDITH	NH	314.2	B+
CLAREMONT SVGS BK	CLAREMONT	NH	241.6	B+
New Jersey				
HUDSON CITY SVGS BK	PARAMUS	NJ	10815.4	A+
KEARNY FSB	KEARNY	NJ	1176.8	A
New Mexico				
WESTERN COMMERCE BK	CARLSBAD	NM	256.6	A-
FIRST NATIONAL BANK - SANTA FE	SANTA FE	NM	339.6	B+
New York				
MASPETH FS&LA	MASPETH	NY	1093.8	A+
SUMITOMO TR & BNKG CO USA	NEW YORK	NY	973.8	A+
North Carolina				
PIEDMONT FS&LA	WINSTON-SALEM	NC	811.0	A
HIGH POINT B&TC	HIGH POINT	NC	567.6	A

Table 19-1 (cont'd)

North Dakota				
GATE CITY BANK	FARGO	ND	676.6	B+
FARMERS & MRCH BK VALLEY CIT	VALLEY CITY	ND	87.5	B+
Ohio				
PEOPLES BK NA	MARIETTA	OH	1165.4	A-
FARMERS NB OF CANFIELD	CANFIELD	OH	642.6	A-
Oklahoma				
FIRST NB&TC MCALESTER	MCALESTER	OK	440.0	A
RCB BK	CLAREMORE	OK	574.6	A-
Oregon				
KLAMATH FIRST FS&LA	KLAMATH FALLS	OR	1419.2	B+
WEST COAST BK	LAKE OSWEGO	OR	1384.2	B+
Pennsylvania				
OMEGA BK NA	STATE COLLEGE	PA	628.5	A+
FIRST NB&TC	NEWTOWN	PA	501.1	A
Rhode Island				
CENTREVILLE SVGS BK	W WARWICK	RI	645.5	A
FIRST B&TC	PROVIDENCE	RI	173.5	A-
South Carolina				
ENTERPRISE BK S CAROLINA	EHRHARDT	SC	252.6	A+
CONWAY NB	CONWAY	SC	512.0	A-
South Dakota				
PIONEER B&TC	BELLE FOURCHE	SD	269.6	A
FIRST WESTERN BANK	STURGIS	SD	260.8	A-
Tennessee				
HOME FEDERAL BANK OF TN	KNOXVILLE	TN	1427.2	A
FIRST FARMERS & MERCHANTS NB	COLIMBIA	TN	824.8	A-
Texas				
CITIZENS 1ST BK	TYLER	TX	505.8	A+
AMARILLO NB	AMARILLO	TX	1372.9	A-
Utah				
MORGAN STANLEY DEAN WITTER B	W VALLEY CITY	UT	2709.6	A-
ADVANTA BK CORP	DRAPER	UT	1003.2	A-
Vermont				
MERCHANTS BK	BURLINGTON	VT	784.7	B+
UNION BK	MORRISVILLE	VT	224.9	B+
Virginia				
BURKE & HERBERT B&TC	ALEXANDRIA	VA	854.8	A+
AMERICAN NB&TC	DANVILLE	VA	564.3	A+
Washington				
WASHINGTON FS&LA	SEATTLE	WA	6991.1	A+
HORIZON BK	BELLINGHAM	WA	743.4	A+
West Virginia				
BANK OF CHARLES TOWN	CHARLES TOWN	WV	167.7	A
WESBANCO BK	WHEELING	WV	2451.1	A-
Wisconsin				
NATIONAL EXCHANGE B&TC	FOND DU LAC	WI	721.4	A
TRI CITY NB	OAK CREEK	WI	583.4	A
Wyoming				
WELLS FARGO BK WY NA	CASPER	WY	2542.1	B+
PINNACLE BK WY	TORRINGTON	WY	316.6	B+

Table 19-1 (cont'd)

STRONGEST LARGE BANKS IN AMERICA			
Source: Weiss Ratings, Inc. (based on 9/30/01 data)			
Bank Name	State	Weiss Safety Rating	Total Assets (in millions of $)
Apple Bk for Svgs	NY	A-	6,117
Bancorpsouth Bk	MS	B+	9,390
Bank of Tokyo Mitsubishi TC	NY	A-	4,128
Capital Federal Savings Bank	KS	A	8,423
Central Carolina B&TC	NC	B+	9,489
Citibank-Delaware	DE	B+	6,160
Columbus B&TC	GA	A-	3,353
Comerica Bk-Texas	TX	B+	3,803
Commerce Bk NA	MO	B+	9,867
Emigrant Svg Bk	NY	A	8,535
First Charter NB	NC	B+	3,061
First Commonwealth Bk	PA	B+	3,430
First Source Bk	IN	A-	3,148
Hudson City Svgs Bk	NJ	A+	9,618
Israel Discount Bk of NY	NY	B+	5,695
Mercantile Safe Deposit & TC	MD	A	3,489
North Fork Bk	NY	B+	14,685
Sanwa Bk Calfornia	CA	B+	9,013
Trustmark NB	MS	A-	6,822
Union Bk of CA NA	CA	B+	35,467
United States TC of NY	NY	B+	3,988
Valley NB	NJ	B+	7,957
Washington FS&LA	WA	A+	6,990
Whitney NB of New Orleans	LA	B+	6,630

Table 19-2   *(see updated list in Appendix B)*

There are other independent and reliable bank rating sources. Among them, Veribanc, Inc. has been in the ratings business the longest. The service covers banks, S&Ls and credit unions. The company's classifications rank financial institutions not just on their present standing but also on their future outlook, which is what you should care about. Using a clear, simple rating system, it assesses capital strength, asset quality, management ability, earnings sufficiency, liquidity and sensitivity to market risk.

IDC Financial Publishing, Inc. also publishes highly specific and easy-to-interpret quarterly financial ratings that track the financial safety of U.S.-based banks, savings and loan institutions and credit unions. You will find their contact information below:

See Appendix A for updated contact information

Veribanc, Inc.
Website: www.veribanc.com
Email: service@veribanc.com
Address: P.O. Box 1610, Woonsocket, RI 02895
Phone: 800-837-4226/800-442-2657
Fax: 781-246-5291

See Appendix A for updated contact information

IDC Financial Publishing, Inc.
Website: www.idcfp.com
Email: info@idcfp.com
Address: P.O. Box 140, Hartland, WI 53029
Phone: 800-525-5457 and 262-367-7231
Fax: 262-367-6497

If, despite all your precautions, you come to suspect that any of your chosen banks face the risk of closure, move your money to a safer bank immediately. If you cannot identify a safer bank, then do not hesitate to withdraw all of your money in cash. If you are not first in line, you may forfeit the opportunity.

Safe Banking Worldwide

A free market in banking would provide every imaginable service, from 100% safekeeping for a fee to 100% lending with a large return. To preserve their reputations, bankers would have an incentive to be extremely careful with your money. Monopoly money and regulated banking have produced quite another result. Nevertheless, there still exist a few banks in the world that mainly provide a wealth preservation service as opposed to interest income and daily transactional conveniences. If you want the utmost safety for capital storage, if a bit less convenience, you must use these banks. The safest banking institutions in the world reside in countries that (1) do not have, and are unlikely to impose, exchange controls or wealth transfer restrictions and (2) have a low ratio of illiquid debts to deposits. Not surprisingly, the top candidates are the same as those with the safest debt: Switzerland and Singapore.

Nevertheless, do not fall into the trap of choosing any Swiss bank just because it's Swiss. Today's largest Swiss banks, with their fat portfolios of derivatives, are at immense risk of failure if a depression occurs. Furthermore, they have branches worldwide and are thus vulnerable to the whims of numerous governments. The best course of action is to locate smaller, safer local Swiss banks. Austria's low debt per capita makes it a good backup alternative. If you want to find a safe bank, these jurisdictions are the place to begin.

Using stringent bank-rating requirements, SafeWealth Group has identified banks in these countries that earn its highest rating for survivability in a global depression. This "Class 1" rating requires an aggressively discounted liquidity ratio of at least 75 percent, an otherwise nearly unheard-of 35 percent net liquid equity ratio (i.e., the percentage of a bank's capital that is free and accessible at all times), a low derivatives/capital ratio, no derivatives held for the bank's account on a speculative basis, a low amount of deposits held at other banks and that the bank operate in a single nation so that the rules it must follow are clearly defined.

A 75 percent aggressively discounted liquidity ratio means that deposits are held in such liquid investments that even if the bank were suddenly faced with demands from depositors to withdraw 75 percent of the total money in the bank, given a few days or weeks, it could do so. There are even a very few banks in the world with liquidity ratios at or above 100 percent. In other words, they could pay off *all* their depositors, *in full*, on very short notice. Many banks couldn't pay off 10 percent of their depositors quickly, and the world's weakest banks would be hard-pressed to service *any* above-normal level of simultaneous withdrawals. And that is in *today's* benign financial environment, never mind a depression environment.

If you are serious about safety and can meet a recommended bank's account minimum, you should set up a relationship with a Class 1 bank. SafeWealth Group can help you cut through red tape to establish relationships with such banks and other institutions. The reason you need to go through a representative is that these private Swiss banks do not readily accept accounts from any individual, corporation or trust representative that walks through the door, a policy that reflects their general conservatism. They will accept a new account only if its ownership and purpose are completely above board and will not endanger the bank's reputation. If you meet these standards, SafeWealth Group can secure the proper introductions for you in most cases and guide you through the process. (See Chapter 18 or the final section of this book for contact information and typical minimums.) If you are a Swiss or Singaporean resident and have ready access to such institutions, by all means stay put as long as local politics remain stable.

Act While You Can

When it comes to safety, it is always best to act early. Due largely to aggressive governmental policing of illegal activities such as the drug trade, money laundering, tax evasion and terrorist financing, average honest people do not enjoy the free, ready access to financial institutions that they did a few years ago. Some banks are now obliged to meet with prospective clients in person to satisfy suitability rules. There can be little doubt that if a crisis climate comes to pass, you could face many more obstacles if not outright denial of service. If you are truly intent on preserving your wealth, you should resist the temptation to procrastinate under the presumption that you can rely on the status quo. Opportunities close down all the time. For example, the two safest banks in London no longer accept non-British clients. In the U.S., the bank deemed the safest in the nation two years ago no longer takes out-of-state accounts. A few of my prudent subscribers got in after I recommended it, but now the procrastinators have to look elsewhere. This is a lesson. Don't delay, or the institutions now available to protect your savings may close their doors to you. Another word of warning: Bank ratings can change. The smart approach is to keep in touch with the services that rate banks seriously to make sure your bank(s) continue to qualify for a high safety rating.

Once you move the bulk of your investment funds into the safest cash equivalents, and after you have chosen a safe bank or two for savings and transactions, then and only then should you consider speculating in the stock market with a small portion of your capital. That is the subject of the next chapter.

Chapter 20:

Should You Speculate in Stocks?

Perhaps the number one precaution to take at the start of a deflationary crash is to make sure that your investment capital is *not* invested "long" in stocks, stock mutual funds, stock index futures, stock options or any other equity-based investment or speculation. That advice alone should be worth the time you spent to read this book.

In 2000 and 2001, countless Internet stocks fell from $50 or $100 a share to near zero in a matter of months. In 2001, Enron went from $85 to pennies a share in less than a year. These are the early casualties of debt, leverage and incautious speculation. Countless investors, including the managers of insurance companies, pension funds and mutual funds, express great confidence that their "diverse holdings" will keep major portfolio risk at bay. Aside from piles of questionable debt, what are those diverse holdings? Stocks, stocks and more stocks. Despite current optimism that the bull market is back, there will be many more casualties to come when stock prices turn back down again.

Don't presume that the Fed will rescue the stock market, either. In theory, the Fed could declare a support price for certain stocks, but which ones? And how much money would it commit to buying them? If the Fed were actually to buy equities or stock-index futures, the temporary result might be a brief rally, but the ultimate result would be a collapse in the value of the Fed's own assets when the market turned back down, making the

Fed look foolish and compromising its primary goals, as cited in
Chapter 13. It wouldn't want to keep repeating that experience.
The bankers' pools of 1929 gave up on this strategy, and so will
the Fed if it tries it.

Short Selling Stocks and Trading in Futures and Options

Short selling is a great idea at the onset of a deflationary
depression, at least from a *timing* standpoint. Shares of vulnerable banks and other financial companies in particular are a
great downside bet. The current stock-market rally, so far a piti-
fully weak response to record Fed-induced liquidity in 2001, is
providing a great general short-selling opportunity, per all the
evidence in Chapters 6 and 7. You should avoid shorting special
situations such as defense and natural resource stocks, which
can move counter-trend, or at least fall less precipitously, when
international tensions rise. Buying "leaps," which are long-term
puts, on stocks and stock indexes would be a fine speculation.
If you do not already know by experience what the terms "short
selling" and "leaps" mean, I recommend that you avoid engaging
in these activities.

Unfortunately, there could well be *structural* risks in
dealing with stocks and associated derivatives during a major
retrenchment. Trading stocks, options and futures could be extremely problematic during a stock market panic. One reason is
that trading systems tend to break down when volume surges and
the system's operators become emotional. When the exchange
floor became a hurricane of paper in 1929, it would sometimes
take days to sort out who had bought and sold what and then
determine whether investors and traders could afford to pay for
their positions. You can experience the turmoil vicariously in
any good history of the 1929 crash. To give you a flavor of what
goes on, read this description, from one of my subscribers, of the
tumult during a comparatively mild panic forty years ago:

I worked for Merrill Lynch in New York in 1962 during the collapse. I well recall the failure of the teletype in our office and inexperienced clerks calling in the orders to the main office. I recall many of the screw-ups: buys called in as sells and vice versa. Some stocks had nicknames like Bessie (Bethlehem Steel), Peggy (Public Service Electric and Gas), and I recall the clerks calling in the orders by the stocks' nicknames and the person on the other end not knowing what the hell they were talking about. All the while, the market was collapsing.

Do you think investors and brokers will behave differently now that so much stock trading is done on-line? I don't. Do you think the experience will be "smoother" because modern computers are involved? I don't. In fact, today's system — much improved, to be sure — is nevertheless a recipe for an even bigger mess during a panic. Investors will be so nervous that they will screw up their orders. Huge volume will clog website servers, disrupting orders entered on-line. Orders may go in, but confirmations may not come out. A trader *might not know* if his sale or purchase went through. Is he in or out? Quote systems will falter at just the wrong time. Phone lines from you to the broker and from the broker to the floor will be jammed, and some will go down. Computer technicians will be working overtime while being distracted worrying about their own investments. Brokers will be operating on little sleep and at peak agitation, since most brokers are themselves bullish speculators. They will be entering orders wrong. Firms will begin to enact and enforce tighter restrictions on trading and margin. Price gaps will trigger stops at prices beyond the ability of some account holders to pay. You, the wise short seller, could survive all these problems only to discover that your broker has gone bankrupt or has been shut down by the SEC or that its associated bank has had a computer breakdown or that its assets are depleted or frozen.

Unless you are prepared for such an environment, don't get suckered into this maelstrom thinking that the bear market will be business as usual, just in the other direction. If you want to try making a killing being short in the collapse, make sure that you are not overexposed. Make sure that if the system locks up for days or weeks, you will not be in a panic yourself. Make sure that in a worst-case scenario, the funds you place at risk are funds you could lose.

Inverse Index ("Short") Mutual Funds

A somewhat more conservative speculation would be to invest in inverse index funds, also called short funds or bear funds, which are bets on falling stock indexes. These funds go up in value as stock index futures fall in value, and vice versa. I recommended inverse index funds in *The Dick Davis Digest* for both 2000 and 2001, and they beat everything else both years. The stock market should have several more down years ahead, and bigger ones at that.

In the U.S., you will find inverse S&P index funds at Rydex and ProFunds. Rydex has Ursa, which is the largest inverse index fund available, and ProFunds has the Bear ProFund. Rydex also has Arktos, which moves inversely to the NASDAQ 100 Index.

For seasoned speculators who can time the market well, Rydex offers Tempest, which is *doubly* short the S&P index, and Venture Fund, which is doubly short the NASDAQ 100. Also, they may be traded twice a day, not just at the close. ProFunds has the UltraBear fund and the UltraShort OTC fund, which are doubly short the S&P and NASDAQ 100, respectively. I am serious about using such funds *only if you are already a seasoned speculator*. You must be extra careful any time you use leverage, because leverage heightens your emotions, making them an even worse enemy to success.

The companies that offer short funds also offer money market funds and "long" index funds too, so with a brief phone call, you can easily move your money to take advantage of swings in either direction or "park" it for safety. Speaking of parking, Rydex's money market fund owns only instruments issued, guaranteed or backed by the U.S. government or its agencies or instrumentalities, making it safer than the average money market fund.

For information on these two mutual fund companies, contact the following:

See Appendix A for updated contact information

Ursa Fund, Arktos Fund, Tempest Fund, Venture Fund
Website: www.rydexfunds.com
Address: Rydex Series Funds, 9601 Blackwell Rd,
Suite 500, Rockville, MD 20850
Phone: 800-820-0888 and 301-296-5406
Minimum: $10,000

See Appendix A for updated contact information

Bear ProFund, UltraBear, UltraShort 100
Website: www.profunds.com
Address: ProFunds, 7501 Wisconsin Ave, Suite 1000,
Bethesda, MD 20814
Phone: 888-776-1970 or 240-497-6400
Minimum: $15,000

Before you invest in bear index funds, you need to understand something important about how they work, which can be a good or bad thing, depending upon the market environment. Holders of shares make money depending upon the short-term *percentage change* that the market undergoes each day or half day. In a persistently trending market, this situation is better than a short sale. Theoretically, the market can go down five percent per week indefinitely. If the market does fall a long way in a straight line, these funds could compound your return well beyond that of a normal short sale, which at most can gain 100 percent. Also, while the shares of these funds lose value in an up market, they do not lose all of their value, as a short sale can when a stock doubles.

On the other hand, this attribute in some circumstances can present a big problem. To understand it, follow this example: You invest $100,000 in a doubly leveraged short S&P 500 fund with the index at 1000, which is a $200,000 short S&P 500 exposure. The next day, the index rises 10%, so you have lost $20,000. The short fund automatically resets your exposure to twice your equity at the end of the day, so your new exposure is short $160,000. The next day, the index returns to 1000, but your equity rises only to $94,545 because the percentage decline from the higher level is only 9.09 percent, and you didn't have enough exposure on the way back to make up your initial loss. The index is unchanged, but you lost money. The same negative result occurs when the index initially goes your way and then returns to its starting point. Critics call this attribute "beta slippage." This problem is compounded when markets are in a trading range and further when leveraged funds reset twice a day. Since markets do tend to fluctuate a lot, this is usually a negative attribute for long-term investors. To make these funds work in all environments, you have to be a short-term market timer. Being a successful one when you are restricted to trading in and out only once or twice a day *at a particular time* is nearly impossible. If you can do it, then use these vehicles. If not, there is an alternative to the rescue.

Customized Dynamic Index Allocation

The brainchild of Stanford M.B.A. Robert R. Champion, Bermuda-based Invesdex, Ltd has developed an Internet-based instrument called MarketPlus, which is a liquid, fully asset-backed over-the-counter investment contract that has the look and feel of an online trading account. It offers a selection of major world equity and debt indexes, currencies, commodities, and a money-market index. You create your own return parameters by customizing your contract to the performance of one or more of these assets, long or short. You also get to choose the leverage you want, from zero (conservative) up to 3-to-1. To avoid beta slippage, your exposure is normally not reset unless and until you choose to do so. You can adjust allocations as often as every half-hour, far more often than index funds allow. This frequency is somewhat restricted compared to a futures account, but with MarketPlus, you cannot lose more than your investment because the system resets your exposure to your initial ratio if your loss exceeds certain limits. What's more, all gains — even when indexed to the money-market rate — are capital gains and are not taxed until funds are withdrawn from the instrument. To invest in MarketPlus, you must be a professional financial adviser, money manager or experienced "Qualified Investor," which means that you must have a net worth in excess of US$1 million and be able to invest at least US$100,000 in the contract. Currently available only to non-U.S. investors, MarketPlus is due to become available to U.S. investors later in 2002. For information, contact the following:

Invesdex, Ltd
Website: www.invesdex.com
Email: info@invesdex.com
Address: P.O. Box HM 1788, Hamilton HM HX,
        Bermuda
Phone: 441-296-4400
Fax: 441-295-2377
President & CEO: Valere B. Costello
Minimum: $100,000

See Appendix A for updated contact information

Managed Bear Funds

You may also wish to consider a portfolio of short or hedged stocks, managed by an expert. Actively managed bearish stock funds are designed to benefit from a declining stock market.

There are very few around today because the stock mania of the 1990s drove most of them out of business. The public hasn't been interested; in fact, it has moved money out of bear funds since the 2000 top! A few courageous money managers have maintained this alternative.

One example in the U.S. is the Prudent Bear Fund, which maintains short positions in individual stocks and indexes and also buys put options. The fund is about 70 percent short. This short percentage typically does not vary greatly, says president David Tice. The fund maintains some long positions, which account for up to 15 percent of its assets. Longs include special situations such as shares of certain small-cap companies and natural resource stocks such as gold and silver mining companies. The fund is no-load. It is about $200 million in size. Tice is fully apprised of the long-term risk in the stock market and the financial world.

Another example is the Comstock Capital Value Fund, which is positioned to profit from a declining market with a combination of index puts and shorts of both individual stocks and stock futures. With the leverage of puts taken into account, the fund is the equivalent of over 100 percent short. The fund also has positions in long-term U.S. Treasury bonds and the Euro currency. The firm's other fund is the Comstock Strategy Fund, which is conservatively positioned to benefit from a bear market, using puts to approximate a 70% net short position. The funds' managers, Charles Minter and Martin Weiner, have been writing free web commentary which (amazingly) calls for a long-term bear market in a deflationary environment. You can read it free on their website.

Another bear fund is the Gabelli Mathers Fund. Manager Henry van der Eb takes a conservative approach, making it attractive if you are unconvinced of the bear's imminence or ultimate severity. The fund also offers tax-sheltered gains due to tax-loss carry-forwards, "earned" during the bull market.

For information on these funds, contact the following:
Prudent Bear Fund
Website: www.prudentbear.com
Email: info@prudentbear.com
Address: 8140 Walnut Hill Lane, Suite 300,
Dallas, TX 75231
Phone: 800-711-1848 and 214-696-5474
Manager: David Tice
Minimum: $2000

Comstock Capital Value Fund and Strategy Fund
Website: www.comstockfunds.com
Email: info@comstockfunds.com
Address: 24 S. Main St, Yardley PA 19067
Phone: 215-493-7076
Fax: 215-493-8083
Managers: Charles Minter and Martin Weiner
Minimum $1000

Gabelli Mathers Fund
Website: www.gabelli.com/mathers.html
Email: info@gabelli.com
Address: One Corporate Center, Rye NY 10580
Phone: 800-422-3554
Manager: Henry van der Eb
Minimum: $1000

Insurance-Based Manager Combinations

Well-heeled investors in the United States have an interesting option. Access Fund Management LLC ("AFM") offers qualified purchasers multi-manager portfolios within private-placement insurance products. AFM utilizes the Performex® Proprietary Analytical System, which maintains the track records of thousands of managers and among them profiles a number of theoretically idealized allocations.

AFM has set up what it calls *market-neutral* strategies. Its methodology allocates assets among several equity and hedge fund managers, including those with a successful record of selecting securities to buy long and others with a successful record of selecting securities to sell short. The expectation is that those managers investing in the direction of the market do extremely well, while the other managers' selection expertise mitigates losses on their counter-trend positions. Ideally, the market is thereby "neutralized," so you get good stock selection on both sides without one-sided exposure to market-trend risk.

According to its reports, Performex®-based investment structures have had strong gains in both rising and falling markets in recent years. Of course, such performance can change.

The insurance product embodying multi-manager allocations provides tax-deferred growth for qualified purchasers. Under current law, some states also provide asset protection from creditors within this type of insurance product. Although I am convinced that the safest insurance companies are in Switzerland, AFM says it chooses only North American insurance companies with high financial ratings. It further points out that each policy's assets are held in separate custodial accounts at stock exchange member firms utilized by the individual investment managers. These separate accounts are not subject to claims by general creditors of the insurance companies, increasing the qualified buyer's overall safety. When choosing such products, make sure that its specific arrangements meet your safety requirements.

The minimum investment for this insurance alternative is high, at $1,000,000. These portfolio structures are also available for taxable and retirement accounts (IRAs, 401Ks, etc.), which have a minimum investment level of half that amount. Access Fund Management LLC can be reached as follows:

See Appendix A for updated contact information

Access Fund Management, LLC

Address: 28050 Highway 19 North, Suite 301,
          Clearwater, FL 33761

Phone: (800) 638-5760

Fax: (877) 577-6744

Contact name: Michael V. Williams

Email: info@AccessFundManagement.com

Portfolio Managers Who Are Not Afraid To Be Bearish

You can also find portfolio managers who are not afraid to be bearish. There are surely many in the world. I personally know of only a few, and they may or may not be the best. In the U.S., examples are Lang Asset Management (www.langasset.com), which selects medium-to-large-cap stocks that look overpriced and shorts them, staying reasonably fully invested, sometimes "hedging" with options or by other means. In Asia, Marc Faber Ltd. (www.gloomboomdoom.com), and in Europe, Zulauf Asset Management AG (Grafenauweg 4, CH-6300 Zug, Switzerland; phone: (US: 011) 41-41-724-57-01), provide bearishly oriented management. Minimum funding requirements range between $100,000 and $3 million. [*Note for 2009: See Appendix A for five newly added management services.—Ed.*]

To find more leads, check out the Hedge Fund Association at http://www.thehfa.org and Planet Hedge Fund at http://planethedgefund.com/catlinks/indi.html. Hedge funds are only as good as their managers. Some fund managers use huge leverage and can "blow up," losing everything on a bad bet. The more spectacular of those make the newspapers; there are others that just go quietly. If you want to go this route, choose wisely and make sure that you satisfy yourself that the money manager you choose deals with safe banks. I have not investigated that aspect of any of these funds.

Temporary Opportunity?

The opportunity to make money on the downside in a deflationary crash can hardly be overstated, because *you will be making more dollars as the value of dollars* is soaring. It's a double benefit. Will it always be there?

I recall only one time when authorities banned buying in a bull market. The Comex futures exchange banned orders "to open" in silver futures in January 1980 to save their own skins, since many exchange members were short. Most investors were long, so their only allowed course was to sell. By changing the rules, the exchange profited and investors got killed. (For more on that story, read *Silver Bonanza*, by James Blanchard and Franklin Sanders, published by Jefferson Financial, 2400 Jefferson High-way, Suite 600, Jefferson, LA 70121, phone 504-837-3033.)

In a bear market, bullish investors always come to believe that short sellers are "driving the market down," when in fact, the decline is almost entirely due to selling from within their own over-invested ranks. Sometimes authorities outlaw short selling. In doing so, they remove the one class of investors that *must* buy. Every short sale (except when stocks go to zero) must be *covered*, i.e., the stock or derivative contract must be purchased to close the trade. A ban on short selling creates a market with no latent buying power at all, making it even less liquid than it was. Then it can dribble down day after day, unhindered by the buying of nervous shorts. Like all other bans on free exchange, a ban on short selling hurts those whom it is designed to help.

The Japanese government is currently discussing a ban on short selling. If authorities in your country decide to disallow short selling, the bad news is that this option will be closed to you. The good news is that they usually take such actions near major bottoms, so it will probably be about the proper time to cover shorts and start composing your "buy" list anyway.

Chapter 21:

Should You Invest in Commodities?

Figures 21-1 through 21-9 show what happened to commodities in dollar terms from 1929 through 1938. Pay particular attention to what happened in 1929-1932, the three years of intense deflation in which the stock market crashed. As you can see, commodities crashed, too.

You can get rich being short commodity futures in a deflationary crash. This is a player's game, though, and I am not about to urge a typical investor to follow that course. If you are a seasoned commodity trader, avoid the long side and use rallies to sell short. Make sure that your broker keeps your liquid funds in T-bills or an equally safe medium.

There can be exceptions to the broad trend. A commodity can rise against the trend on a war, a war scare, a shortage or a disruption of transport. Oil is an example of a commodity with that type of risk. This commodity *should* have nowhere to go but down during a depression. From 1929 to 1933, for example, after oil had already fallen substantially over preceding years, it plummeted another 80 percent in price. The odds of a repeat performance, however, are lessened by the fact that 4/5 of the world's known oil reserves are in Asia. Aside from France, political entities in general have squandered their nations' forty-year opportunity to have responsible companies replace the cumbersome, costly and dangerous old models of energy production

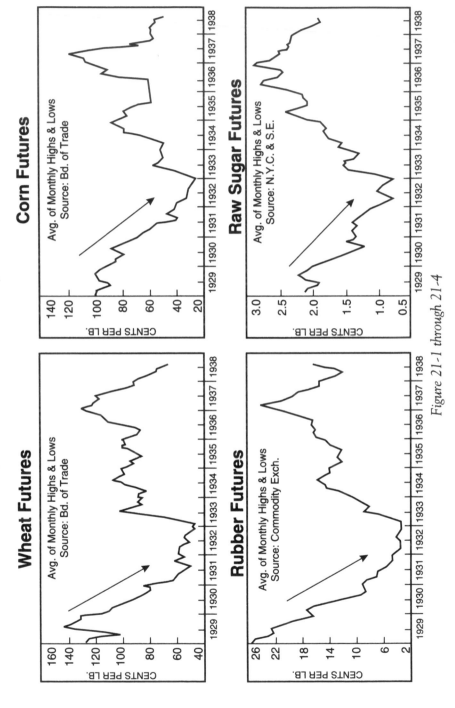

Prices of Commodities, 1929 — 1938

Wheat Futures

Avg. of Monthly Highs & Lows
Source: Bd. of Trade

CENTS PER LB.

Corn Futures

Avg. of Monthly Highs & Lows
Source: Bd. of Trade

CENTS PER LB.

Rubber Futures

Avg. of Monthly Highs & Lows
Source: Commodity Exch.

CENTS PER LB.

Raw Sugar Futures

Avg. of Monthly Highs & Lows
Source: N.Y.C. & S.E.

CENTS PER LB.

Figure 21-1 through 21-4

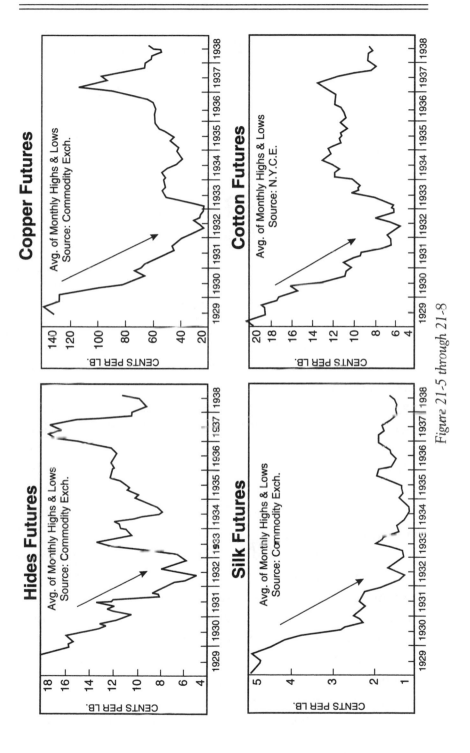

Figure 21-5 through 21-8

Figure 21-9

with nuclear power plants, which (absent politics) can produce multiples more energy at far less cost, risk and pollution. Because of these policies, many nations are deeply vulnerable to a cessation of oil shipments from unstable nations. So oil may be a good short, but it's a risky one. Be careful with any commodities that could experience shortages.

Some people today who are concerned about economic upset are touting commodities, mostly because they look for a replay of the inflationary 1970s. Commodities have been jumping higher since October, and advocates are vehement. I do not buy this argument, at least not as of today. As shown in Figure 21-10, the Commodity Research Bureau (CRB) commodity index has tracked the S&P, with a slight lag, since mid-1998. Gold and silver have also joined in the latest stock rally. As I see it, this correlation means that most assets lately are moving up and down more or less together, probably as liquidity expands and contracts. If so, then any deflation will crush hard-asset prices right along with share prices, just as it always has.

Even if I came to expect the prices of hard assets to rise, I still would not put commodities on the top of my list. I would buy gold and silver, for three reasons: First, unless you own an oil company or the like, you can't own physical commodities; you

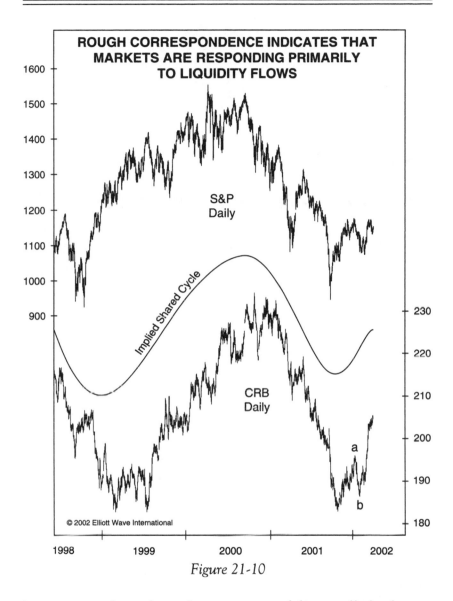

Figure 21-10

have to own them through a promise to deliver, called a futures contract. With respect to gold and silver, you can own the physical asset. Second, gold and silver are cheap, and third, they have monetary value. If there truly is a panic into real goods, I cannot imagine a scenario in which those two would be excluded.

Chapter 22:

Should You Invest in Precious Metals?

Precious metals are likely one day to become the most important asset class to own. From the mid-1970s to the mid-1980s, investors were dedicated to owning gold and silver for safety. Today, people are utterly disinterested in gold or silver, which is what sets the stage for an opportunity.

First, some brief background. Currencies today are utter fictions, but few realize it. Sometime during this century, people will question the validity of the fiat money system. The 1970s may prove to have been just a warm-up in a world battle for real money. Governments may exercise their powers to keep the fiat paper money system afloat, defending their currencies with various schemes and legal restrictions, but in the end, gold will win.

Why is gold such a desirable commodity? At the top of the list is its impeccable utility as a store of value. Relentless inflating has caused chronic value losses in currencies. The U.S. dollar has dropped in value by an estimated 94 percent (exact values depend upon the benchmark) since the Fed came into being. These collapses have destroyed the financial security of the working class, the middle class and retirees. Had modern money a tangible basis, then workers could have saved for their retirement in a true store of value, and retirees would have far more buying power in their golden years. It is already a pity to observe hard-working people unable to save a penny. It will be heart wrenching to see innocent people suffer during the ultimate resolution of central banks' credit-expansion policies. Gold also contributes to long-run productive stability. By setting up central banks with monopoly powers dedicated to paper money, governments traded that stability for an international casino in which money manipulators thrive at the expense of both producers and savers.

It is dangerous to entrust any service crucial to survival to a statutory monopoly or government regulation. When the Russian government handled food production and distribution, central planners reported over seven straight decades of "bad weather," food shortages and starvation. Similarly, with the Bank of England, the Fed and their worldwide counterparts in charge, central planners report decades of "rising prices," monetary debasement and the impoverishment of savers. Periodic credit inflation would occur in a free market as well, but its effects would be limited because real money cannot be inflated, and prudent people and institutions could choose to opt out of a credit binge in favor of real money. A free people would choose the best money, and I have no doubt that it would be gold.

Is the Precious Metals' Bear Market Over?

Despite the verity of gold as the best form of money, there is a right time for everything. Advisors who have insisted upon inflation's inevitability have kept their followers in gold and silver for 21 years as they plummeted 70 percent and 93 percent respectively in dollar terms, while the dollar was losing purchasing power at the local store. This is no mean feat insomuch as no other commodity has accomplished it. These losses, even forgetting the massive opportunity costs, have been staggering.

Right now, I think it likely that gold and silver will fall into their final dollar price lows at the bottom of the deflation because that is what happened to silver in the last great deflation.

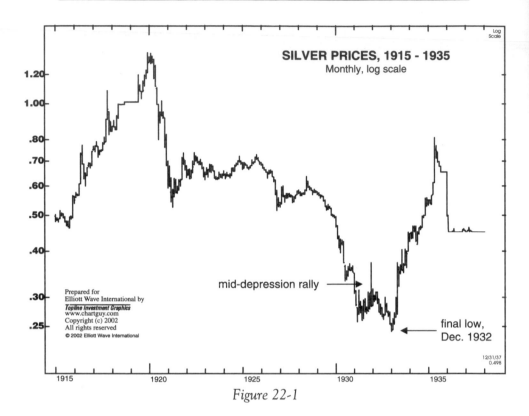

Figure 22-1

Figure 22-1 shows that although silver had undergone most of its bear market by the time of the 1929 high in the stock market, it still followed commodities and paper assets down during the deflation to a final low in December 1932. There is rarely sufficient reason to bet heavily on cycles doing something different from what they have typically done, and this cycle's history implies that the precious metals' bear market is not quite over yet. If this deflation acts like the last one, then at the coming bottom, we will have a great buying opportunity for gold and silver — maybe the greatest ever.

Most gold bugs today assert that gold and silver are a "deflation hedge," a "war hedge," and a "depression hedge," claims that the record does not convincingly support. The price history of 1931 is instructive in showing that there was a year-long mid-depression rally in the price of silver, which ended on a spike, indicating brief panic buying. Investors of that time were likewise convinced that silver would provide counter-trend solace during monetary difficulty. They were remembering silver's positive performance during the preceding difficult times of 1914-1919, which were inflationary. Similarly, today's precious metals enthusiasts have the inflationary 1970s in mind. However, the actual troubles in the 1930s were, and in this case are expected to be, deflationary.

The fact that people "rushed into gold" in the early 1930s has been a mainstay of the gold advocates' argument. They rarely tell the whole story. I suspect that people bought gold then because the U.S. government had fixed the price, at $20.67 per ounce. While everything else collapsed, gold was soaring in relative value, and its value gains were guaranteed. Who wouldn't buy it? If the government had fixed the price of any other substance, people would have invested in that instead. Like silver in the 1930s, gold today is free to trade at market price, which means that it can go down during a dollar deflation. I cannot guarantee that it will; I can only state that there is no good case to be made that history indicates otherwise.

Buy Gold and Silver Anyway

You might be surprised to find that I advocate holding a healthy amount of gold and silver anyway. There are several reasons for this stance:

First, it could be different this time, for some reason I cannot foresee. In a world of fiat currencies, prudence demands hedging against a rush to tangible money.

Second, these metals should perform well on a relative basis compared to most other investments. Unlike so many commodities, they will not fall 90 percent from today's prices, much less to zero, like so many stocks and bonds. These metals are downright inexpensive compared to their top values in 1980. Silver today costs only about 8 percent of its peak dollar value. Relative to home prices and stock prices, the metals have never been cheaper. So even if the precious metals continue to decline, they will fall much less in percentage terms than most other assets because they have already fallen so far.

Third, the question of whether there will be further bear market in the metals is really one for speculators and quibblers. Gold and silver have declined in dollar value for over two decades, which is between 90 percent and 100 percent of the total time I had expected them to fall. It may not be prudent to try to finesse the final months.

Fourth, the metals should soar once the period of deflation is over. Notice in Figure 22-1 that silver rebounded ferociously after it bottomed in 1932, tripling in just two years, rewarding those who continued to hold it. If deflation again keeps precious metals prices down, the rebound after the bottom should be no less robust. Given the likely political inflationary forces, it could well be much stronger. So by all means, you want to own precious metals prior to the onset of the post-depression recovery.

Fifth and foremost, if you buy gold and silver now, *you'll have it*. If investors worldwide begin to panic into hard assets, locking up supplies, if governments ban gold sales, if gold and silver prices go through the roof, you won't be stuck entirely in paper currency. You will already own something that everyone else wants.

Be aware that the present legalities of gold and silver ownership could change. This political risk isn't fantasy, even in the Land of the Free. In 1933, President Roosevelt outlawed gold ownership for U.S. citizens and imposed a ten-year prison sentence on anyone who refused to surrender his gold to a Federal Reserve Bank within 25 days. (The following year, the government began a long campaign of fixing the price of newly mined silver, though each level was temporary and closely reflected market forces.) The ban on gold stayed in place for over four decades, until President Ford lifted it on the first day of 1975.

Should you buy gold and silver now? The answer depends on how much you are willing to pay for the added breadth in your portfolio and for their current availability. If you are willing to see the dollar value of the precious metals drop another 30 percent or more before they rise substantially, then I would say, that's the price you're willing to pay for its current availability and for the "insurance" of greater portfolio stability under an unexpected inflation scenario. If you want to arrange for capital safety in every way that you can manage, then diversification into real money is a necessary part of that effort.

How To Buy Gold and Silver

I do not advocate buying gold and silver in paper form by way of futures contracts, gold-backed bonds from the Russian government or ownership certificates connected to commingled accounts at storage facilities. After all, which is better — owning actual gold or some entity's promise to pay it? For maximum safety, you should own gold and silver in physical form, outright.

One-kilo bars are widely traded globally, but "standard bars" of 400 fine ounces are the primary form of gold and silver used by central banks and recognized by the U.S. Comex, the London Bullion Market Association and the Tokyo Commodity Exchange (TOCOM). So that is the most liquid medium for storing substantial wealth in gold.

Coins are a good medium for smaller portfolios. Even larger ones should include their share of coins, because some day tangible money could once again become a medium of exchange, at least temporarily. To that end, be sure to avoid rare coins that have a "collectibility" premium. Many dealers recommend paying up for rare coins because in 1933 some collectible gold coins were exempt from U.S. government confiscation. The "cutoff" point for rarity was never codified, though, and there is no guarantee that any such law, much less exactly the same law, will go into effect in your jurisdiction. Any future confiscation in your country may include gold coins with a small collectibility premium because investment strategies built around them are well known. By all means, though, if the argument makes sense to you, pay the premium and sleep better for it.

The best-known and most liquid "bullion" style gold coins are American Eagles, South African Krugerrands, Canadian Maple Leafs and Australian Nuggets. As for silver, Americans should own a bag or two of circulated U.S. silver coins. Most coin dealers can get you these items. After you have a core position, accumulate the metals at a pace with which you are comfortable, preferably on price declines. Every time myopic central banks and panicked debtors push the price of gold and silver down, buy some more.

It is probably not as good an idea to invest in gold stocks, either. In common stock bear markets, stocks of gold mining companies have more often gone down than up except in relatively rare five to ten-year periods of accelerating inflation. Few people know that from the top day in the Dow in 1929 to the bottom day in 1932, gold mining shares rose only slightly *even though the U.S. government propped up the companies' product by fixing its price.* Mining shares did not soar in value until the stock market as a whole turned up. Today the government does not fix the price of gold, so in the deflation we currently face, gold mines will enjoy no false advantage over any other companies. Their stocks will probably rally when the overall stock market rallies (as they are doing now), but they have no built-in support as they did in the 1930s, so they are likely to disappoint those who invest in them. (Of course, if the government's policy on gold changes, then so might the outlook for mining share prices.)

Also be aware that there are risks attending the independence of mining companies. Owning gold shares means betting that no government will nationalize the mines whose shares you own. Owning gold shares is fine at the top of a Kondratieff economic cycle when inflation is raging, such as occurred in the 1970s, but not in its final years when deflation is raging and political tensions are their most severe.

In 1933, Roosevelt's Executive Order stated, "Your possession of these proscribed metals and/or your maintenance of a safe-deposit box to store them is known to the Government from bank and insurance records. Therefore, be advised that your vault box must remain sealed, and may only be opened in the presence of an agent of The Internal Revenue Service." Most banks were only too happy to comply because gold prohibition promised their salvation, or so they believed. If your government decides to confiscate gold, your country's banks will be recruited in the operation. If it happens sometime in the coming crash, the reason will probably be "fighting terrorism." By the way, this potential is a good reason to refrain from keeping any important personal papers in bank safe deposit boxes in any jurisdiction where such an action is possible. Otherwise, you may have to wait a while for permission to access the contents.

If you would like to buy gold and silver, your options are much more limited than they were twenty years ago, when everyone seemed to be in the business. Here are some suggestions. If you want to buy at least $100,000 worth of gold and/or silver bars and store them in one or more of the safest depositories in the world, contact SafeStore, Ltd., via the SafeWealth Group. If you want to buy bullion-style gold coins or circulated silver coins inside the U.S. and store them domestically, check out the dealers listed below. (Fidelitrade also offers an exchange-approved depository.) Be sure to cross-check prices before buying.

See Appendix A for updated
contact information

Fidelitrade
Website: www.fidelitrade.com
Email: info@fidelitrade.com
Address: 3601 North Market Street,
        Wilmington, DE 19802
Phone: 800-223-1080 and 302-762-6200
Fax: 302-762-2902
CEO: Mike Clark

See Appendix A for updated
contact information

Hancock & Harwell
Website: www.raregold.com
Email: info@raregold.com
Address: Suite 310, 3155 Roswell Rd.,
        Atlanta, GA 30305
Phone: 888-877-1782 and 404-261-6566
CEO: Robert L. Harwell

See Appendix A for updated
contact information

Investment Rarities, Inc.
Website: www.gloomdoom.com
Email: jcook@investmentrarities.com
Address: 7850 Metro Parkway, Suite 213,
        Minneapolis, MN 55425-1521
Phone: 800-328-1860 and 612-853-0700
CEO: James R. Cook

See Appendix A for updated
contact information

Miles Franklin Ltd.
Website: www.milesfranklin.com
Email: milesf@ix.netcom.com
Address: 3601 Park Center Building, Suite 120,
        St. Louis Park, MN 55416
Phone: 800-822-8080 and 952-929-7006
Fax: 952-925-0143
CEO: David M. Schectman

See Appendix A for updated contact information

Straight Talk Assets, Inc.
Website: www.coinmoney.com
Email: straighttalk@mindspring.com
Address: P.O. Box 1301, Gainesville, GA 30503
Phone: 800-944-9249 and 770-536-8045
CEO: Glenn R. Fried

Well-heeled investors should round out their holdings with platinum. Platinum is a precious metal, and in recent decades, its coinage has established it as an emerging monetary metal as well. Platinum has several advantages over gold and silver, not the least of which is that it packs more value per ounce. If you can afford to diversify to this extent, ask your metals dealer about platinum bars and coins.

Chapter 23:

What To Do With Your Pension Plan

As most of us know, banks and mortgage companies lend money to consumers via credit cards, auto loans and mortgages. You may not know that they then package and re-sell those loans as investments to pension funds (perhaps yours) as well as portfolio managers, insurance companies and even trust departments at other banks. The issuing banks keep most of the interest paid by the consumers in exchange for guaranteeing a small interest payment (today less than 2.5 percent) on the package. These investments are called "securitized loans," and banks and mortgage companies have issued $6 trillion worth of them. This high sum implies that if you have a managed trust, invest in a debt fund or have insurance or a pension, you are almost surely dependent upon some of these deals.

When banks sell the packages, they get back as much money as they lent out in the first place, so guess what. They can go right out and roll the same percentage of their deposits out again and again as new consumer loans. Investors in the packages are, in a sense, new depositors.

If the issuing banks get in trouble some day and can't pay, the owners of the debt packages will then have dibs on the interest payments from the consumers. If those payments dry up, they have that great collateral to fall back on: vacant homes, used cars and household junk. If a depression is on, what will that collateral be worth?

If such deals don't sound that solid to you, then why are so many institutions making these investments? Because they're buying them with OPM: Other People's Money...your money.

And besides, it's "guaranteed" and backed by "collateral"!

This scheme, like so many others in existence today, works only as long as the debtors and the economy can keep up the pace of interest payments, some of which are as high as 17 percent. In a major economic downturn, this credit structure will implode.

Make sure you fully understand all aspects of your government's *individual* retirement plans as well. In the U.S., this includes such structures as IRAs, 401Ks and Keoghs. If you anticipate severe system-wide financial and political stresses, you may decide to liquidate any such plans and pay whatever penalty is required. Why? Because there are strings attached to the perk of having your money sheltered from taxes. You may do only what the government allows you to do with the money. It restricts certain investments and can change the list at any time. It charges a penalty for early withdrawal and can change the amount of the penalty at any time.

What is the worst that could happen? In Argentina, the government continued to spend more than it took in until it went broke trying to pay the interest on its debt. In December 2001, it seized $2.3 billion dollars worth of deposits in *private pension funds* to pay its bills.

In the 1930s, the world heard a lot of populist rhetoric about why "rich" people should be plundered for the public good. It is easy to imagine such talk in the next crisis, directed at requiring wealthy people to forfeit their retirement savings for the good of the nation.

With the retirement setup in the U.S., the government need not be as direct as Argentina's. It need merely assert, after a stock market fall decimates many people's savings, that stocks are too risky to hold for retirement purposes. Under the guise of protecting you, it could ban stocks and perhaps other investments in tax-exempt pension plans and restrict assets to one category: "safe" long-term U.S. Treasury bonds. Then it could raise the penalty of early withdrawal to 100 percent. Bingo. The government will have seized the entire $2 trillion — or what's left of it given a crash — that today is held in government-sponsored, tax-deferred 401K private pension plans. I'm not saying it will happen, but it could, and wouldn't you rather have your money safely under your own discretion?

By the way, if you are normally in a high tax bracket and find yourself in a year with zero income or significant business losses, you can cash out part or all of your plan with either less tax (since you will be in a lower tax bracket) or no tax, if your earned-income losses cancel out the income from the plan. If you are under the age of 59½, you will normally have to pay a penalty, which is currently 10 percent of the value of the distribution. If you use the funds to pay for college tuition, though, you can even avoid the penalty. When you cash out your plan, you can still keep the money in the same investments if you wish, but then they will be in your own name, not in the name of a plan. Be sure to consult a tax advisor before proceeding.

Perhaps you have no such opportunity for tax saving and do not want to pay the penalty attached to premature withdrawal. If your balance is high enough, you may wish to consider converting your retirement plan investments into an annuity at a safe insurance company (see Chapter 24). It is highly likely (though not assured) that such investments would be left alone even in a national financial emergency.

If you have money in a personally directed corporate or government employee retirement plan with limited options, move it out of stock and bond funds. Park it in the safest money market fund available within the plan. Investigate the rules that pertain to cashing out and decide your next course of action.

If you or your family owns its own small company and is the sole beneficiary of its pension or profit sharing plan, you should lodge its assets in a safe bank or money market fund. As an alternative, depending upon your age and requirements, you may consider converting it into an annuity, issued by a safe insurance company. Such insurance companies are few and far between, but the next chapter shows you where to find them.

Chapter 24:

What To Do With Your Insurance and Annuities

If you believe that your fortunes are not dependent upon junk bonds, you might be in for a surprise. If you have life insurance, especially if you have a "guaranteed rate of return" insurance policy, your policy may be dependent upon the performance of junk bonds. Many large insurance companies failed in the comparatively mild recession of the early 1990s because they backed their policies with junk bonds. The economic contraction that insurance companies now face is *three degrees larger* than that one (Grand Supercycle as opposed to Primary). Your insurance nest egg, to put it bluntly, may be at risk.

Some insurance companies guarantee a minimum return on "equity-indexed annuities" while letting you participate in the market's gains but not its losses. An article in a major financial magazine calls these plans "a bear-proof way to ride the market" that "removes downside risk," but the way it's done involves zero-coupon bonds, index options and other exotic vehicles. This scheme will surely blow up, and if it does, the guarantee will stress the insurance companies that sell these policies.

Even traditionally safe insurance companies are massively exposed to losses during a major deflation because they invest in standard vehicles such as stocks, bonds and real estate. Some venerable insurance companies in Europe have become compromised not from their own investments but because banks that today are awash in leveraged derivatives purchased them some time in the past ten years.

A deflationary vise will put double pressure on the solvency of insurance companies. As the values of most investments fall, the value of insurance companies' portfolios will fall. Conversely, as the economy weakens, more and more people will decide to cash out their policies. Insurance companies become hard-pressed to honor the value of whole-life policies when there is a net outflow of cash at the same time that their property and stock investments are declining in value.

When insurance companies implode, they file for bankruptcy, and you can be left out in the cold. I know, because my insurance broker placed our insurance with, of all the companies in the world, Confederation Life. In 1994, it collapsed, along with Baldwin United and First Executive Corporation, which were huge institutions. See what happened when I didn't do the necessary research? If you think that you can rely on your broker to recommend a safe insurance company, think again. Brokers shop mainly for price, and when they do look into safety, they rely on rating services that don't do a good job (see Chapter 25). As it turned out, I was lucky. Government and industry leaders in both the U.S. and Canada worked for three years to distribute the policies to other companies. When my policy moved, it carried another full year's cash-out restriction, and all the while, I was still required to pay the premiums. The only reason that the deal finally made it through was that the North American financial boom continued throughout the 1990s, and other insurance companies felt safe taking on the additional obligations.

When a bust is in force, few insurance companies are willing or able to take over a stressed company's policy obligations, which have little collateral behind them. If your insurance company fails, your investment of a lifetime will be gone. It's happened to many people and will happen to many more.

Whole-life policies are almost always a terrible idea under a fiat money system. During inflationary times, their real value grows far more slowly than it appears, if at all, because the purchasing power of the monetary unit declines. During deflationary times, the policy your family is counting on to protect against death or old age can disappear if the company fails.

One option is to cash out such policies and buy term insurance instead. With term insurance, you can keep an eye on the fortunes of various companies and switch from one to another. Talk to your insurance broker about the courses of action open to you.

On the other hand, an interesting "deflation bonus" can also come available if you're careful. If you have whole-life insurance or an annuity with a *sound company*, you can actually come out way ahead because *the values and payouts are denominated in currency*. During deflation, the value of cash rises, so in terms of purchasing power, each dollar of value in your policy will be able to purchase more goods and services than it previously did. All you need to do is find a sound company.

Where To Buy Your Insurance Policies

At minimum, you should move your whole-life insurance policy or annuity to a sound insurer as soon as possible. If you delay one day too long in moving your policy, and the company's assets are frozen, you will have no recourse.

As far as I can tell, Weiss Ratings, Inc. produces the most reliable ratings of U.S. insurance companies. Their system is also simple and straightforward. Unlike the maze of gradations such as "Bbb+" and so on that other services use, the Weiss system simply reads like a report card, from A+ down to F, adding only a set of "E" grades prior to F. Weiss considers any company rated B- or above to have "good" financial safety but recommends that you do business with companies rated B+ or better. In normal times, that assessment is probably all you need. However, if you believe that there is a reasonable risk of that rare and devastating event, a deflationary crash and depression, why not demand the absolute best? Table 24-1 lists all U.S. insurance companies that Weiss rates A+. The three companies on this list that are also on Weiss' list of the 25 largest insurance companies rated B+ or higher are marked with an asterisk. To investigate a larger list of companies, see Weiss' book, *The Ultimate Safe Money Guide.*

Of course, as prudent as these judgments may be, these ratings do not fully take into account other considerations that will be crucial in a depression. For example, what bank(s) does

THE SAFEST U.S. INSURERS			
Source: Weiss Ratings, Inc. (based on 12/31/01 data)			
Company Name	**Domicile State**	**Weiss Safety Rating**	**Total Assets (in millions of $)**
LIFE & HEALTH INSURERS			
American Family Life Ins Co	WI	A+	2,541.2
Country Life Ins Co	IL	A+	4,118.9
Northwestern Mutual Life Ins Co*	WI	A+	99,660.8
State Farm Life & Accident Asr Co	IL	A+	991.2
State Farm Life Ins Co*	IL	A+	29,344.9
Teachers Ins & Annuity Asn Of Am *	NY	A+	124,606.7
PROPERTY & CASUALTY INSURERS			
Alfa Mutual Ins	AL	A+	1,136.6
Amica Mutual Ins	RI	A+	2,912.4
Associates Ins	IN	A+	529.6
Auto-Owners Ins	MI	A+	5,514.3
Canal Ins	SC	A+	661.2
Government Employees Ins	MD	A+	8,157.9
Home-Owners Ins	MI	A+	323.6
Interins Exch of the Automobile Club	CA	A+	3,366.1
Kentucky Farm Bureau Mutual Ins	KY	A+	1,108.2
Protective Ins	IN	A+	412.6
State Farm Mutual Automobile Ins	IL	A+	73,397.5
Tennessee Farmers Asr	TN	A+	470.0
Tennessee Farmers Mutual Ins	TN	A+	1,212.3
United Services Automobile Asn	TX	A+	10,278.6
USAA Casualty Ins	TX	A+	3,145.5

*These are among the largest 25 insurers rated B+ or higher.

Table 24-1   *(see updated list in Appendix B)*

your insurer use to hold its assets and make transactions? If an insurer's main bank implodes, its situation could become chaotic. This one factor could override even an insurer's A+ credit rating. Ratings can change for all sorts of reasons. For maximum confidence, keep abreast of Weiss' ratings as they pertain to the companies you choose. (See contact information in the last section of this book.)

As if there were not already enough to worry about, the currency denomination of your policy may also prove crucial. If the currency in which you expect to be paid collapses in value, so will your plans for retirement.

Again, SafeWealth Group specializes in minimizing all these risks by identifying the safest insurance companies in the world as well as those among them that use safe banks as custodians of their funds. Better yet, it can identify the ones that also allow you to designate the currency denomination(s) of your choice within their policies. Such provisions for ultimate safety are particularly important for annuity arrangements, estate planning and capital-preservation programs that utilize insurance contracts.

The main point is to make sure that you assess the vulnerability of your insurance policies and annuities now. If you are satisfied, fine. If not, then you can take appropriate action before your insurance company, its bank, or you, become too stressed to adapt.

Chapter 25:

Reliable Sources for Financial Warnings

Safety Ratings for Financial Institutions

The most widely utilized rating services are almost always woefully late in warning you of problems within financial institutions. They often seem to get news about a company around the time that everyone else does, which means that the price of the associated stock or bond has already changed to reflect that news. In severe cases, a company can collapse before the standard rating services know what hit it. When all you can see is dust, they just skip the downgrading process and shift the company's rating from "investment grade" to "default" status.

Examples abound. The debt of the largest real estate developer in the world, Olympia & York of Canada, had an AA rating in 1991. A year later, it was bankrupt. Rating services missed the historic debacles at Barings Bank, Sumitomo Bank and Enron. Enron's bonds enjoyed an "investment grade" rating four days before the company went bankrupt. In my view, Enron's bonds in particular were transparently junk well before their collapse. Why? Because the firm employed an army of traders in derivatives, which is an absolute guarantee of ultimate failure even when it's *not* a company's main business.

Sometimes there are structural reasons for the overvaluation of debt issues. For example, investors buy the debt offerings of Fannie Mae, Freddie Mac and the FHLB because they think that the U.S. government guarantees them. It doesn't. All that these companies have is the right to borrow money from the U.S. Treasury, $2.5 billion in the case of Fannie and Freddie and $4 billion in the case of the FHLB. That credit line represents less than ¼ of 1 percent of each company's outstanding mortgage loans, so it is a drop in the bucket. Worse, because of that advantage, the bonds that these companies issue are exempt from SEC registration and disclosure requirements because they are simply *presumed* to be safe. Managers of these companies are going to be utterly shocked when a depression devastates their portfolios and their earnings. Investors in these companies' stocks and bonds will be just as surprised when the stock prices and bond ratings collapse. Most rating services will not see it coming.

A few companies take a stringent approach to rating institutional safety. I listed three good U.S. bank-rating firms in Chapter 19. Weiss Ratings, Inc. has quite reliable, detailed ratings on a broader range of U.S. institutions. For example, while most analysts never saw the Enron disaster coming, Weiss placed Enron on its "Corporate Earnings Blacklist" in April 2001 and cited the company as being "highly suspect of manipulating its earnings reports." Two quarters later, the scandal broke, and countless employees and investors — people who hadn't the foggiest notion about taking the precautions I'm suggesting to you in this book — lost everything.

SafeWealth Group uses an even more stringent "survivability indicator" for financial institutions globally, taking not just the present balance sheet and corporate structure into account but also the institution's projected viability in a financial crisis or depression. SafeWealth is not in the ratings publishing business, but in response to inquiries, it will introduce qualified individuals, companies and trusts to its highest-rated institutions.

Investment Advice from Brokers

Throughout my career, I have advised people not to trust a brokerage firm's "fundamental" (as opposed to technical) analysts to warn you about anything. Brokerage firm analysts are notoriously poor at market timing. Besides being beholden to their corporate clients, which gives them an extreme bullish bias, most of these analysts use the wrong tools. Even when they are independent thinkers, they are usually not students of market psychology and thus have no idea how to figure out when a stock is probably topping. In fact, brokerage firm analysts are typically cheerleaders for a stock just as it is topping out and during most of its fall. Over 20 years ago, when I worked as a Technical Market Specialist at Merrill Lynch, I watched as an analyst kept a "buy" rating on a maker of CB radios while its stock dropped from 19 to 1. Nothing has changed. According to reports, 11 out of 16 analysts covering Enron had a "buy" (some even emphasized "strong buy") on the stock four weeks before the company declared bankruptcy and well after the decline in the stock price had wiped out its investors. As most people have subsequently learned, brokerage firm analysts almost never use the word "sell." If they really think a company's stock is dangerous, they label it a "hold." The problem with trying to follow this guideline, though, is that they usually label a stock that way after its bear market has run most or all of its course. To avoid being hurt by these strategists, you need independent market analysis.

Useful Newsletters in a Bear Market

Most newsletters these days are wet behind the ears. Their focus is touting stocks to buy. That was fine for the bull market, but it probably isn't now. At all times ideally, but particularly in a global bear market, you need input from seasoned analysts who cover the financial world with healthy skepticism and are as good at warning you about what investments to avoid as they are at suggesting what actions to take. Besides my own company's publications (see final section of this book), here are a few that I like:

The Gloom, Boom & Doom Report
Website: www.gloomboomdoom.com
Email: info@gloomboomdoom.com
Address: 3308 The Center, 99 Queens Rd. Central,
        Hong Kong
Phone: (U.S. dial 011) 852-2-801-5410
Fax: 852-2-845-9192
Editor: Marc Faber

Grant's Interest Rate Observer
Website: www.grantspub.com
Email: webmaster@grantspub.com
Address: 30 Wall Street, New York, NY 10005
Phone: 212-809-7994
Fax: 212-809-8426
Editor: James Grant

The International Speculator
Website: www.internationalspeculator.com
Email: info@internationalspeculator.com
Address: P.O. Box 84911, Phoenix AZ 85071
Phone: 800-528-0559 and 602-252-4477
Fax: 602-943-2363
Editor: Doug Casey

Safe Money Report
Website: www.safemoneyreport.com
Email: wr@weissinc.com
Address: Weiss Research, P.O. Box 31689,
        Palm Beach Gardens, FL 33420

See Appendix A for updated contact information

See Appendix A for updated contact information

See Appendix A for updated contact information

See Appendix A for updated contact information

Phone: 800-236-0407 and 561-627-3300
Fax: 561-625-6685
Editor: Martin D. Weiss

SafeWealth Report
Email: clientservices@safewealthadvisory.com
Address: SafeWealth Advisory Ltd. – Service Center,
            P.O. Box 1995, Windsor, Berkshire SL4 5LL, U.K.
Phone: (in U.S., dial 011) 44-1753-554-461
Fax: (in U.S., dial 011) 44-1753-554-642
Production Manager: Jane V. Scott

See Appendix A for updated contact information

All that most of these services can do is offer you ideas. In the
end, you will have to make up your own mind with the evidence
that they present.

Chapter 26:

How To Ensure Your Physical Safety

In essence, bull and bear markets are social mood trends. Social mood trends have consequences.

A positive social mood has positive social consequences. The great bull market of the past quarter-century created a wonderful world. Major antagonists in the areas of politics, religion and race kissed and made up. The Cold War ended. Communism collapsed. Markets became global and sophisticated. The world embraced, to one degree or another, capitalism and freedom. The Information Age was born. Even country music got raucous and happy. In the 1990s, people felt secure, and today wealth abounds.

Generally speaking, that environment has been safe, profitable and fun. However, social mood trends are a two-way street. When the positive trend ends, a negative one takes over for a while. Those trends have social consequences, too: destructive ones, which affect finance, the economy, politics and all kinds of social relationships.

This book focuses mostly on finance. If you get out of investments that will lose most of their value in a crash and keep your money safe, you will be quite wealthy in terms of your purchasing power. Unfortunately, that's not all there is to a major bear market. Depressions are a mess. You may have money, but certain goods might be scarce or rationed. You might be financially smart yet get caught in a war zone.

It may not be much fun to contemplate the social effects of downtrends, but it is important. It's true that if you become financially devastated, you can't take advantage of great investment opportunities. But if you encounter physical risk, you may not even be around to try.

In order to profit from and enjoy an uptrend, you and your family must be fully protected during the preceding downtrend. Then, at the bottom, you can rise above the general despair and take full advantage both financially and emotionally of the next expansive increase in positive social mood.

Elliott waves portend many social changes, and you can anticipate them to some degree by understanding what I call socionomics. There is not room to explain the idea in this book. For a taste of how useful socionomics can be, review these comments on one result of social mood change that the forecasted bear market was expected to exhibit:

"Foreigners will commit terrorist acts on U.S. soil...."
— *At the Crest of the Tidal Wave* (1995)
Chapter 21, p.435

"The impulse to build shows up in the construction of record-breaking skyscraper buildings at social-mood peaks. At troughs, few buildings are built, and many of those already in place may be burned or bombed out of existence."
— *The Wave Principle of Human Social Behavior and the New Science of Socionomics* (1999)
Chapter 14, pp.229-230

"The Middle East should be a complete disaster. You've got at least three major religions in that area that all dislike each other, and the truce of the bull market has already been tenuous, so that area is going to blow up."
— *The Elliott Wave Theorist*, August 2001 issue

The 9/11/01 attack on the World Trade Center and the ensuing war in Afghanistan have borne out these observations, and we are as of yet only two mild years into the bear market.

By the way, some commentators write as if the terrorist attack caused the recession, but the stock market topped out a year and a half earlier, and the economy began contracting half a year earlier. Attacks such as this *result* from negative social-mood trends, which is why a socionomist can generally anticipate the tenor of behavior that manifests in such acts. Such manifestations are always a matter of frequency and degree. There is always some social unrest, even in the late stages of a bull market, but conflict always escalates in a bear market. For more on this theme, please see Chapters 14-16 of *The Wave Principle of Human Social Behavior and the New Science of Socionomics*. For a fuller discussion of what to expect socially in the bear market, please read Chapter 21 of *At the Crest of the Tidal Wave*.

Polarization and Conflict

The main social influence of a bear market is to cause society to polarize in countless ways. That polarity shows up in every imaginable context — social, religious, political, racial, corporate and by class. In a bear market, people in whatever way are impelled to identify themselves as belonging to a smaller social unit than they did before and to belong more passionately. It is probably a product of the anger that accompanies bear markets, because each social unit seems invariably to find reasons to be angry with and to attack its opposing unit. In the 1930s bear market, communists and fascists challenged political institutions. In the 1970s bear market, students challenged police, and blacks challenged whites. In both cases, labor challenged management and third parties challenged the status quo. In bear markets, rallies, marches and protests become common events. Separatism becomes a force as territories polarize. Populism becomes a force

as classes polarize. Third parties, fourth parties, and more, find
constituents. Bear markets engender labor strikes, racial conflict,
religious persecution, political unrest, trade protectionism, coups
and wars. In the area of personal behavior, part of the population gets more conservative, and part gets more hedonistic, and
each side describes the other as something that needs reform.
One reason that conflicts gain such scope in depressions is that
much of the middle class gets wiped out by the financial debacle,
increasing the number of people with little or nothing to lose
and anger to spare.

The Erroneous Timing of Previous Concerns

In the late 1970s and early 1980s, survival was a big topic.
There were million-seller books about where to buy electric gen-
erators, how to choose bulletproof vests, storing dried foods and
so on. This occupation of course coincided with an approaching
major bottom in a 16-year bear market (in inflation-adjusted
terms). By then, you shouldn't have been wasting your time with
it; you should have been buying stocks and bonds. The ideal time
to address safety concerns is at the beginning of a downtrend,
not at the end.

In 1999, near the all-time high in stocks, many people
were again concerned for their physical safety, but this time, it
was for the wrong reason. They feared that the "Y2K" computer
glitch would shut down the civilized world. In the heat of the
international obsession over this issue and in answer to many
emails to the Message Board on our website, I answered that the
free market would take care of that problem. Until the social
mood trend turned down, as evidenced by a major downturn in
the stock averages, there was little to fear on that scale.

Anticipated events such as those rarely cause global
disruption. Major trends of increasing pessimism, anger and
fear do cause global disruption, and that's what a bear market

is. After January 1, 2000, all the worriers over Y2K evaporated. Complacency reigned again, just when financial risk was at its greatest. That's also when physical safety should have become a real concern. The eruption of terrorist activity in recent months is a product of a bear market, so you see my point.

Some Thoughts on Preparedness

Exactly what to do about your physical safety is a difficult problem. Living in a populous area or near a military installation or an important infrastructure site is somewhat dangerous in times of social unrest. If you are physically tied to a job in such a spot, decisions about relocating are even more difficult than otherwise.

I know people who have farmland in the country, a retreat in the mountains or a self-sufficient home. Others buy guns or learn self-defense. These are fine ideas if you can fit them into the requirements and desires of your life. But for such preparations to be useful, you have to find yourself in a position where you need them. Usually in a major bear market, you are less likely to encounter a mob, a criminal or a terrorist than to face state-sponsored controls within your own country or military attack from without, and there may be little that a retreat or karate can do for you in those situations.

Nevertheless, if you determine that you need this type of preparation, now is a good time to dig out that old list of "Y2K" items and buy from it whatever you would like to have — such as an electric generator, a few months' worth of emergency dried foods, a video surveillance system, defensive weapons, etc. — some at half the prices that they were selling for in late 1999. Being prepared for terrorism is hardly an unreasonable idea.

Here are some web locations to help you with aspects of physical preparedness. Some of them link to other sites, so once you get in the loop, you will find many more resources.

Disaster Preparedness
> http://www.oism.org/nwss/s73p908.htm
> http://www.fema.gov

Basic Survival
> http://www.survivalcenter.com
> http://www.ki4u.com/nuclearsurvival/list.htm

Home Security, Disaster Information
> www.joelskousen.com

Dried Foods
> www.alpineaire.com
> www.freezedryguy.com
> www.fcs.uga.edu/pubs/current/FDNS-E-34-CS.html
> http://foodsafety.nal.usda.gov/

Self Defense
> www.kravmagainc.com

Some disaster-related literature can be more upsetting than helpful. Always stop and think: Is this course of action necessary? Is there a more sensible alternative? There is little point in taking much time and effort and cost to prepare for disastrous events that are highly unlikely or which can be judiciously avoided.

Chapter 27:

Preparing for a Change in Politics

The Elected Leader's Fortunes

Figure 27-1 uses U.S. electoral history to show that when the stock market is rising, reflecting a positive social-mood trend, voters tend to maintain the incumbent leader. When stocks collapse, the leader is thrown out in a landslide or by other means; though the instances are rare, there are no exceptions to this rule. Voters do not appear to care which party is in power at such times; they just throw whomever they perceive to be in charge, and his party, out of power.

National leaders always make things worse for themselves by (1) claiming credit when the economy does well, thereby implying that it's their fault when it doesn't, and (2) vowing to enact economy-boosting measures when the economy weakens, thereby supporting the fiction that they can control it, which puts their opponents in a position to claim that those policies failed.

A leader doesn't control his country's economy, but the economy mightily controls his image. When the economy contracts, that image suffers, and the voters throw him out. This is true of elected rulers all over the earth. For an instructive case in point, study the fortunes of U.S. president Richard Nixon, who won a second term in a landslide in late 1972 at a major top and was hounded from office less than two years later as the Dow

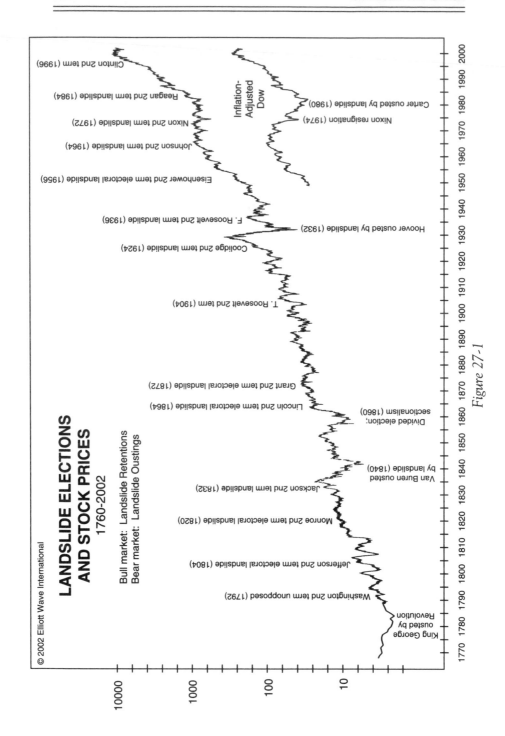

LANDSLIDE ELECTIONS
AND STOCK PRICES
1760-2002

Bull market: Landslide Retentions
Bear market: Landslide Oustings

© 2002 Elliott Wave International

King George ousted by Revolution

Washington 2nd term unopposed (1792)

Jefferson 2nd term electoral landslide (1804)

Monroe 2nd term electoral landslide (1820)

Jackson 2nd term and landslide (1832)

Van Buren ousted by landslide (1840)

Lincoln 2nd term electoral landslide (1864)

Divided election; sectionalism (1860)

Grant 2nd term electoral landslide (1872)

T. Roosevelt 2nd term (1904)

Coolidge 2nd term landslide (1924)

F. Roosevelt 2nd term landslide (1936)

Hoover ousted by landslide (1932)

Eisenhower 2nd term electoral landslide (1956)

Johnson 2nd term landslide (1964)

Nixon 2nd term landslide (1972)

Nixon resignation (1974)

Reagan 2nd term 2nd term landslide (1984)

Carter ousted by landslide (1980)

Clinton 2nd term (1996)

Inflation-Adjusted Dow

Figure 27-1

suffered its largest decline since 1937-1938. Or consider George Bush, who enjoyed record presidential approval ratings in 1991 yet lost the election just a year later amidst the deepest slide in S&P companies' earnings since the 1940s. In Argentina, which recently has suffered financial ruin after a deflationary crash, the president saw his public approval drop from 70 percent to 4.5 percent in just two years. The country then ran through four successive presidents in a matter of weeks. Those voters wanted all the bums thrown out.

If there is a deflationary crash, the incumbent leader of your nation, no matter how popular he is early in his term, will not win re-election if stock prices are much lower on election day. The financial and economic decline during his term and the defeat that follows will not be primarily his fault, though the majority will insist that they are. If the decline is a drawn-out affair, more than one successive leader could suffer defeat at its hands.

The Public, Not the President, Controls the Trend

People who hear me say in speeches that the markets and the economy affect the election of the leader more so than vice versa invariably gasp in incredulity. In the U.S., Republicans say, "How can you say that Ronald Reagan's conservative policies cannot be credited for the economic improvement of the 1980s, which led to 8 out of 10 years of expansion?" To which I reply, "Then do you also credit Franklin Roosevelt's liberal policies for the economic improvement of the 1930s, which led to 11 out of 12 years of economic expansion?" (You can switch these lines when a Democrat asks you the question.) Or more poignantly, "Do you credit Adolf Hitler for the dramatic economic upturn in Germany after he assumed power in 1933?"

What is really happening is that these leaders got into power because the people, despairing over their depression, demanded the ouster of the incumbents. The trend turned, and the new leader got the credit. Sometimes, voters at market bottoms do elect leaders with better economic policies. Usually, they don't.

Conversely, leaders in power during financial collapses are rarely directly at fault. Usually years of mismanagement by others set the stage. The leaders in power at the time, though, always appear inept, because they take actions designed to "help the economy," which fail, or they decline to take actions and are blamed for fiddling while Rome burns. Regardless of what they do or don't do, the public blames them and their party and kicks them out.

Political Stresses in Major Bear Markets

As we discussed in Chapter 26, bear markets create social polarization; in the political realm, that means radical politics. That much I can guarantee in the upcoming depression. Who wins the battles or the war is not scripted beforehand, except that the incumbents perceived to be in power lose.

In recent years, voter turnout has been low, races have been lackluster and close, and politics have been middle-of-the-road, with little difference between the major parties. Get ready for dramatic political changes.

In the U.S. stock collapse of 1835-1842, a brand-new political party (the Whigs) won the presidential election in 1840 and another (the Democrat Republicans), which had held power for forty years, soon afterward dissolved. In the election of 1860, following the stock bottom and deep recession of 1859, politics were so polarized that many states did not list all the presidential candidates on their ballots. A new party (Republican) won its first election. The following year, the Civil War broke out. The election of 1932, near the bottom of the Great Depression, was less tense but still a watershed, which led to the transformation of the United States into a semi-socialist state.

Given the projected size of this bear market, look for nations and states to split and shrink. Look for regional governments to challenge national ones. There is no way to know exactly where such splits will erupt, but they will erupt somewhere.

International politics will become increasingly dangerous. The number of annual nuclear explosions, whether for testing or attack, waxes and wanes inversely with the stock market. (For a graph, see Chapter 16 in *The Wave Principle of Human Social Behavior*.) Look for an increased number of nuclear explosions during the bear market.

Debt and fiat money create political risks. Overseas investors and central banks own 45 percent of the U.S. Treasury's bonds in the marketplace. The largest investors are Japan and China. Ultimately, the turmoil of a record-breaking debt liquidation could force the Treasury or the Fed to renege on some of its obligations, which could have extreme political consequences and turn global sentiment viciously against the U.S. On the other hand, an irony arises in the area of currency. The Fed's September 2001 bulletin reports that an estimated 90 percent of the new $100 bills ordered by the Federal Reserve Bank of New York are used to "satisfy foreign demand." According to a 1994 *New York Times* article, "In Russia, Romania, Tajikstan, China, Vietnam and other countries [the U.S. dollar] has become 'the official unofficial tender.'" Since 70 percent of dollar currency is overseas, a major dollar-based credit deflation would transfer 70 percent of the surviving dollars' expanding purchasing power to non-U.S. holders of dollar bills. Americans hold a larger percentage of IOUs, while others hold a larger percentage of the real thing, that is, to the extent that it is real. What political decisions such a situation may cause are anyone's guess, and so are the consequences.

What To Do If You Have Political Aspirations

If there is a major stock market crash, you want to run for office near the bottom. You will be revered by the public and historians if you win. George Washington, Abraham Lincoln, Franklin Roosevelt and Ronald Reagan were all elected at or near the bottom of severe downtrends, and all have an exalted place in American history.

Third parties do well in tough times; so do outsiders and radicals; incumbents do poorly. So if you are a non-incumbent political animal, you can plan now to take advantage of the situation. If you want to be a politician, plan to run for office on any party ticket but that of the leader(s) in your country who rode the trend down.

Why Politics Matter in the Context of This Book

At some point during a financial crisis, money flows typically become a political issue. You should keep a sharp eye on political trends in your home country. In severe economic times, governments have been known to ban foreign investment, demand capital repatriation, outlaw money transfers abroad, close banks, freeze bank accounts, restrict or seize private pensions, raise taxes, fix prices and impose currency exchange values. They have been known to use force to change the course of who gets hurt and who is spared, which means that the prudent are punished and the thriftless are rewarded, reversing the result from what it would be according to who *deserves* to be spared or get hurt. In extreme cases, such as when authoritarians assume power, they simply appropriate or take *de facto* control of your property.

You cannot anticipate every possible law, regulation or political event that will be implemented to thwart your attempt at safety, liquidity and solvency. This is why you must plan ahead and pay attention. As you do, think about these issues so that when political forces troll for victims, you are legally outside the scope of the dragnet.

Chapter 28:

How To Identify a Safe Haven

As I said in Chapter 26, the real risk of social unrest will probably involve not so much roving itinerant bands looting your home — a classic fear that is rarely realized — as much as *international conflict* and *domestic repression*. In a bear market, both international and domestic tensions increase, and the resulting social actions can be devastating.

Far more people in the past century had their lives wrecked or terminated by domestic implosions than by war. Whether you lived in Russia in the 1920s, Germany in the 1930s, Europe in the 1940s, China in the late 1940s, Cuba in 1959 or Cambodia in the 1970s, the smart thing to do early was to get out of Dodge. However, if you ever make such a decision, you will have to be lucky as well as smart. The people in Europe who decided in 1937 to move away before things got worse were the prudent ones. But one or two of them might have said, "Let's go somewhere far away and safe. Let's go out to the Pacific and live on one of those sleepy islands in the Philippines." In other words, you might guess wrong.

One good guide to the world's developing crisis spots is Richard Maybury's *Early Warning Report*. If you are an Asian, African or Middle Eastern resident, his analysis is especially pertinent. Maybury has also published some excellent primers on inflation and justice. You may contact him through the following means:

See Appendix A for updated contact information

Early Warning Report
Website: www.richardmaybury.com
Email: pmc701@aol.com
Address: P.O. Box 84908, Phoenix, AZ 85701
Phone: 800-509-5400 and 602-252-4477
Fax: 602-943-2363
Editor: Richard Maybury

If you live in a country with unstable politics, you should think about where you might go if things get oppressive. Like everything in a developing crisis, it is imperative to be prepared well before you have to make a final decision.

Some readers, admittedly only a few, may find merit in the idea of spending some time outside of their home countries while a depression unfolds. After researching the international scene for free and stable Western-style English-speaking countries, I find five top candidates: the United States, Canada, Australia, New Zealand and Ireland.

The world's #1 choice for refuge is the United States. Indeed, the philosophical foundation of the United States and its (sometimes dormant) embodiment by many of its citizens may bode well for a low likelihood of severe domestic repression. Nothing is impossible, of course, and some people argue that the history of civilizations suggests that, on a multi-century basis at least, the peak of U.S. world power is at hand and repression will follow. Potentially more dangerous is the international threat. The U.S.'s penchant for involving itself in other countries' disputes has made it a prime target for terrorists and certain governments. Any sustained or coordinated effort by America's enemies could make domestic life highly unstable. Alternatively, if authoritarians assume power at the federal level near the bottom of a depression (which happened throughout Europe and Asia in the 1930s and 1940s), difficulties could arise from domestic sources.

Simply *preparing* to move might not prove to be enough. Before you actually take that crucial action, your country of choice might shut its borders. Your country of *origin* might shut its borders. If terrorists infect a city in your nation with a biological warfare agent, you may be banned from entering any other nation. If you ever reach the point that you are sure you want a foreign refuge, you should move right then. If you choose a safe haven, and if the threats pass, you can always return to your home country.

At minimum, make sure that your passport is current, since demand for passports may increase later and delay processing. Another great idea is to obtain a "green card" or permanent resident visa in the country to which you would probably move if you came to such a decision. Usually they are issued for a period of five years or so, at which time you must renew them from inside that country. Permanent-resident visas generally cost about $US 4000 in legal fees to obtain, although most attractive countries have do-it-yourself forms available on the Internet. Like everything else, though, getting an extended visa takes time. You have to fill out forms and meet fairly stringent requirements. Even if you are quick and efficient, your legal representative or your host government might not be. Silly roadblocks can crop up that require another piece of paper, and so on. The point is, to get what you want, act early. Before actually packing up to move, you should consult an attorney in your chosen country so that you understand its laws.

A great way to get to know other countries from your armchair is by way of the *Eyewitness Travel Guides,* by Dorling Kindersley Publishing. They are not only packed with information, like most travel guides, but they are also loaded with breathtaking and informative photos. Their current cost is $24.95 each. For specific information about these countries' visitation and extended visitation policies, investigate the following websites:

United States: www.bcis.gov
Canada: www.cic.gc.ca/english
Australia: www.immi.gov.au
New Zealand: www.immigration.govt.nz
Ireland: www.justice.ie

Some of these sites are easier to use than others; you may have to poke around to find what you want. Sometimes web addresses change. If any of these sites move, or if you wish to investigate countries other than those listed above, just perform an Internet search on key words. Most immigration offices have their own websites.

I thought about filling up a couple of chapters with the pros and cons of these and other nations, but in the end, what really matters is what matters to *you*. Some of these countries have a better set of laws, others better weather, others a better culture, others better infrastructure, others more convenience. I am unfamiliar with non-English speaking countries that other people have been recommending, such as Argentina, Chile and Costa Rica, partly for the reason that I am unconvinced that they would be stellar havens of peace in a global depression. There are also many beautiful small island countries around the world, which rarely seem to be the focus of international conflict. You will have to sift through the data, the books and the brochures and decide for yourself. Of course, the best way to approach such a question is to visit selected locations personally. They make great vacation spots, so you will hardly regret it. Who says contemplating a depression can't have its pleasures?

Chapter 29:

Calling in Loans and Paying off Debt

People and institutions that best weather the system-wide debt liquidation of a deflationary crash and depression are those that take on *no debt* and extend *no risky credit*. This is the ideal situation for most people most of the time, anyway.

Handling Credit

In this book, we have already covered many topics that pertain to the problem of risky credit. Make sure that you do not lend your money to a weak debt issuer, whether corporate, governmental or any other entity. If you have already done so, trade it for something better.

There is also the question of personal credit extension. Have you lent money to friends, relatives or co-workers? The odds of collecting any of these debts are usually slim to none, but if you can prod your personal debtors into paying you back before they get further strapped for cash, it will not only help you but it will also give you some additional wherewithal to help those very same people if they become destitute later.

Handling Debt

If at all possible, remain or become debt-free. Being debt-free means that you are freer, period. You don't have to sweat credit card payments. You don't have to sweat home or auto repossession or loss of your business. You don't have to work 6 percent more, or 10 percent more, or 18 percent more just to stay even.

If you can afford it, the best mortgage is none at all. If you own your home outright and lose your job, you will still have a residence. When banks are throwing others out of their homes, you will still have a place to live. If you can't pay the rent on your business space, you can move your business into your house. And so on. I would rather own a crackerbox outright than have a mansion with mortgage payments I can barely make.

Consider the bank's situation in times of financial stress. Suppose you have paid off enough of your mortgage so that you own 50 percent of your home, which reflects the average equity held by homeowners nationwide. Suddenly, you find that you can't make further payments because of money problems in a depression. At that point, even if house prices had fallen by a whopping 50 percent, your bank would see it as no drop at all. It can place your property (actually *its* property) on the market. If the house sells for only 50 percent of its peak value, the bank gets 100 percent of its outstanding loan back. You can see why banks are pressured to sell properties in such situations. Of course, you end up homeless after slaving to pay off half the mortgage on the house over many years. That's what happens to many homeowners in a depression.

I suppose it might be possible to be creative in an otherwise impossible situation. Some people might decide to borrow as much of the home's value as possible, put the proceeds in a safe money-market fund and use those funds to meet the mortgage, thus assuring no missed payments for the duration. The problem with this idea is that many people are their own worst enemies, and they lack the discipline to protect the needed cash. They can find themselves both broke and homeless either way.

One way out of a debt load is personal bankruptcy. I don't recommend it because it isn't honest. People lent you their hard-earned money; you should pay it back. If you truly are a victim of unforeseen circumstances and must declare bankruptcy, apologize to your creditors and tell them that you hope the experience taught them a lesson about under-collateralized lending.

Chapter 30:

What You Should Do If You Run a Business

Avoid long-term employment contracts with employees. Try to locate in a state with "at-will" employment laws. Red tape and legal impediments to firing could bankrupt your company in a financial crunch, thus putting everyone in your company out of work.

If you run a business that normally carries a large business inventory (such as an auto or boat dealership), try to reduce it. If your business requires certain manufactured specialty items that may be hard to obtain in a depression, stock up.

If you are an employer, start making plans for what you will do if the company's cash flow declines and you have to cut expenditures. Would it be best to fire certain people? Would it be better to adjust all salaries downward an equal percentage so that you can keep everyone employed?

A cynic might recommend that if you are an employer, you should try to pay in stock or options, but if you share the expectations presented in this book, that course of action would be dishonest. Besides, an employee who gets gypped is hardly going to serve your company well. Don't forget, depressions don't last forever; when the next upturn comes, you will want a loyal staff to help you prosper in it, and they will want a healthy company to help them prosper, too. To encourage that result, pay what and how you need to for the talent you require.

If you manage a bank, insurance company, money management firm or other financial institution, try to work out of your speculative derivative positions, particularly bullish ones. Reduce stock market risk as much as possible. If you must be heavily invested in stocks — for example if you manage a stock mutual fund — hedge your positions with options. Tidy up your mortgage portfolio. Get rid of all second-tier debt paper. If you have invested in municipal bonds, consumer debt, real estate debt, junk bonds or anything other than top-grade paper, sell it at today's lofty prices. Get on a solid footing with investments that are high quality, liquid and commonly understood.

Perhaps most important, plan how you will take advantage of the next major bottom in the economy. Positioning your company properly at that time could ensure success for decades to come.

Chapter 31:

What You Should Do with Respect to Your Employment

Over the past decade, more and more companies have been compensating employees with stock options instead of money. In 2001, over half of America's large public companies were paying over half of their employees in stock options. As a market analyst, I am fascinated with the value of these figures as a reflection of society-wide stock-market optimism. As someone trying to help you, I see them as a trap that you should avoid.

If you have no special reason to believe that the company you work for will prosper so much in a contracting economy that its stock will rise in a bear market, then cash out any stock or stock options that your company has issued to you (or that you bought on your own).

If your remuneration is tied to the same company's fortunes in the form of stock or stock options, try to convert it to a liquid income stream. Make sure you get paid actual money for your labor.

If you have a choice of employment, try to think about which job will best weather the coming financial and economic storm. Then go get it.

If you are entrepreneurial, start thinking of ways to serve people in a depression so that you will prosper in it. For example,

I am writing this book. Think about what people will need when times get hard. Some people automatically think that providing services for strapped people is the right choice when they think "depression." Certainly, opportunities are there. At the same time, that's not where much of the money is. Many people will *not* have their assets tied up in the stock market or other risky investments, and if deflation occurs, their real purchasing power will soar. At the bottom of the Great Depression, 70 percent of the population had jobs, and they were quite well off. You can prosper by providing services to the solvent and the wealthy. Offering services to creditors may also yield steady employment. For example, because so much of today's debt is consumer debt, the repo business will probably thrive. There will also be a boom in bankruptcy services in a depression; maybe you can keep out of debt by helping others manage theirs.

If you have charitable impulses, this is the time to exercise them. Government services will shrink in a depression, and many people will be suffering. If you are *really* creative, find a way to help destitute people and make money doing so.

Unfortunately, I don't have all the answers for your situation. You know your skills and tastes better than I do. Now is the time to take account of them.

Chapter 32:

Should You Rely on Government To Protect You?

In one sense, the answer is yes. You always have to live somewhere. If you are fortunate enough to live in a safe, free country, you can probably tell that those benefits are greatly a product of its philosophy of government. To that extent, you should rely on the best government you can find. Other than that, government can be a disappointing guardian.

Compounding the Problems

Government is rarely prepared for national financial calamities or economic depressions, and when it is, they are unlikely to occur. This is not a result of personal failures so much as an aspect of collective human nature. People are often prepared for the past but rarely for the future.

Generally speaking, the intelligent way for an individual to approach the vagaries of his or her financial future is to have *savings* or buy *insurance*. Governments almost invariably do the opposite. They spend and borrow throughout the good times and find themselves strapped in bad times, when tax receipts fall. Like their counterparts around the world, the Social Security, Medicare, Medicaid and "welfare" systems in the U.S. have been dispersing billions of dollars throughout decades of mostly good times. Even today, political forces are trying to raise the government's payouts, for example to include coverage of mental as well as physical illness, which seems to be another express ticket to insolvency.

When the bust occurs, governments won't have the money required to service truly needy people in unfortunate circumstances. They are likely then to make things worse by extending "unemployment benefits," which sucks money away from employers and makes them lay off more workers, by raising the cap on retirement benefit taxes, which takes money away from employees and makes them unable to save and spend, and by increasing taxes generally, which impoverishes productive people so that they cannot spend and invest. It's sad, but the pattern is almost always the same.

Dependencies To Avoid

Don't rely on government programs for your old age. Retirement programs such as Social Security in the U.S. are wealth-transfer schemes, not funded insurance, so they rely upon the government's tax receipts. Likewise, Medicaid is a federally subsidized state-funded health insurance program, and as such, it relies upon transfers of states' tax receipts. When people's earnings collapse in a depression, so does the amount of taxes paid, which forces the value of wealth transfers downward. Every conceivable method of shoring up these programs can lead only to worse problems. A "crisis" in government wealth-transfer programs is inevitable.

Don't rely on projected government budget surpluses. A couple of years ago, the U.S. government declared a budget surplus, projected it years into the future and predicted healthy trends for its wealth-transfer programs. Was that a proper conclusion? Well, in 1835, after over two decades of economic boom, U.S. government debt became essentially fully paid off for the first (and only) time. Conventional economists would cite such an achievement as a bullish "fundamental" condition. (Any time an analyst claims to be using "fundamentals" for macroeconomic or financial forecasting, run, don't walk, to the nearest exit.) In actuality, that degree of government solvency occurred the very year of the onset of a 7-year bear market that produced two back-to-back depressions. Government surpluses generated by something other than a permanent policy of thrift are the product of exceptionally high tax receipts during boom times and therefore signal major tops. They're not bullish; they're bearish and ironically portend huge deficits directly around the corner.

Don't rely on any government's bank-deposit "insurance." The money available through the FDIC, for example, is enough to cover only a small fraction of U.S. bank deposits. As Japan's troubles increase, its government has proposed lowering the value of insured deposits; that could happen in any country. The whole idea of having other banks and taxpayers guarantee bank deposits is theft in the first place and thus morally wrong and thus ultimately practically wrong. Government sponsored deposit insurance has lulled depositors into a false sense of security. After the 1930s, when thousands of banks failed, depositors became properly wary of profligate banks. Today they don't know or care what their bank officers are doing with their money because they think that the government insures their deposits. Deposit insurance will probably save accounts in the first few distressed banks, but if there is a system-wide money and credit implosion, this insurance won't protect you.

Don't rely incautiously on government's obligations to you if you are a retired government worker. In Argentina in recent weeks, the government suspended state pension payments to 1.4 million retired state employees. It had no money to pay because times got tough, and it had never saved when times were good. The same thing could happen to many governments around the world, whether national, state or local, which pay billions of dollars annually in pensions. All of them are dependent either upon wealth transfer or upon managed funds that may or may not be properly invested.

Don't rely on all governments to pay their debts. In the 1930s, Fulton County, Georgia, where I grew up, was formed from two bankrupt counties that defaulted on their bonds. By 1938, state and local municipalities had defaulted on approximately 30 percent of the total value of their outstanding debt. Much of it was eventually resolved; some wasn't. U.S. investors today own billions of dollars worth of municipal bonds, thinking they are getting a great deal because that bond income is tax-exempt. This tax break may be a bonus in good times, but like so many seemingly great deals, this one will ultimately trap investors into a risky position. Governments that have borrowed to the hilt were running deficits even in the booming 1990s, so the risk of default in a depression is huge. If the issuers of your tax-exempt bonds default, you will have the ultimate tax haven: being broke. Quite a few munis are "insured," which salesmen will tell you means the same as "guaranteed." Such guarantees work fine until defaults drag down the insurers. That is to say, when you really need the supposed guarantees, they can fail. Given the huge extent of today's municipal indebtedness, such failures are inevitable.

Don't rely on your central bank, either. Ultimately, it is not in control of your country's stock market, bond market or interest rates. It mostly reacts to market forces. People think that the Fed "lowered interest rates" in 2001. For the most part, the *market* lowered interest rates. Declining interest rates are not a "first cause" designed to induce borrowing; rather, a dearth of borrowing is a "first cause" that makes interest rates decline. Interest rates on perceived safe debt always fall when an economy begins to deflate. So the record-breaking decline in short-term U.S. interest rates last year was not any kind of "medicine." It was not primarily administered but an effect. Japan's prime interest rate fell to nearly zero over the past decade because of its ongoing deflation. That drop in the cost of borrowing didn't change the economy. Why? Because the economy was in charge of the drop. The most that a central bank can do is distort normal market trends and make credit a bit tighter or looser than it would otherwise be. Unfortunately, every such distortion has a counterbalancing market-induced correction later. The Fed's record-breaking monetary looseness during 2001 has revived the economy and propped up asset markets for a few months, but it probably won't last much longer than that. Ultimately, it will simply serve to make the contraction worse.

Don't rely on government to bail out the banking system. When Barings Bank failed, the Bank of England declined to save Barings' depositors. The World Bank and the IMF did not bail out the banks that collapsed in Southeast Asia in 1997. The Japanese Ministry of Finance has not been bailing out troubled Japanese banks. No one is bailing out Argentina's banks today. The French government bailed out Credit Lyonnais in a series of bailouts from 1994 through 1998 that drained more than $20 billion from France's tax intake. This was not much of an exception, though, because the bank was state-owned. Financial institutions and the U.S. government, through the FSLIC and then the Resolution Trust Corporation, bailed out the Savings & Loan industry a dozen years ago to the tune of $481 billion. These were unfortunate actions. Yes, unfortunate, because they lulled French and American bank depositors, who might otherwise have become wary, into thinking that they are protected against anything. How many more bailouts can France afford? Or the U.S.? If many big banks get in trouble, prudence will dictate that even the richest governments stand aside. If instead they leap unwisely into bailout schemes, they will risk damaging the integrity of their own debt, triggering a fall in its price. Either way, again, deflation will put the brakes on their actions.

Don't expect government services to remain at their current levels. The ocean of money required to run the union-bloated, administration-stultified public school systems will be unavailable in a depression. School districts will have to adopt cost-cutting measures, and most of them will result in even worse service. Encourage low-cost free-market solutions, which will benefit both children and teachers. The tax receipts that pay for roads, police and jails, fire departments, trash pickup, emergency (911) monitoring, water systems and so on will fall to such low levels that services will be restricted. Look for ways to get better services elsewhere wherever it is legal and possible.

Don't rely on government "watchdogs." They rarely foresee disasters. U.S. regulators did not anticipate the Savings & Loan industry collapse. Subsequent investigation revealed several years of immense corruption. Enron created some 850 suspicious partnerships and employed an army of "inventive" accountants. Still, the SEC and the FASB were clueless about anything being amiss. A $68 billion company collapsed, impoverishing countless employees and creditors. Now the watchdogs in Congress are holding "hearings." Do you think this will help the employees and investors who bet the farm on Enron? Well, when the Insull utility trust similarly collapsed in 1931-1932, no investor was reimbursed a nickel; no manager ever went to jail. With 20/20 hindsight, Congress passed a few new laws.

Be smart. Don't let your financial future end up depending upon proceedings covered by C-Span.

Chapter 33:

A Short List of Imperative "Do's" and Crucial "Don'ts"

Recall the old Chinese character that entwines crisis and opportunity in the same glyph. Position yourself to take advantage of what's coming.

Don't:

- Generally speaking, don't own stocks.

- Don't own any but the most pristine bonds.

- Generally speaking, don't invest in real estate.

- Generally speaking, don't buy commodities.

- Don't invest in collectibles.

- Don't trust standard rating services.

- Don't presume that government agencies will protect your finances.

- Don't buy goods you don't need just because they are a bargain. They will probably get cheaper.

Do:

- Fight the inertia that will keep you from taking action to prepare for the downturn. Start taking steps now.

- Involve your significant others in your decisions. Put your home or business partners in tune with your thinking before it's too late.

- Talk to heavily invested parents or in-laws who may be planning to pass on their investments to you. See if you can get them to become safe and liquid.

- Think globally, not just domestically.

- Open accounts at two or three of the safest banks in the world.

- Invest in short-term money market instruments issued by the soundest governments.

- Own some physical gold, silver and platinum.

- Have some cash on hand.

- Make sure that you have insurance policies only with the safest firms and make sure that they deal only with safe banks.

- If you are so inclined, speculate conservatively in anticipation of a declining stock market.

- Sell any collectibles that you own for investment purposes.

- If it is right for your circumstances, sell your business.

- Make a list of things you want to buy at much lower prices when they go on "liquidation sale."

• If you want to have kids, hurry up. Statistics show that fewer people feel like doing so during a bear market.

• Give friends a copy of this book.

• Keep up with our *Bear Market Strategies* page, a continually updated report on-line at http://www.con-querthecrash.com/readerspage.

• *Contact the services mentioned in this book!* I am a market analyst and forecaster, not a banker, insurer, money manager, institution rater or depression strategist. These services can help guide you through the maze. Some of them can help you design your whole strategy in a matter of days.

• Plan how to take advantage of the next major uptrend. For example, go back to school during the decline and come out with extra skills just as the economy begins to recover. Apprentice in a job for low pay and learn enough to start your own business at the bottom so you can ride the next big upwave of prosperity. Investigate troubled businesses to buy at the bottom at deep discounts.

• Smile! because you will not be jumping out of the window; you'll be preparing for the incredible opportunities listed in the next chapter.

Chapter 34:

What To Do at the Bottom of a Deflationary Crash and Depression

At the bottom of a crash and depression, reverse most of Chapter 33's investment "do's" and "don'ts." When the Elliott wave pattern in the major stock market averages indicates that the collapse is over, take a good portion of your safely stored cash and do the following:

•Cover shorts and buy stocks of surviving companies at fire sale prices.

• Buy depressed bonds from issuers that have survived.

• Buy more gold, silver and platinum.

• Buy prime pieces of investment property from distressed banks.

• Buy your favorite uninhabited home or mansion at pennies on the dollar.

• Buy the under-rented office building or the abandoned business facility you need for the cost of back taxes.

•Buy your favorite art and collectibles at bargain prices.

• Buy your own business back, start a business, or buy a distressed business cheap.

• Keep an eye on commodities. Generally, one would wait about two decades, when inflation begins to accelerate as the Kondratieff liquidity cycle approaches its peak, to buy them aggressively. Because a financial crisis could ignite hyperinflationary political forces at the bottom of the deflation, you might decide to buy some commodities then as a safety hedge. If the futures market survives the crash, the Rogers Raw Materials Fund should provide an excellent vehicle. It invests in an international basket of 35 commodities, continually adjusting it to maintain constant percentage weightings for each commodity. These maneuvers are a mechanical method of buying relative weakness and selling relative strength, which helps the fund's profitability. You can learn more about the fund at its website, www. rogersrawmaterials.com or by calling 800-775-9352 or 866-304-0450.

• Choose your location well and remain watchful of world affairs, because wars often break out during or shortly after depressions. (For more specifics, see Chapter 16 of *The Wave Principle of Human Social Behavior*.)

• Sit back and watch the investment markets in which you have invested turn up strongly and surprise the world.

You've survived! Now prosper!

BOOK THREE

(NEW FOR THE SECOND EDITION)

PUBLISHER'S PREFACE

The first edition of *Conquer the Crash* advised readers to stay completely out of trouble by avoiding stocks, bonds, real estate and commodities. It strongly recommended investing primarily in the safest cash equivalents and some gold, along with a bag or two of silver coins for coming emergencies. This was good advice. Cash today buys more stocks, more property and more commodities than it did at these markets' highs over the past four years. Gold has done pretty well, too. Perhaps most impressively, traders enjoyed the start of what could be a once-in-a-century ride on the short side of the stock market.

Despite being a bestseller, *Conquer the Crash* garnered no notice whatsoever from the establishment media during the meltdown of 2005-2009. Perhaps its thesis is too radical for most writers to acknowledge. But reality may soon catch up with it. Since this book was published, the figures on debt and economic performance cited herein as bearish signs have all gotten worse, not better, as Prechter shows in Appendix E. This is one reason why we feel confident in issuing a new edition of this book.

Another reason is the accuracy of the book so far despite its complete divergence from mainstream—and even non-mainstream—economic commentary. Prechter forecast a broad psychological shift from optimism to pessimism, in which creditors and debtors, producers and consumers, and investors worldwide would change their primary orientation from aggressive expansion to defensive conservation. Even details of the forecasts in this book have been accurate so far. It predicted bank failures (which now occur weekly), pension-fund stresses, the implosion of collateralized securities, the formation of government bailout schemes, a collapse in Fannie Mae stock, the failure of the big bond-rating services to issue warnings, government restrictions on short sales, and—most impressively—an exceptionally rare, simultaneous fall in real estate, stocks and commodities, all of which have happened.

But the most dramatic among Prechter's forecasted events are still to come. In other words, you still have time—if you act swiftly—to benefit from this book's recommendations.

To keep the record intact, Book One of this volume (the analytical portion) is republished exactly as it appeared in the original edition. Book Two (the strategy section) is also the same, except that printings in 2003-2005 added some bits of new material, which are retained here.

Book Three, which you are reading now, is new for this edition. In Appendices A and B, Prechter notes some changes to his recommended services, adds some new ones and updates ratings and contact information. Then Appendix C takes over where Book One left off, bringing you in real time through the topping process with excerpts from Prechter's published commentary during the mid-decade reflationary binge. Appendix D adds Prechter's key essays through 2007 on the inevitability of deflation, extending the theme of Chapters 9 through 13 of this book. Finally, Appendix E provides closure by updating Chapter 1 of Conquer the Crash and taking a retrospective look at a decade of optimism. It also revisits Prechter's 1978 scenario for a major bull market followed by a major bust. This very long term forecast seems to be playing out.

Speaking of deflation, as far as we can tell, Prechter is the only published analyst in recent years who has resolutely forecast a historically large, destructive deflation. The vast majority of economists forecasted stability, normalcy and moderate inflation, while bears predicted runaway inflation resulting from the Fed and the government's policies. In the mid-2000s, the former group enthusiastically recommended stocks and property, while the latter group advocated commodities and foreign assets, all of which plunged so severely in 2008 as to set speed records for lost value. Prechter remains steadfast in his forecast—issued back when the world was still in full-on party mode—that there would not be either a stable economy *or* a hyperinflationary boom but a deflationary collapse. So there is no denying that—right or wrong—Prechter's deflationary outlook was, and still is, a distinctly minority view.

If he continues to be right, those select investors who have been surviving and prospering by following the advice in this book will be alone in having funds to invest at the final bottom. It should prove to be one of the greatest buying opportunities of all time.

Appendix A

UPDATED CONTACT INFORMATION FOR SERVICES DESIGNED TO HELP YOU SURVIVE AND PROSPER IN A DEFLATIONARY DEPRESSION

Updated Information on Recommended Services

Suitability and Risk

Many of the services listed in this book are suitable for all investors. Some are suited only for those of a certain level of expertise, wealth and/or income. In pursuing your chain of inquiries, you may occasionally discover some financial services that are unavailable to certain investors who fail to meet legal and financial criteria required by their nations' Accredited, Qualified and/or Professional Investor rules. These rules may prohibit your access to services that authorities deem to be unsuitable for you. Entities that need to comply with such rules should be able to explain which rules, if any, pertain to you. As you explore and judge various courses of action, please forgive any entities that refuse to fulfill your desires because they are following legal requirements.

I have endeavored to provide enough avenues of inquiry in this book so that readers at all strata of wealth — small to large — will find methods for protecting their capital in times of deflation and depression. If you discover any that I haven't mentioned, please let me know so that I may investigate them for possible listing at our continually updated site for readers of this book at elliottwave.com/conquerthecrash.

We have positive information and impressions about the service providers listed in this book and believe them to have integrity. Nevertheless, I cannot endorse or guarantee other people's products or services. Therefore, it is imperative that each reader do his own proper investigation regarding suitability. I have experience with many of these service providers or know their CEOs personally. You will probably get even better service if you mention that you read about them in this book.

Changes to Recommended Services

Some aspects of our recommended services have changed since 2002:

Federated Investors, Inc. has bought the Prudent Bear Fund. David Tice is currently still the manager, but this arrangement may not be permanent. Whether the fund will continue to behave as it did in the past is uncertain. I have kept it on our Recommended Services list, but do your own due diligence.

Asset Allocation Consultants, listed in the original edition, now provides services to Access Fund Management, a discussion of whose services appeared in Chapter 20 of a later printing of the book and is maintained in this edition. Although I think this service is well thought out, I have declined at this time to include it in our Recommended Services list due to the myriad systemic risks that could affect a structure involving multiple managers, brokers, banks and an insurer to boot, all based in the U.S. But the information is in Chapter 20 if you wish to pursue this option, which otherwise is quite brilliantly constructed.

The "beta slippage" described in Chapter 20 for the inverse ("bear") index funds—as with index-tracking inverse ETFs as well—has proved to be a bigger issue than most people, including the fund managers themselves, expected. These funds track the market exceptionally well day by day but not over the long term, especially in choppy and volatile markets. They are therefore unsuited for long term investors. At the same time, the index funds impose difficult time constraints on short-term traders, who would have far more flexibility using futures contracts. Sometimes inverse index funds offer the only available option, for example if one's retirement plan prohibits short sales. But this is why in Chapter 23 I recommended getting out of such government-controlled structures. Only people who understand how these index funds work and can deal with their special features should entertain using them. I have omitted these inverse index funds from the Recommended Services list, but the information remains in Chapter 20 for those who are interested. For a good explanation of the slippage problem, see http://www.altenergys-tocks.com/archives/2009/02/ultrapromises_fall_short.html.

Additions to Recommended Services

GoldMoney: A Special Way to Own and Transact in Real Money

I have run into many people who think their money is safe because it is in bank CDs, corporate bonds, municipal bonds, money-market funds, etc. But most of these investments depend upon the solvency of some creditor institution that will probably not survive the developing depression. *Conquer the Crash* readers should continue to hold most of their liquid wealth in Treasury bills, greenback cash, short term debt of Switzerland, Singapore and New Zealand (see www.stablecurrencyindex.com) and some gold, ideally held in safe depositories such as those identified by SafeWealth Ltd., based in Switzerland.

When the crisis reaches an extreme, people may rediscover the values of using gold as money and give up on the idea of central banking. I want to be among the advance guard of the new monetary era by owning accounts denominated in real money, not the "IOU nothings" offered by banks worldwide under the fiat-enforced, debt-based, money-substitute system. Remember, a bank is a loan-brokering institution that in most cases has handed out, in exchange for promises to pay interest, your money to home buyers, car buyers, property developers, credit card borrowers and other such debtors. If you deposited all your money in a bank and it goes under because its debtors can't pay, you won't have the money to buy food, pay for heat or fill up your car's gas tank. But if you have real money in a vault, you will always have purchasing power.

To that end, there is a way to own gold that should—and someday may—serve as the world's currency. Well-known gold analyst and dealer James Turk has created a patented way to own actual gold—not a promise via certificate or contract—and to use its ownership as digital currency. This currency, unlike government monopoly money, has all three of the necessary virtues: It serves as a unit of account, a store of value and final payment. Through Jim's firm, GoldMoney, you can transfer U.S. dollars, Canadian dollars, euros, British pounds, Swiss francs or Japanese yen electronically from your checking account to buy grams of gold, called "goldgrams." You can choose to receive a currency deposit when you sell goldgrams. Silver is also available. Gold-Money stores your gold or silver in London and Zurich vaults insured through Lloyd's of London. You choose which vault(s) you would like to use. External auditors ensure that the company has the gold that it credits to you. GoldMoney never lends, which means that, unlike a bank, it can never become a participant in a credit bubble and thereby be subject to a bust. GoldMoney nevertheless has the convenience of a bank in that you can use goldgrams as currency simply by "clicking" goldgrams from your account to someone else's GoldMoney account. Essentially, GoldMoney is like online banking except that your account is denominated in goldgrams and mils, not dollars and cents, and represents a real asset—not a government's promise or a bank's construction loans.

There is no minimum account balance. Customers pay a monthly storage charge ranging from 0.15-0.18% per annum, depending on the weight of gold in your account. GoldMoney makes some of its profit from the spread, as customers buy goldgrams for one to three percent above the current spot rate, depending on the amount purchased. Considering what customers usually pay in terms of a premium for coins or bars, it's an attractive rate. Plus, you avoid the added expense of shipping and storing the coins. GoldMoney also generates some profit when you use your account to pay for things, as the company charges one percent of the value of each transaction up to a maximum of 100 mils (about $2.90 today), with a minimum fee of 10 mils (29 cents). This is a great arrangement, because it allows you to use the account even for small transactions without being gouged, yet it triggers only a negligible fee on very large amounts.

An account with GoldMoney is not the same as having physical metal in your hands. But that is both a drawback and an advantage. If you have to leave your jurisdiction someday due to political unrest, you won't have to figure out how to get your gold out, too. All you have to do is remember your account number. And if you do wish to hold physical gold, GoldMoney will ship your gold in bar form to virtually any requested location.

Opening the account is somewhat of a pain. It takes a couple of days to fill out all the required forms. You will have to go through 20 steps across multiple screens. They involve accessing your email account, questions about the source of your money and your investment plans, an identity check through Equifax (requiring your address, phone number, driver's license number and other such information) or by transmission of notarized documents, and eventually a copy of a photo I.D. This is because GoldMoney is a stickler—as it should be—for satisfying the government's requirements for knowing its customers, so it can stay in full legal compliance by shunning money launderers and other lawbreakers.

The main risk is with GoldMoney's associated banks. If you deposit money with GoldMoney and do not purchase metals immediately, the money is deposited in one of three British banks, which needless to say, in my view, are at risk of collapse. So if you decide to use GoldMoney, buy the metals you want as soon as you transfer money to the account. If you want to buy metals later, keep most of your money in a safe institution until you are ready to buy. Whatever your ultimate intentions, it would be a good idea to open the account with at least a small amount now, because when the markets are in chaos, you won't be able to focus, and if key intermediary banks shut down, you won't be able to transfer money at all.

GoldMoney advertises with my firm, and when I told the people there that I was going to recommend their services, they decided to arrange a special deal for you. When you open an account, you can receive six months of free gold storage to kick off your relationship with them. If you want this perk, make sure to sign on at www.goldmoney.com/VIP.

For the record, even though I know Jim Turk personally, believe GoldMoney to be 100 percent safe, have an account there myself and believe that risks in the banking system far outweigh anything I can imagine inside GoldMoney, unforeseen adverse events can always happen in life. Make sure you satisfy yourself that opening an account is the right thing to do. For more information about GoldMoney, see the contact information in the Recommended Services list.

Another Form of Cash

I have recently become aware of a new way to hold cash relatively safely and in large amounts. The "Certificate of Indebtedness" is a Treasury security that does not earn any interest and has no fixed maturity. In these ways, it is very like cash. Normally, there would be no reason to forfeit the interest on a T-bill. But if dealing with rollover transactions were to become problematic temporarily in the next phase of the financial crisis, it might be comforting to know that you are under no obligation to roll over the debt. The "C of I" can be bought, sold and held only in a TreasuryDirect account, which is run by the U.S. Treasury and is open to all investors—even those with as little as $1000 to invest. The intention of the instrument is to provide a temporary vehicle for holding funds designated for future Treasury security purchases. The Treasury does not allow anyone to transfer money from a bank to the C of I, probably because the Treasury does not want to appear as a competitor to banks. But it is O.K. to buy the usual Treasury debt securities, let them lapse, and leave the money in a C of I. The Treasury informed me that there is no limit on funds kept in the C of I, and redemptions can be made at any time. In many ways, this option is like using the U.S. Treasury as the banker for your deposits. To open an account, you will need the following items:

- Social Security number
- Driver's license number or state ID and exp date
- Your bank account number and bank's routing number
- E-mail address
- Password

Corporations and other such entities have a few different requirements. To access the form, go to www.treasurydirect.gov, click on "Open an Account," then "TreasuryDirect," and follow the instructions from there. You may find more information here: http://www.treasurydirect.gov/indiv/help/TDHelp/help_ug_152-CofILearnMore.htm.

Additional Money Managers

For this edition of the book, I am listing five additional money managers. All of them are friends of mine whose integrity and skill, in my experience, have been beyond question. I have not, however, investigated the financial soundness of the institutions with which they deal. You must satisfy yourself about every aspect of the services they offer. I have listed these managers in alphabetical order and added their contact information to the Recommended Services list in the "Money Managers" area.

Cycles expert Peter Eliades has developed a long-only seasonal investment strategy, which is employed by his company, Stockmarket Cycles Management. More than 70 percent of the time, his individually managed accounts earn interest in a money market fund of government-backed securities. The rest of the time, the accounts are long the market on selected days with 2x leverage. His model also has an alert mechanism to identify strong bear market environments, in which case it keeps funds on the sidelines even for those days when they would normally be invested. The program has returned much more than the S&P over the four years he has overseen real-money accounts. It beat the S&P in the rising years, and as the S&P fell over 50 percent from October 2007 to February 2009, his program returned a positive 28.6 percent. There are risks in using leverage, and there is no guarantee that the seasonal patterns he has isolated will continue to work. But so far his clients are making money in bull and bear markets.

Adam Nowak of AW Trading Strategies in Toronto has developed an intermediate-term market-timing model and used it in real time over many years. The model gives buy and sell signals on S&P futures and uses a 2 or 3 percent (depending upon conditions) contrary market move as a stop. The signals tend to be spaced months apart, so there is not a lot of trading. Futures are highly leveraged and carry substantial risk, but the client sets the size of each investment. Adam has a record of his real-time signals, and I have watched them be mostly success-ful for some years. There is no real-money track record due to constant changes in clients' invested funds and their continual interference in the decisions to buy or sell. If you want someone to manage futures trading for you in a brokerage account, you might wish to look into Adam's service.

Tom Rehberger of Private Asset Group spent two decades designing trading systems and trading for hedge funds. In the pro-cess he learned a lot about the essential flaws behind the models they sought to build and struck out on his own to build a better model. The result is the Tactical Investment Model, which takes long-only positions in exchange-traded funds (ETFs). Among the 700 or so ETFs available, Tom typically invests his clients only in the dozen or so with the most bullish indications according to his model. The model is also designed to avoid weak markets. For much of 2008, when all investment prices were falling, his model recommended no investments at all, undoubtedly a rare event. When the model is invested, leverage is available at the client's wishes. The PAG website offers more information and a complete disclosure page.

For the highly safety minded, Michael Smorch of Hillier Advisors is a rare find. Michael got well out in front of the down-trend by embracing *Conquer the Crash*'s message early and helping his clients get their capital liquid and safe. His specialty is capital preservation, and he has flown around the world identifying institutions and short term cash equivalents that he believes are most likely to survive the crash and depression. Hillier manages money only for high-net-worth clients with a minimum of $2 million to invest.

Martin Truax and Ron Miller of The Investment Planning and Management Group are two portfolio managers with over 35 years of experience. They are mostly long, but they raise cash and place hedges on portfolios when their sell signals indicate. They report that their independently monitored, real-money track record substantially beat the S&P over the past ten years. Having read their well-timed advice to clients over the years, I do not doubt their success. They manage stocks for income and growth as well as bond portfolios, currencies and gold. Contact them to discuss their track record and investment approach.

The main issue of concern regarding most money management services in the current environment is the strong probability that many—perhaps even most—banks and brokerage firms will fail before the crash and depression are over. The exceptional track records the above-mentioned trading services have produced in relatively normal times would become moot if the institutions they deal with were to shut down. Therefore, choose management services carefully and investigate second-party risks, while keeping the bulk of your money in safe cash equivalents in safe institutions during the decline. Once the bear market is over and surviving banks and brokers are identified, you may wish to utilize much more fully the excellent talents behind these more active services.

NOTE: *Contact information can change. For the latest updates, please visit http://www.conquerthecrash.com/readerspage*

RECOMMENDED SERVICES

Consultants on the World's Safest Banks, Insurance Companies and Precious Metals Storage Facilities

Introductions to international wealth preservation managers, private banks, insurance companies, general inquiries, etc.:

> SafeWealth Consultants Ltd.
> Email: clientservices@safewealthconsultants.com
> Address: Service Center, Grand-Rue 114, 2nd Level East,
>   CH-1820 Montreux, Switzerland
> Phone: (U.S. dial 011) 41-21-966-7200
> Fax: (U.S. dial 011) 41-21-966-7201
> Contact: Sr. Vice President: Cari Lima
> Contact for wealth preservation private consulting:
>   Vice-President: Robert Fortes
> Contact for insurance company introductions:
>   Corporate Administrator: Cybele Antoun

> Qualified institutions' typical minimums:
>   Insurance companies: 100,000 Sfr
>   Precious metals acquisition & storage: $100,000
>   Banks: 1 million Sfr
>   Asset Managers: 3 million Sfr

Precious metals acquisition and storage:

> SafeStore Ltd. — Service Center
> Email: clientservices@safestoreservices.com
> Delegated Administrator: Emmanuelle Seror

Managed Bear Funds

Comstock Capital Value Fund and Strategy Fund
Website: www.comstockfunds.com
Email: info@comstockfunds.com
Address: 24 S Main Street, Yardley PA 19067
Phone: 215-493-7076
Fax: 215-493-8083
Minimum: $1000 or $250 in an IRA
Managers: Charles Minter and Martin Weiner

Federated Prudent Bear Fund
Website: www.prudentbear.com
Email: info@prudentbear.com
Address: 1001 Liberty Ave, Pittsburgh, PA 15222
Phone: 800-245-4770
Minimum: $2000
Manager: David Tice

GAMCO Mathers Fund
Website: www.gabelli.com/mathers.html
Email: info@gabelli.com
Address: One Corporate Center, Rye NY 10580
Phone: 800-422-3554
Minimum: $1000
Manager: Henry van der Eb

Money Managers with a Safety Orientation

Hillier Advisors, LLC
Website: www.hillieradvisors.com
Email: michael@hillieradvisors.com
Address: 5 Radnor Corporate Ctr, 100 Matsonford Rd.
        Ste. 520, Radnor PA 19087
Phone: 610-977-0248

Fax: 610-964-3630
Minimum: $2 million
Contact: Michael Smorch

Lang Asset Management, Inc.
Website: www.langasset.com
Email: investments@langasset.com
Address: 5605 Glenridge Dr., Suite 1080
    Atlanta, GA 30342
Phone: 800-732-4171 and 404-256-4100
Fax 404-256-1473
Minimum: $200,000
CEO: Robert B. Lang

Money Managers with Timing and/or Allocation Models

AW Trading Strategies
Website: www.pfgcanada.ca
Email: anowak@pfgcan.com
Peregrine Financial Group Canada
Address: 1290 Central Parkway West, Ste 200
    Mississauga, ON L5C4R3 Canada
Phone: 905-896-4102
Fax: 905-896-8806
Minimum: $250,000
Contact: Adam M. Nowak, Futures Specialist

The Investment Planning & Management Group
Website: www.truaxmiller.mkadvisor.com
Email: martin.truax@morgankeegan.com
    ron.miller@morgankeegan.com
Address: 1100 Abernathy Road, Bldg. 500,
    Ste 1850, Atlanta GA 30328
Phone: 866-813-9911 or 770-673-2177

Fax: 770-673-2150
Minimum: $50,000 for managed accounts
Managing Directors: Martin Truax and Ron Miller

Stockmarket Cycles Management, Inc.
Email: garrett111@comcast.net
Address: 1805A Wagner Lane, Petaluma, CA 94954
Phone: 925-820-0161
Minimum: $500,000 commitment
CEO: Peter Eliades
Contact: Garrett Jones

Tactical Investment Models
Website: www.investpag.com
Email: investpag@gmail.com
Private Asset Group LLC
Address: 7465 W. Lake Mead Blvd, Ste. 103
        Las Vegas, NV 89128
Phone: 800-598-0631 or 702-932-8626
Fax: 800-598-0631 or 702-562-1228
Minimum: $50,000
President: Thomas J. Rehberger

Newsletters for Staying Globally Informed

Casey's International Speculator
Website: www.caseyresearch.com
Email: info@caseyresearch.com
Address: P.O. Box 84900, Phoenix, AZ 85071
Phone: 888-512-2739/602-445-2736
Editor: Doug Casey

The Gloom, Boom & Doom Report
Website: www.gloomboomdoom.com
Email: info@gloomboomdoom.com

Address: Suite 3311-3313, Two Int'l Finance Ctr,
        8 Finance St, Central, Hong Kong
Phone: (U.S. dial 011) 852-2-801-5410
Fax: 852-2-845-9192
Editor: Marc Faber

Grant's Interest Rate Observer
Website: www.grantspub.com
Email: webmaster@grantspub.com
Address: 2 Wall Street, New York, NY 10005
Phone: 212-809-7994
Fax: 212-809-8492
Editor: James Grant

The Long Wave Analyst
Website: www.longwavegroup.com
Email: igordon@longwavegroup.com
Long Wave Group Inc.
Address: Long Wave Analytics
        202-15388 24th Ave, South Surrey, BC
        V4A 2J2 Canada
Phone: 778-294-4286
Editor: Ian A. Gordon

Rosen Numismatic Advisory
Email: mauricerosen@aol.com
Numismatic Counseling, Inc.,
Address: P.O. Box 38, Plainview, NY 11803
Phone: 516-433-5800
Fax: 516-433-5801
CEO: Maurice Rosen

Safe Money
Website: www.moneyandmarkets.com
Email: elettter@moneyandmarkets.com
Address: Weiss Research Inc.
　　15430 Endeavor Drive, Jupiter, FL 33478
Phone: 800-291-8545 and 561-627-3300
Fax: 561-625-6685
Editor: Martin D. Weiss

SafeWealth Report
Email: clientservices@safewealthadvisory.com
Address: SafeWealth Advisory Div. — Service Center
　　SafeWealth Services, Grand-Rue 114,
　　2nd Level East, CH-1820 Montreux,
　　Switzerland
Phone: (in U.S., dial 011) 41-21-966-7200
Fax: (in U.S., dial 011) 41-21-966-7201

U.S. & World Early Warning Report
Website: www.chaostan.com
Email: pmc701@aol.com
Address: P.O. Box 84908, Phoenix, AZ 85701
Phone: 800-509-5400 and 602-252-4477
Fax: 602-943-2363
Editor: Richard Maybury

Physical Safety

This is a diverse field. See Chapters 26 and 28 for leads.

Real Money (Gold) Account

GoldMoney
Website: www.goldmoney.com/VIP

Email: support@goldmoney.com
Address: 12-14 David Place, St Helier,
        Jersey JE2 4TD, British Channel Islands
Phone: (U.S. dial 011) 44-1534-511-977
Fax: (U.S. dial 011) 44-1534-511-988
Director: James Turk

Safety Ratings for U.S. Banks and Insurance Companies

for institutions only:
Egan-Jones Ratings and Analytics
Website: www.egan-jones.com
President: Sean J. Egan

IDC Financial Publishing, Inc.
Website: www.idcfp.com
Email: info@idcfp.com
Address: P.O. Box 140, Hartland, WI 53029
Phone: 800-525-5457 and 262-367-7231
Fax: 262-367-6497

TheStreet.com Ratings Inc.
Website: www.thestreetratings.com
Address: 15430 Endeavour Dr., Jupiter FL 33478
Phone: 800-289-9222
Fax: 561-354-4497

Veribanc, Inc.
Website: www.veribanc.com
Email: service@veribanc.com
Address: P.O. Box 1610, Woonsocket, RI 02895
Phone: 800-837-4226
Fax: 401-766-2777

U.S. Gold, Silver and Coin Dealers

American Federal Rare Coin & Bullion
Website: americanfederal.com
Email: info@americanfederal.com
Address: PO Box 5810, Carefree, AZ 85377-5810
Phone: 800-221-7694
Fax: 480-553-5290
President/CEO: Nick Grovich

Fidelitrade
Website: www.fidelitrade.com
Email: info@fidelitrade.com
Address: 3601 North Market Street, Wilmington,
    DE 19802
Phone: 800-223-1080 and 302-762-6200
Fax: 302-762-7570
President/CEO: Jonathan Potts

Hancock & Harwell Rare Coins & Precious Metals
Website: www.raregold.com
Email: info@raregold.com
Address: Suite 310, 3155 Roswell Rd,
    Atlanta, GA 30305
Phone: 877-217-1776 and 404-261-6565
Fax: 404-237-6500
CEO: Robert L. Harwell

Investment Rarities, Inc.
Website: www.investmentrarities.com
Email: jcook@investmentrarities.com
Address: 7850 Metro Parkway, Ste 213,
    Minneapolis, MN 55425-1521
Phone: 800-328-1860 and 952-853-0700
CEO: James R. Cook

Miles Franklin Ltd.
Website: www.milesfranklin.com
Email address: andy@milesfranklin.com
Address: 801 Twelve Oaks Center Drive, Ste 834
        Wayzata, MN 55391
Phone: 800-822-8080 and 952-929-7006
Fax: 952-476-7971
CEO: Andy and David M. Schectman

Straight Talk Assets, Inc.
Website: www.coinmoney.com
Email: straighttalk@mindspring.com
Address: P.O. Box 1301, Gainesville, GA 30503
Phone: 800-944-9249 and 770-536-8045
CEO: Glenn R. Fried

Watching the Fed

Federal Reserve Board
Website: www.federalreserve.gov
Phone: 202-452-3819

Ludwig von Mises Institute
Website: www.mises.org
Email: contact@mises.org
Address: 518 West Magnolia Avenue,
        Auburn, AL 36832
Phone: 334-321-2100
Fax: 334-321-2119
Book catalog: www.mises.org/store/Books-C1.aspx

The Money Market Observer
Website: www.wrightson.com
Email: sales@wrightson.com
Wrightson Associates

Address: Harborside Financial Center, Plaza V
       Jersey City NJ 07311
Phone: 212-815-6540
Fax: 212-341-9103
Editor: Lou Crandall

TrimTabs.com Investment Research
Website: www.trimtabs.com
Email: service@trimtabs.com
Address: 1505 Bridgeway, Ste 121, Sausalito, CA 94965
Phone: 415-331-4400
Fax: 415-324-5873
Editor: Charles Biderman

Wave Analysis and Economic Forecasting

Elliott Wave International, Inc.
Website: www.elliottwave.com
Email: customerservice@elliottwave.com
Address: P.O. Box 1618, Gainesville, GA 30503
Phone: 800-336-1618 and 770-536-0309
Fax: 770-536-2514
Paid services: Financial periodicals, global market
       coverage, opportunity alerts, intraday market
       forecasts, books, online courses
Free services: EWI Independent, Weekly Select,
       Club EWI
Free for readers of this book: Special offers and free
       updates on services designed to protect you and
       your finances: www.conquerthecrash.com/
       readerspage
Associated websites:
       www.robertprechter.com
       www.socionomics.net
       www.socionomics.org
CEO: Robert R. Prechter, Jr.

UPDATED LISTS OF BANKS, INSURERS AND TREASURY-ONLY MONEY MARKET FUNDS IN THE U.S., TOP-RATED FOR SAFETY

Introduction

Chapter 19 of *Conquer the Crash* recommended only three financial rating services. This edition has added a fourth. Observe that the biggest, best-known and most widely followed rating services, which had long been sanctioned by government regulators, are *not* among them. The ratings posted by these firms blew up in 2008-2009, crushing the finances of the people who relied on them. Generally speaking, it pays to deal with independent judges who have no obligation to those they judge and no special privileges granted by government.

Weiss Ratings, Inc. provided one of the most reliable bank and insurance-company rating services in America. The company has been sold to TheStreet.com Ratings, whose ratings we use in the following tables. Although these lists are a valuable resource, be advised that I cannot be held responsible for the ratings accuracy of an outside service. I encourage you to research financial firms carefully on your own before committing funds.

(Note: The following lists are updated with information available as of September 2009.)

Treasury-Only Money Market Funds
(updating the lists from Chapter 18)

Banks are coming under pressure of insolvency, just as *Conquer the Crash* predicted, and bank runs and mass closings may not be far off. A better alternative for capital protection is money market funds that invest only in short-term Treasuries. You can even write checks against these accounts, which could be a handy service if banks close. For a review of how T-bill money-market funds work, see Chapter 18.

When I wrote *Conquer the Crash*, Vanguard's Treasury-only Admiral fund was the best bargain available. Now Vanguard accepts no new investors in either of its Treasury-only funds. As I warned in Chapter 19, you have to act while you can. Readers of the original book secured their accounts when they were available.

Below is a list of sizeable, still-available funds that hold no mortgages, asset-backed "securities," corporate debt, municipal bonds or anything aside from Treasuries. To the best of my knowledge, these are the only major money market funds that have committed to invest solely (or in one case primarily) in short-term Treasury debt. New York Mellon Bank owns Dreyfus, which could prove problematic. American Century is independent. Fund policies change over time, so be sure that you completely understand a fund's investment strategy and prospectus before committing any money.

STILL-AVAILABLE TREASURY-ONLY MONEY MARKET FUNDS WITH NO TRANSACTION CHARGES OR LIMITS		
Fund Name	**Toll-Free No.**	**Web Address**
American Century Capital Presv Fund I	(800) 345-2021	www.americancentury.com
Dreyfus 100% US Treasury MMF	(800) 782-6620	www.dreyfus.com

Table B-1   *(updating Table 18-1)*

Highest-Rated Banks in America, per TheStreet.com (updating the lists from Chapter 19)

In 2002, *Conquer the Crash* noted that depositors would soon become concerned about bank risks and move their money from weak banks to strong banks, making the weak banks weaker and the strong banks stronger. This is happening now. A recent Washington Post article notes that one of the banks listed in CTC has received a windfall from migratory deposits. (Read the article at elliottwave.com/wave/wp.)

Nevertheless, do not assume that once you find a relatively safe bank you can simply move all of your funds to it and sleep soundly. The entire U.S. banking system faces problems, and the environment is changing rapidly. Many U.S. banks are at risk, some in ways that even the best ratings firms may be unable to recognize or track. To illustrate the problem, consider that Lehman Brothers Commercial Bank was rated B+ on a list dated 6/30/08 from TheStreet.com Ratings, Inc. Just a few months after that list was published, Lehman Bros. filed for bankruptcy.

Because of such uncertainty, banks in general are not the safest place to put the bulk of your money right now. Observe, for example, that there is not one A or A+ rated bank on the list of top-rated large ($5b.+ in assets) U.S. banks, and there are six fewer B-or-higher-rated banks listed than there were in 2002. Obviously the first phase of the credit crisis crippled many banking institutions. Some smaller U.S. banks have been better at staying out of trouble, but the safest banks, by far, reside in Switzerland. Readers with substantial capital should place a comfortable amount of it in the safest institutions there, per the leads in Chapter 19. Those of lesser means who must bank in risky systems in their home territory should keep, even in relatively strong local banks, only enough money on deposit to cover living expenses and whatever additional funds you trust the bank to hold. Keep a comfortable amount of cash currency on hand

HIGHEST-RATED LARGE BANKS IN AMERICA

Source: TheStreet.com Ratings, Inc. Based on 3/31/09 data. Reprinted with permission

Company	State	TheStreet.com Financial Strength Rating	Total Assets ($MIL)
Bancorpsouth Bk	MS	B+	13,454
Bank of Hawaii	HI	B	11,427
Capitol Federal Svgs Bk	KS	B	8,292
Citizens Business Bk	CA	B+	6,411
Eastern Bk	MA	B	6,681
First Citizens B&TC	SC	B	6,904
First Hawaiian Bk	HI	B	13,366
First Niagara Bk	NY	B	9,491
Frost NB	TX	B+	15,376
GE Capital Fncl	UT	B+	11,512
International Bk of Commerce	TX	B	10,182
Northern Trust NA	FL	B	11,872
Peoples United Bk	CT	B	18,534
Silicon Valley Bk	CA	A-	10,277
State Street B&TC	MA	B+	142,458
UBS Bk USA	UT	B	33,959
UMB Bk NA	MO	B	8,699
USAA Savings Bk	NV	B	6,473
WestAmerica Bk	CA	B	5,388

Large banks have at least $5 billion in assets
A=Excellent; B=Good; C=Fair; D=Weak; E=Very Weak

Table B-2   *(updating Table 19-2)*

in case your bank shuts down. Also keep some non-numismatic gold and silver coins. Place a substantial portion of your liquid wealth in safe cash equivalents such as directly-held T-bills and Treasury-only money market funds. The T-bill money-market funds listed in the previous section allow you to write checks above a certain minimum (generally a few hundred dollars), so you can pay larger bills directly from the funds. At the right time you should also diversify into the currencies and short-term debt of the governments of Switzerland, Singapore and New Zealand, per our Stable Currency Index (stablecurrencyindex.com).

Highest-Rated Banks in America by State, per TheStreet.com (updating the list from Chapter 19)

The longer a bank stays on this list, the more it implies a consistent policy of relative safety. I suggest you compare this list with that in Chapter 19 to see which banks have maintained a consistent safety rating over this time.

Quarterly ratings are reported with a four-month time lag. As with all the lists in this Appendix, the ratings reported here are the latest available. They carry through the first quarter of 2009, when financial institutions suffered the most stressful conditions to date. In other words, these lists should provide a pretty good indication of relative bank safety in stressful times. The next wave down, however, should be far more severe, so keep an eye on updated ratings at www.conquerthecrash.com/readerspage or directly from the ratings firm at www.thestreet.com.

THE TWO HIGHEST-RATED BANKS IN EACH STATE
Source: TheStreet.com Ratings, Inc. (based on Q1 2009 data) Printed with permission.

Name	City	State	Total Assets in millions	TheStreet Safety Rating
Alabama				
FIRST NB OF TALLADEGA	TALLADEGA	AL	355.4	A
CITIZENS BANK OF WINFIELD	WINFIELD	AL	197.9	A
Alaska				
MOUNT MCKINLEY BK	FAIRBANKS	AK	271.4	A
FIRST NB ALASKA	ANCHORAGE	AK	2400.8	B+
Arizona				
NORDSTROM FSB	SCOTTSDALE	AZ	174.3	A-
FOOTHILLS BK	YUMA	AZ	140.5	B+
Arkansas				
FIRST NB IZARD CTY	CALICO ROCK	AR	137.0	A+
FIRST NATIONAL BANK & TRUST	MOUNTAIN HOME	AR	386.9	A
California				
FARMERS & MERCHANTS BK CTRL CA	LODI	CA	1731.6	A
FIRST SECURITY BUSINESS BANK	ORANGE	CA	361.9	A
Colorado				
DOLORES ST BK	DOLORES	CO	105.7	A
FIRST NATIONAL BK ESTES PARK	ESTES PARK	CO	89.4	A
Connecticut				
CITIZENS NB	PUTNAM	CT	291.6	A
LIBERTY BK	MIDDLETOWN	CT	2896.7	A-
Delaware				
APPLIED BANK	WILMINGTON	DE	230.1	A+
FIRST BANK OF DELAWARE	WILMINGTON	DE	113.4	A-
District of Columbia				
NATIONAL CAPITAL BK OF WA	WASHINGTON	DC	273.4	A+
CITY FIRST BK OF DC NA	WASHINGTON	DC	130.2	C-
Florida				
DRUMMOND COMMUNITY BK	CHIEFLAND	FL	185.0	A+
PEOPLES BANK OF GRACEVILLE	GRACEVILLE	FL	68.5	A
Georgia				
WEST CENTRAL GEORGIA BANK	THOMASTON	GA	94.5	A
PELHAM BANKING COMPANY	PELHAM	GA	61.4	A
Hawaii				
BANK OF HAWAII	HONOLULU	HI	11,427.2	B
TERRITORIAL SAVINGS BANK	HONOLULU	HI	1221.7	B
Idaho				
BANK OF COMMERCE	AMMON	ID	759.4	A
FARMERS NB OF BUHL	BUHL	ID	395.9	A
Illinois				
FIRST NB OF DWIGHT	DWIGHT	IL	107.4	A+
GERMANTOWN TRUST & SVGS BK	BREESE	IL	311.2	A
Indiana				
FIRST FINANCIAL BK NA	TERRE HAUTE	IN	2215.0	A-
MERCHANTS BANK OF INDIANA	LYNN	IN	242.5	A-
Iowa				
CITIZENS FIRST NB	STORM LAKE	IA	190.6	A
IOWA TRUST &SAVINGS BK	CENTERVILLE	IA	144.4	A

Table B-3   (*updating Table 19-1*)

Kansas				
FARMERS & DROVERS BK	COUNCIL GROVE	KS	124.9	A+
BANK OF TESCOTT	TESCOTT	KS	211.2	A
Kentucky				
KENTUCKY-FARMERS BK	ASHLAND	KY	137.0	A+
EDMONTON ST BK	EDMONTON	KY	397.4	A
Louisana				
M C BANK & TRUST CO	MORGAN CITY	LA	271.2	A
GULF COAST BK	ABBEVILLE	LA	253.9	A
Maine				
FRANKLIN SVGS BK	FARMINGTON	ME	309.0	A
CAMDEN NATIONAL BANK	CAMDEN	ME	2273.9	B-
Maryland				
ROSEDALE FS&LA	BALTIMORE	MD	614.5	A+
MIDDLETOWN VALLEY BANK	MIDDLETOWN	MD	132.4	A+
Massachusetts				
BROOKLINE BANK	BROOKLINE	MA	2573.4	A-
EVERETT CO-OP BANK	EVERETT	MA	252.7	A-
Michigan				
UPPER PENINSULA ST BK	ESCANABA	MI	166.9	A
CENTURY BANK & TRUST	COLDWATER	MI	244.8	A-
Minnesota				
FIRST NB OF BEMIDJI	BEMIDJI	MN	470.8	A
VERMILLION ST BK	VERMILLION	MN	416.3	A
Mississippi				
FARMERS & MERCHANTS BK	BALDWYN	MS	191.2	A+
BNA BANK	NEW ALBANY	MS	392.1	A
Missouri				
NEW ERA BK	FREDERICKTOWN	MO	265.5	A+
FIRST NATIONAL BANK	CAMDENTON	MO	263.5	A+
Montana				
YELLOWSTONE BK	LAUREL	MT	437.2	A
FIRST STATE BANK OF MALTA	MALTA	MT	110.5	A
Nebraska				
WORLDS FOREMOST BK	SIDNEY	NE	843.7	A
FIRST NATIONAL BANK OF GORDON	GORDON	NE	140.5	A
Nevada				
CREDIT ONE BANK NA	LAS VEGAS	NV	103.4	A
HERITAGE BANK OF NEVADA	RENO	NV	362.5	A-
New Hampshire				
LEDYARD NATIONAL BANK	HANOVER	NH	376.4	B
LAKE SUNAPEE BK FSB	NEWPORT	NH	863.0	B-
New Jersey				
SUMITOMO TR & BKG CO USA	HOBOKEN	NJ	623.8	A
FIRST INVESTORS FED SAVINGS BK	EDISON	NJ	51.3	A
New Mexico				
WESTERN COMMERCE BK	CARLSBAD	NM	320.2	A
CITIZENS BANK OF CLOVIS	CLOVIS	NM	230.4	A
New York				
MASPETH FS&LA	MASPETH	NY	1466.8	A
BROOKLYN FSB	BROOKLYN	NY	514.9	A
North Carolina				
SURREY BANK & TRUST	MOUNT AIRY	NC	207.2	A-
INDUSTRIAL FEDERAL SAVINGS BK	LEXINGTON	NC	164.1	A-

Table B-3 (cont'd)   *(updating Table 19-1)*

North Dakota				
BANK OF TIOGA	TIOGA	ND	78.1	A
SARGENT COUNTY BK	FORMAN	ND	77.4	A
Ohio				
ST HENRY BK	ST HENRY	OH	182.9	A+
WORLD FINANCIAL NETWORK NB	COLUMBUS	OH	1552.5	A
Oklahoma				
OKLAHOMA B&TC	CLINTON	OK	131.5	A+
FIRST NB&TC	CHICKASHA	OK	348.8	A
Oregon				
FIRST FEDERAL SAVINGS & LOAN	MCMINNVILLE	OR	339.8	A-
PIONEER TRUST BK NA	SALEM	OR	267.5	A-
Pennsylvania				
FIRST NATIONAL BANK &TRUST	NEWTOWN	PA	658.5	A
WAYNE BANK	HONESDALE	PA	511.5	A
Rhode Island				
WASHINGTON TRUST CO	WESTERLY	RI	2945.3	B
TALBOTS CLASSICS NB	LINCOLN	RI	9.8	B
South Carolina				
FIRST PIEDMONT FS&LA	GAFFNEY	SC	282.0	A
BANK OF CLARENDON	MANNING	SC	182.7	A
South Dakota				
FIRST FIDELITY BK	BURKE	SD	245.1	A+
FIRST PREMIER BK	SIOUX FALLS	SD	901.4	A
Tennessee				
ELIZABETHTON FSB	ELIZABETHTON	TN	332.9	A+
CITIZENS BANK	CARTHAGE	TN	495.8	A
Texas				
CITIZENS 1ST BK	TYLER	TX	684.8	A+
COMMUNITY NATIONAL B&T	CORSICANA	TX	317.3	A+
Utah				
HERITAGE BANK	ST GEORGE	UT	92.9	A+
OPTUMHEALTH BK INC	SALT LAKE CITY	UT	1054.7	A
Vermont				
MERCHANTS BK	SOUTH BURLINGTON	VT	1353.4	B
UNION BK	MORRISVILLE	VT	421.0	B
Virginia				
VIRGINIA BANK &TRUST	DANVILLE	VA	152.0	A+
BURKE & HERBERT BANK &TRUST	ALEXANDRIA	VA	1807.9	A
Washington				
VALLEY BANK	PUYALLUP	WA	219.8	A-
SOUTH SOUND BK	OLYMPIA	WA	167.8	A-
West Virginia				
PENDLETON COMMUNITY BANK	FRANKLIN	WV	206.0	A
LOGAN BANK & TRUST	LOGAN	WV	235.0	A-
Wisconsin				
NATIONAL EXCHANGE BANK & TRUST	FOND DU LAC	WI	1156.4	A+
WAUKESHA STATE BANK	WAUKESHA	WI	754.3	A+
Wyoming				
FIRST ST BK OF NEWCASTLE	NEWCASTLE	WY	127.1	A+
HILLTOP NATIONAL BANK	CASPER	WY	462.4	B+

Table B-3 (cont'd)   *(updating Table 19-1)*

Highest-Rated Insurance Companies in America per TheStreet.com (updating the lists from Chapter 24)

Although there have been some changes since 2002, most of the highest-rated insurers are still on this list. This consistency is a sign that the rater has not (as yet) been caught off-guard with hidden weaknesses, as has happened with some banks.

HIGHEST-RATED U.S. INSURERS

Source: TheStreet.com Ratings, Inc. Ratings and data based on First Quarter 2009. Reprinted with permission.

Life and Health Insurers

Company	Domicile State	TheStreet.com Financial Strength Rating	Total Assets ($Mil)
AMERICAN FAMILY LIFE INS CO	WI	A+	3,898
COUNTRY LIFE INS CO	IL	A+	7,329
PHYSICIANS MUTUAL INS CO	NE	A+	1,445
STATE FARM LIFE INS CO	IL	A+	44,978
STATE FARM LIFE & ACCIDENT ASR CO	IL	A+	1,691
TEACHERS INS & ANNUITY ASN OF AM	NY	A+	194,589

Property and Casualty Insurers

Company	Domicile State	TheStreet.com Financial Strength Rating	Total Assets ($Mil)
DAIRYLAND INS CO	WI	A+	1,222
HASTINGS MUTUAL INS CO	IN	A+	586
INTERINS EXCH OF THE AUTOMOBILE CLUB	CA	A+	5,435
UNITED SERVICES AUTOMOBILE ASN	TX	A+	19,905
USAA CASUALTY INS CO	TX	A+	6,714

Table B-4   (updating Table 24-1)

For periodic updates to these lists, visit www.conquerthecrash.com/ readerspage. For more comprehensive reports, contact TheStreet.com.

COMMENTARY FROM THE ELLIOTT WAVE THEORIST LEADING TO THE FINAL MARKET TOPS

Introduction

Conquer the Crash was completed in March 2002, at the peak of a six-month, 2000-point rally in the Dow. From a high that month of 10,673, the Dow fell 33% to a low of 7198 in October. As it turned out, that decline completed only "wave **a**" of the bear market, and there was one last phase of optimism-fueled credit inflation left to go. Thanks to a few more years of extreme borrowing, lax lending standards, phony debt insurance, inflated safety ratings, record leverage and, as a result, a plummeting dollar, many stock indexes and other dollar-denominated assets such as real estate climbed to new highs.

But as shown in the pages ahead, all these gains were in fact non-existent when measured in real money (gold). The dollar lost so much value from 2001 to 2008 that the real value of stocks, which started down in 1999, and real estate, which started down in 2001, continued to fall throughout the entire time. *The Elliott Wave Theorist* called this period "the Silent Crash." To most investors, the run-up felt real, but in the end credit finally contracted and exposed the whole sham.

Appendix C chronicles this "wave **b**" rally via excerpts from *The Elliott Wave Theorist*. As this wave matured, investments began rolling over one by one even in dollar terms: real estate in 2005, the stock market in 2007 and commodities in 2008. Thus began the great deflation.

(Note: Figures from The Elliott Wave Theorist *have been renumbered to fit this book's format. —Ed.)*

The Next Stage of the Bear Market

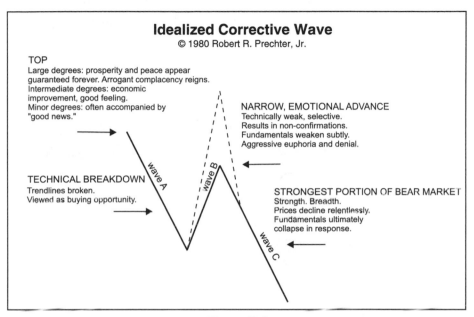

Idealized Corrective Wave
© 1980 Robert R. Prechter, Jr.

TOP
Large degrees: prosperity and peace appear
guaranteed forever. Arrogant complacency reigns.
Intermediate degrees: economic
improvement, good feeling.
Minor degrees: often accompanied by
"good news."

NARROW, EMOTIONAL ADVANCE
Technically weak, selective.
Results in non-confirmations.
Fundamentals weaken subtly.
Aggressive euphoria and denial.

TECHNICAL BREAKDOWN
Trendlines broken.
Viewed as buying opportunity.

STRONGEST PORTION OF BEAR MARKET
Strength. Breadth.
Prices decline relentlessly.
Fundamentals ultimately
collapse in response.

wave A

wave B

wave C

Figure C-1

Figure C-1 is from Chapter 2 of *Elliott Wave Principle*. It displays a typical progression of prices and psychology in a bear market. See if the stock market environment of 2000-2002 fits the classic description of an A wave:

> During the A wave of a bear market, the investment world is generally convinced that this reaction is just a pullback pursuant to the next leg of advance. The public surges to the buy side despite the first really technically damaging cracks in the individual stock patterns.

To anticipate the ultimate resolution of the bear market, we can again refer to the description in *Elliott Wave Principle* regarding the second major wave of decline:

Declining C waves are usually devastating in their destruction. They are third waves and have most of the properties of
third waves. It is during these declines that there is virtually
no place to hide except cash. The illusions held throughout
waves A and B tend to evaporate, and fear takes over. C waves
are persistent and broad.

Get ready for a change in that direction.

The Elliott Wave Theorist, June 13, 2005

Figure C-2 shows that starting in 1998, the year that
the Value Line geometric average topped out, advisors became
consistently on-balance bullish. Amazingly, despite a 50% drop

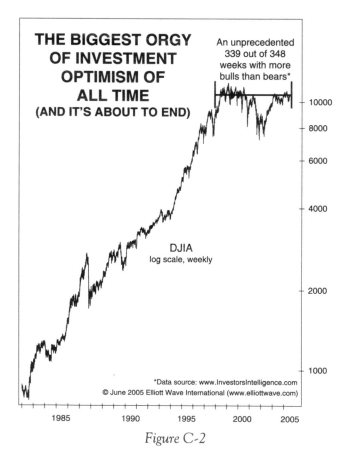

Figure C-2

in the S&P and a 78% drop in the NASDAQ, they have stayed that way in all but nine out of 348 weeks (including last week, not yet reported). Nothing like this has ever happened. It is the biggest top of all time, an amazing feat of levitation fueled psychologically by optimism and financially by credit. This amazing streak is nearly over.

Undoubtedly many analysts will try to call a market bottom at the first sign of pessimism, but we may be confident that no important stock market bottom will occur until advisors are net bearish for a long, long time. In 1994, they were net bearish almost all year despite only a Minor-degree correction. How long will they have to be net bearish before a Supercycle degree bottom occurs? More than a year, that's for sure.

The Elliott Wave Theorist, November 17, 2005

The Big Picture in the Stock Market Has Changed Only for the Worse

You may recall that in 1999, prominent economists and academics wrote editorials in The Wall Street Journal declaring boundless optimism. On October 26, 2005, another editorial, by a world famous economist, uses language not seen since George Gilder's famous paean to the bull market, "The Faith of a Futurist," on December 31, 1999. The economist writes, "I have never witnessed or even read about an economy that comes close to the excellence of the current U.S. economy. It just doesn't get any better."[1] These are two vitally important statements. The first sentence is important because it is so wrong; the economy expanded at a much faster rate in the 1950s and 1960s than now. (To review the statistics, see Chapter 1 of *Conquer the Crash*.) The implications of the long term slowing in the rate of expansion are ominous, because a slowing economy cannot support record debt. The second statement is important because if the economy truly

cannot get any better than this, then all it can do is get worse.
If his assessment is accurate, and if one believes in anything but
perpetual social nirvana, then one should expect the pendulum
to swing the other way.

The optimism reflected in this quotation is not isolated
to a few contrarians; quite the opposite is the case. Figure C-3,
for example, shows the percentage of cash held by institutions.
As you can see, it recently hit its lowest level on record, which
is probably the lowest level ever. This reading means that money
managers and their clients are as bullish on the market as it is
possible to get. Many other indicators, including price/dividend,
price/book value, and long-term TRIN, also reflect unequivocally
the environment of a major peak in optimism. Alan Newman
adds, "Dollar trading volume is at levels that exceed any year

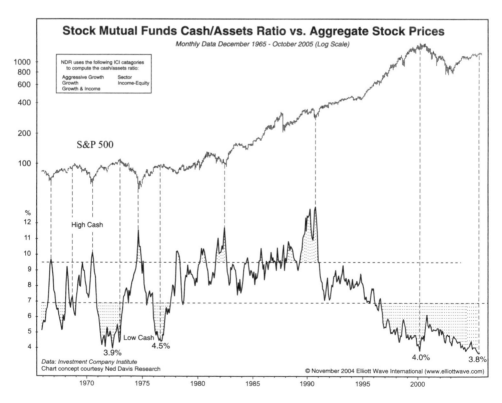

Figure C-3

except the blowoff peak established in 2000."[2] We must judge every near- and intermediate-term technical indication against this background indicating a historic market high.

NOTES

[1] Laffer, Arthur. (2005, October 26). "Ben Bernanke Is the Right Person at the Right Time," *The Wall Street Journal*.

[2] Newman, Alan, "Still on Overdrive," Internet, Cross-currents.net.

The Elliott Wave Theorist, December 16, 2005

Real Estate

It took a long time, but evidence is piling up that the real estate bubble has finally burst.

We have caught some flak in the past year for not piling on to this mania and for warning that disaster was around the corner. People who bought property on huge margin, representing a substantial portion of the American population, have their backs against the wall. People who have been leveraging into more expensive properties or borrowing equity from their homes at a record rate are going to regret the decision. Manias always look good on the left side; it's the right side that causes the problems, and, generally speaking, people who don't get out early don't get out at all.

The Elliott Wave Theorist, March 21, 2006

Bull or Bear Market?

Since 2002, has it been a bull market or a bear market? The "Year 2000" edition of *At the Crest* showed a long term graph of the Dow plotted annually in terms of gold. The wave labeling for that chart has proved an accurate predictor of subsequent action, as the ratio has been down ever since. (See Figure C-4.) Incredibly, the Dow in terms of gold made a new low for the bear market just last month. (See Figure C-5.) If gold were our money, the major stock market indexes would have declined relentlessly from 2000 to the present, with a muted bounce in 2003. There would be no arguing the point of whether a bull or bear market was in force. When viewing Figure C-5, it is obvious why the measure of presidential popularity has just hit a new post-2000 low. These two indicators of social mood are in sync. The loss in dollar value relative to gold since 2001 hides this confluence.

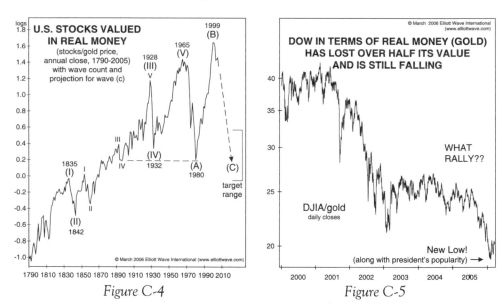

Figure C-4   Figure C-5

A significant difference between the Dow/$ ratio and the Dow/gold ratio previously occurred in 1970-1973. Climbing upward from its collapse into May 1970, the nominal DJIA made a new all-time high in January 1973, but the Dow in terms of gold was below the orthodox top of the bull market in February 1966, as you can gather from Figure C-4. This type of analysis confirms the validity of the Wave Principle in having identified February 1966 as the end of the upward impulse, i.e. the true end of the bull market from 1942. In January 1973 the bear market in real terms was still going strong, exactly as Elliott wave analysis indicated. I believe that the even more severe difference today confirms the validity of our analysis identifying 2000 as the orthodox top of the bull market, as outlined in *View from the Top* and *Beautiful Pictures*.

The only reason that people even think that stocks are back in a bull market is that their measuring unit, the dollar, has lost value by various measures since 2000. Ironically, one of the reasons that the dollar has been falling in value is that it is a credit-based currency, and people have been borrowing dollars not only for consumption but also to speculate in real estate and stocks. So the borrowing of dollars is pushing up prices and lowering money values at the same time! Isn't "modern" finance great? When the house of cards falls, deflation will rule, for reasons set out in Chapters 9-13 of *Conquer the Crash*. Until then, we have to put up with the nonsense of rising stock indexes in dollar terms, which is a complete sham.

The Approaching Crash

Figure C-6 shows the Saudi Arabian stock market index for the past eight months. It shows better than I can explain what lies ahead for the Dow and S&P. The U.S. stock market has continued to climb almost mystically, defying sentiment extremes, momentum divergences, cycles and completed wave patterns on a short term basis. Likewise the Saudi index had been advancing relentlessly as if on a mission. Yet the SASE index just lost 28 percent of its value in 2½ weeks. This is equivalent to waking up just a dozen trading days from now to see the Dow back at its October 2002 low. Can you cite any obvious indication at the high that the Saudi market would reverse and plummet? Fundamentally, oil [upon which the Saudi economy relies] has been trading near all-time highs. Technically, there was no top formation, no head

Figure C-6

and shoulders pattern, no slowing of the market's ascent; in fact, the index accelerated in its final two months of rise and then further in its final few days of rise. As with the U.S. market in the late 1990s, one would have counted the waves in real time only with extreme difficulty because the corrections during the rise were exceptionally shallow. At the top all we had for certain was an extended mania, and that was enough.

The Elliott Wave Theorist Special Report, May 11, 2006

Primary Topping Years of the Decade: 6, 7 and 9

Over the past century, the key years for major tops during a decade were the 6th, 7th and 9th years. The style of the advance has been related to the year of the peak.

The 6th year of the decade has marked the Dow's high for the decade four times, in 1906, 1946, 1966 and 1976 (in the latter case within 3 percent of the 1973 high). The 7th year of the decade has marked the most significant high for the decade twice, in 1937 and 1987, and both times led to a crash.

The 9th year of the decade marked the Dow's high for the decade five times, in 1919, 1929, 1959, 1989 and 1999. (In two cases—1959 and 1999—the impulse-wave high occurred days later, in early January of the 0 year.) Four of these were "runaway" decades, in which prices rose persistently almost the entire time, much or most of it in new all-time high territory. In four of those decades there were also significant interim peaks in the 6th year—1916, 1926 and 1956—or the 7th year—1987. Among these decades, the most significant 6th-year peak occurred in the 'teens, which was not a runaway decade. In two other decades in which there was a significant peak in the 6th year, there was also a significant peak in the 9th year—1909 and 1969 (in the latter case within one month, since the peak price occurred in December 1968; in May 1969 the Dow approached the high).

We can summarize this record as follows: In non-runaway decades, the 6th year marked a top, but if it didn't, the market crashed from a peak in the 7th year; this description covers six of the past ten decades. In runaway decades, the 9th year marked the high; this description covers four of the past ten decades. (The 1980s sported both events: a crash in the 7th year and higher prices in the 9th.) The 'teens were not a runaway period, but that decade's two crucial tops occurred in the 6th and 9th years. Figure C-7 summarizes these observations.

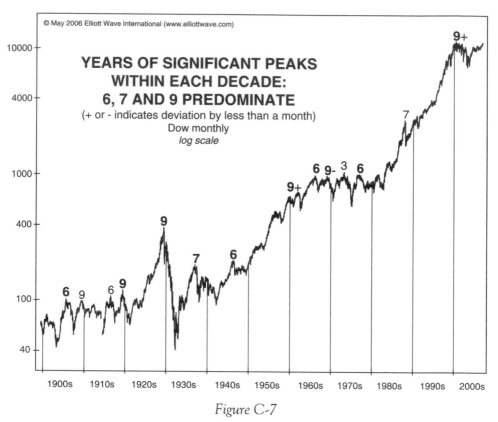

Figure C-7

Implications for the Current Decade

The current decade is not of the runaway type. The Dow has been in a choppy advance, and none of it (to date) has been in new all-time high territory. If this decade holds to pattern, then the most likely year for the high is 2006. The next most likely year is 2007, in which case the market should resolve in a crash. The Dow should not persist in a rising trend into 2009. But if 2006 marks a significant high, then the history of the 'teens and '60s allows for a rebound into 2009 to form a double top. There are two reasons, however, to bet against such a test of the highs: Secondary issues have already had a 3.5-year period of upside leadership, dwarfing the similar '60s experience of 2.2 years from October 1966 to December 1968; and stock-market optimism has already been stretched beyond previous historic extremes in terms of both time and value.

The Elliott Wave Theorist, October 2, 2006

The Real Purchasing Power of Stocks

One of the biggest scams ever perpetrated is the idea that the stock market has made people rich over the past 80 years. Almost the entire gain in the Dow is due to debasement of the currency. Figure C-8 shows the DJIA (reconstructed prior to 1890) priced in dollars, and Figure C-9 shows the Dow priced in real money—gold—since the founding of the Republic. If you look closely, you can see that both charts are identical for well over a century, through 1933. Then they utterly diverge. Now look at the bullets in Figure C-9. The Dow today buys less gold—and by extension less in the way of goods and basic services—than it did in 1929. Because gold was fixed at $20.67 per oz. until January 1934, we may take the first three decades of the century as the nominal Dow's benchmark, because during

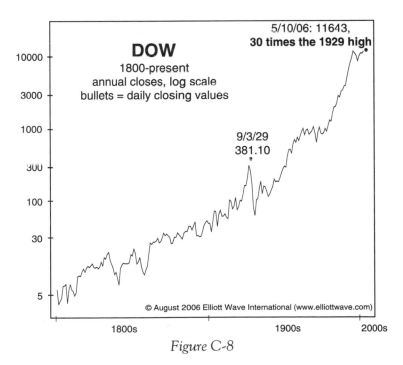

Figure C-8

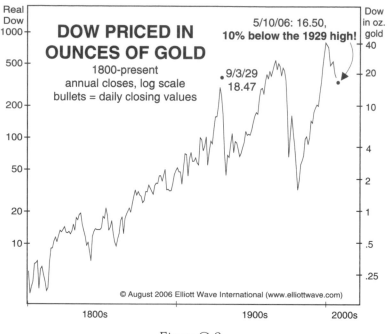

© August 2006 Elliott Wave International (www.elliottwave.com)

Figure C-9

those years the nominal Dow and the Dow/gold ratio moved precisely together. Had the dollar remained worth 1/20.67 of an ounce of gold, then today the Dow would sell at 340. That's right: not 11,700 but 340. That is what it *does* sell for today when it is denominated in constant, gold-valued dollars. The entire net gain from 1929 to today is an illusion. The real price should be no surprise. Our railroads are rusted out, the auto companies are failing, and except for computers American industry in general is so crippled by regulation that it can't compete successfully in the global marketplace. This is the legacy of 93 years of expanding indebtedness, fostered by a wave of runaway optimism and fueled by a paper money monopoly in the form of the Federal Reserve System.

The illusion of the Dow's value since 2000 hardly pales by comparison. Investors have broken out party hats in anticipation of celebrating a new Dow high, but in terms of real money, the

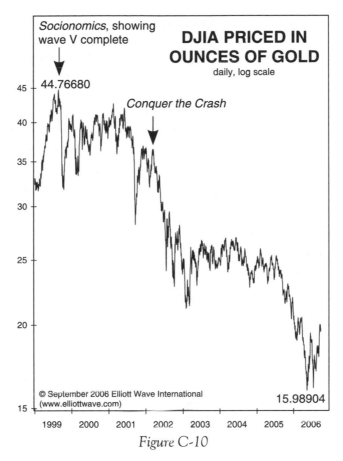

Figure C-10

Dow has crashed since 2000. Figure C-10 shows that at the May low the Dow in terms of gold was down 64.28 percent from its 2000 high! In other words, you can buy 1/3 the amount of gold now with your 30 Dow shares that you could have in 2000. You can buy even less oil and copper. Yet people think the Dow is unchanged. If we were to normalize the Dow to its 1999 peak in gold terms, it would be in the 4000s today.

If deflation occurs as we expect, these values will fall substantially back in line, and the Dow will decline in dollar terms as well. Credit bubbles always lead to collapses. We hear from many quarters—both from bulls and bears—that "this time it's different." Time will tell.

The Elliott Wave Theorist Special Report, October 27, 2006

Devastation in Real Value Confirms a Bear Market Pattern

Elliott waves define bull and bear markets. Real bull markets make new highs in real terms. A major fifth wave has never failed to make a new high in real terms as well as nominal terms. Many corrective-wave rallies also make new highs in real terms, but a *failure* to do so happens only in corrective-wave rallies. The wave **b** label fills this bill.

The declines in real value for the Dow, S&P and NASDAQ appear devastating enough on semilog scale, but it helps to view them on arithmetic scale to understand why they are not possibly part of the old bull market. Figures C-11 through C-14 show the entire bull market and the ensuing action in real terms on arithmetic scale from 1980 to the present for the strongest and weakest of these indexes. There is no question that a major trend change in the purchasing power of the Dow and S&P occurred in 1999 (2000 for the NASDAQ). This decline is clearly of larger degree than the corrections in 1981-82 and 1987. The crash that EWT and *Conquer the Crash* predicted is in fact already well advanced, but almost no one knows it because it has happened so far primarily in terms of the purchasing power of stock shares rather than in dollar value. It is also clear from these graphs that the correct wave count is five waves down, which must be part of the bear market structure of Grand Supercycle degree.

The Personality of a B Wave

We know that this new high in the Dow has been a phony. The S&P and NASDAQ are below their old highs, and the Dow is well below its high in real terms. The market is being propelled by hedge funds leveraging to the hilt with lines of credit on other people's money. Sentiment measures indicate record optimism

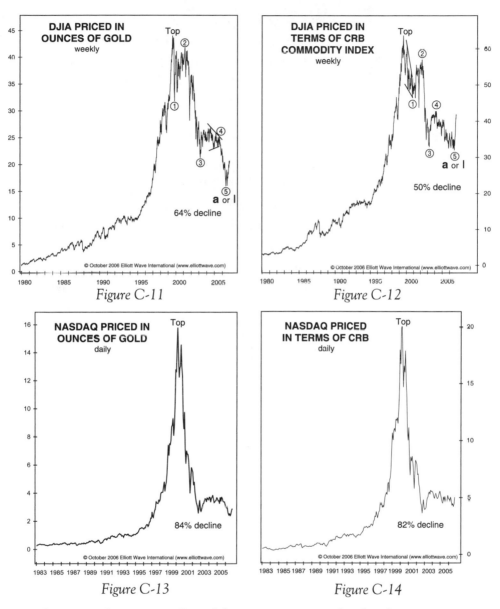

Figure C-11

Figure C-12

Figure C-13

Figure C-14

by several measures. See if this environment fits the description of B waves, from *Elliott Wave Principle* (1978) pp. 81-83:

> **B waves** — B waves are phonies. They are sucker plays, bull traps, speculators' paradise, orgies of odd-lotter mentality or expressions of dumb institutional complacency (or both). They

often involve a focus on a narrow list of stocks, are often "un-confirmed" by other averages, are rarely technically strong, and are virtually always doomed to complete retracement by wave C. If the analyst can easily say to himself, "There is something wrong with this market," chances are it's a B wave.

Valuation

EWT has often showed a graph of S&P valuation on the basis of book value and dividend yield relative to corporate bond yield. Figure C-15 shows just the Dow's dividend yield. This is the most important measure for determining stock values, because dividends are the way the investor gets paid. It shows that stocks are still historically expensive. It also shows that dividend yield—as with book value and the bond/stock yield ratio—has

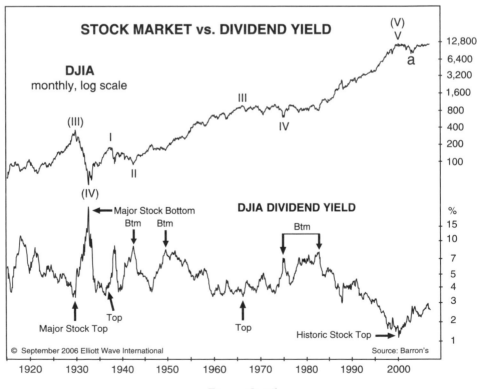

Figure C-15

not accompanied the Dow to a new extreme. I think this is because the orthodox top of the bull market is past. The onset of the bear market in 2000 started a revaluation of dividends back to higher levels. Wave **b** is delaying the ultimate resolution, but it will not change it.

Expanded Flat Wave (a) Developing in the Nominal Dow

There is at least one precedent for the shape of the bear market so far in the nominal Dow. *At the Crest of the Tidal Wave* covered this possibility, correctly expressing its unlikelihood while nevertheless carefully painting the picture to make sure readers understood all potential outcomes. This labeling has been in the arsenal, tucked way in the back behind the bows and arrows. It's time to bring it out and use it. To get oriented, read this discussion from pp.78-79 of *At the Crest* (1995):

> **The Comparative Uncertainty in Forecasting the Path of a Corrective Pattern**
>
> The scenarios displayed in Figure 5-4 [not shown] are the most likely candidates for wave ⓘⱽ. Indeed, I would say that they are the only candidates were it not for the experience of 1987. In that year, an expanded flat correction was stretched so dramatically in terms of price and contracted so dramatically in terms of time that there is no remotely comparable event in the stock price record.
>
> Figure 5-7 shows what the Primary wave ④ correction of 1987 would look like at Grand Supercycle degree.

The size of the formation in Figure C-16 (Figure 5-7 from the book) is one degree larger than the one I am proposing now, so the time and price elements will be far smaller. Instead of the entire Grand Supercycle taking this expanded flat shape, only Supercycle wave (a) is taking this shape.

As illustrated in *At the Crest of the Tidal Wave* (1995):

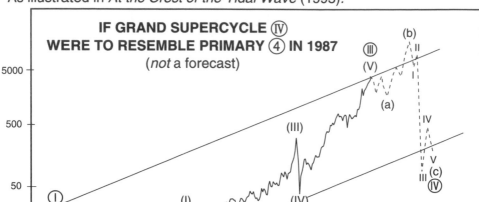

Figure C-16

Maintaining the Original Interpretation of the Bull Market

Conquer the Crash ran a chart (Figure 4-4) showing that the bull market of 1974-2000 is a dead ringer for the one that took place in the 1920s. This was, and remains, strong evidence that wave V ended in 2000. These two bull markets have the same label: Cycle wave V, and each one of them ended a decades-long advance of Supercycle degree. Figure C-17 shows their positions as terminal waves within the larger Grand Supercycle. The many Fibonacci relationships that converge at the 2000 high, as detailed in *Beautiful Pictures*, confirm this as the correct interpretation.

As Figure C-18 shows, wave V sports alternation (wave ② is a zigzag, wave ④ a flat), and wave ⑤ peaked at the upper end of a parallel trend channel. Figure C-19 updates its standing within Supercycle wave (V).

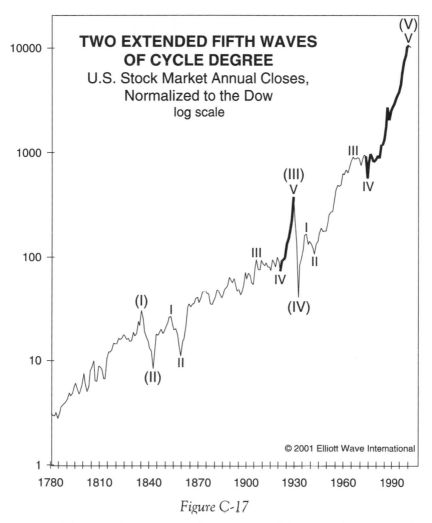

Figure C-17

Observe the action of waves **a** and **b** around two trend-lines. You can see in Figure C-18 that the decline of 2000-2002 broke the lower line of the channel for wave V. Since then, that line has been resistance for this rally. If you look closely, you will see that wave **b** rose to touch that line in 2004. Now notice in Figure C-19 that wave **a** stopped right on the upper line of the trendchannel for Supercycle wave (V). This line served as support for wave **a**, and the one in Figure C-18 is serving as resistance for wave **b**.

Figure C-18

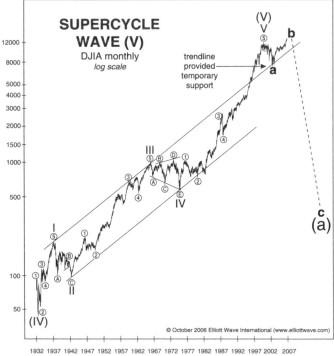

Figure C-19

It is difficult to catch the top of a B wave. This one could top any time, but the most that it should be able to do is to touch the resistance trendline again. With the Daily Sentiment Index reporting a vastly unprecedented 19 out of 25 trading days (through 10/26) with 90% or more bulls among traders in the S&P, NASDAQ or both, one should not be anything but a fully committed bear. Wave **b** could be peaking this week; if it takes months longer and stretches higher, nothing important will change. Being prepared and positioned for wave **c** is all that matters.

The Approaching Resolution of the Pattern

The upcoming wave **c** will take the form of a crash. Because the corrective pattern is of such large degree, wave **c** will be huge by historical standards and probably bring the Dow back into triple digits, ideally under 400. As shown in Figure C-9, the Dow has already fallen below 400 in real terms, i.e. when we use the stable gold-value of both the dollar and the Dow as established in the first three decades of the 20th century.

The only way a value this low can be achieved in nominal terms for the Dow is for the credit supply to collapse in a huge deflation. The crash and debt implosion will not only bring dollar values down but also devastate the very industries that the stock market values, bringing on an exceptionally deep and broad economic depression.

The Elliott Wave Theorist, February 16, 2007

BIG PICTURE INDICATORS

T-bills have outperformed the S&P (including dividends), for the past eight years. With short term interest rates at their highest level in six years and the stock market over-bulled and overbought, there is every reason for investors to stay locked into safe, interest-bearing cash equivalents, which are currently paying an excellent return.

After the Dow Jones Industrial Average went above 11,770 last October, EWT recommended that aggressive speculators stand aside until one of three things occurred: a break of 11,770, a daily closing high in the 12,937-13,007 range, or a new Dow high within four days of March 13, 2007. None of these three events has occurred, and the Dow has clawed its way 1000 points higher, so far ignoring what in the past would have been repeated signs of imminent termination.

Inverted Yield Curve

Short term interest rates have been above long term interest rates—as measured by 3-month vs. 30-year U.S. Treasury debt—for six months. Such conditions occur at extremes in short term lending for investment purposes. This condition in turn implies a peak in financial markets, which today more than ever rely upon speculative borrowing to keep them rising. Many observers have discounted the implication of the current "inverted yield curve" because it has been in effect for a number of months with no reversal in stocks. History shows, however, that the indicator's timing is almost always within a matter of months. Every passing month gives a reason to be more concerned about this condition, not less.

Figure C-20 demonstrates the utility of this indicator. When the yield curve was negative in 1978-1980, the stock market underwent three "massacres" and persistently lost value in real terms. The stock market peak of April 1981 occurred after six months of a negative yield curve. The peak of 1989 in the Value Line Composite and Dow Jones Transports occurred four months after this condition began, and the high in the New York Composite index of September 2000 occurred two months

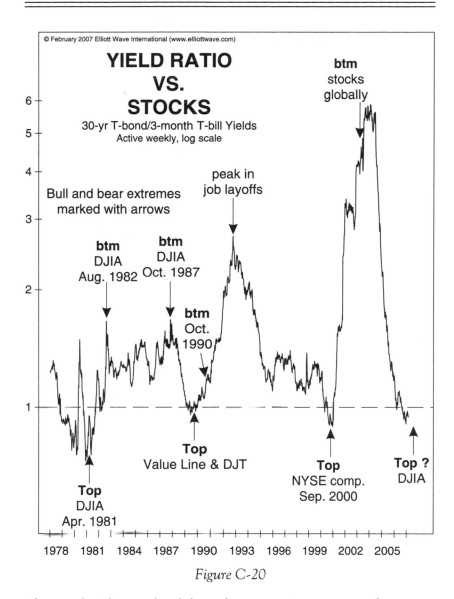

Figure C-20

afterward. After each of these latter two junctures, at least one market index fell at least 47 percent. The yield curve has now been inverted for six months. Essentially, it is right in the normal area when a reversal in the stock market usually occurs.

All the Same Markets

One can hardly peruse a financial periodical or posting these days and not read about how "liquidity is driving up all the markets." As far as we know, we were the first firm to introduce this idea. *Conquer the Crash*, completed in March 2002, presented this illustration and accompanying commentary:

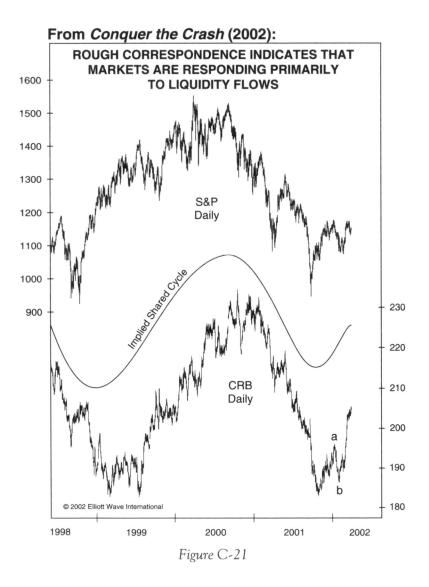

Figure C-21

As shown in this chart [C-21], the Commodity Research Bureau (CRB) commodity index has tracked the S&P, with a slight lag, since mid-1998. Gold and silver have also joined in the latest stock rally. As I see it, this correlation means that most assets lately are moving up and down more or less together, probably as liquidity expands and contracts.

We began following up on this idea in *The Elliott Wave Theorist* and *The Elliott Wave Financial Forecast*, showing graphs of financial markets that were tracking each other. We published the idea in an article for Barron's in May 2004.

Our main focus has been to recognize the topping phase of this liquidity binge. We have been wrong in continually expecting the big party to end. When stocks turn down, it will signal a major liquidity contraction, and all major asset classes should decline together.

The Real Estate Bust

The optimism that fostered liquidity creation for property speculation has turned to caution. On Thursday, the National Association of Realtors said that in the final three months of last year, sales of existing homes fell in 40 states, and home prices dropped in 49 percent of the cities it surveyed. This is the widest price decline in the history of the survey. Today the Commerce Dept. reported that construction of new homes and apartments fell by 14.3 percent in January. This "bigger-than-expected drop" brought the seasonally adjusted annual rate of construction to its lowest level in nearly a decade. Crashes do not typically occur in straight lines. Even they have a structure, with periods of bounce and recovery. Each positive sign will probably be taken as the bottom.

The Elliott Wave Theorist, April 30, 2007

LONG TERM PERSPECTIVE ON THE STOCK MARKET

Extreme Optimism in the Face of Looming Disaster

I just returned from a speaking engagement at a financial conference. The conference began years ago as a hard-money-oriented group, and the theme was usually bearish. What a difference today! According to several attendees and one of the conference organizers, there were no super bears on the stock market until I showed up. They had difficulty finding speakers who would volunteer for the bear side in a panel debate, but they finally found three. So while investors have bought into the idea of perpetual liquidity, so have most of the experts. The record readings reported in *The Elliott Wave Financial Forecast* of 90 percent bulls among traders and the unprecedented duration of net bullishness among advisors are not just numbers; they reflect exactly how lopsided market opinion is these days. And the market is so blissfully convincing; the Dow has closed higher in 19 out of the past 21 trading days, an event that had never occurred in 120 years of Dow history. As one would expect, some such periods have occurred around the "third of a third" wave (see *Elliott Wave Principle*, p.80), but the most similar string of days ended in July 1929, two months before the start of the biggest stock market slide in two centuries. These days, just as in the summer of 1929, investing seems so easy: Just buy anything, and it will go up forever. But as a general observation, the financial world does not work this way; and as a specific observation, today's financial world, built upon debt, will definitely not work out this way. To quote Joe Granville's immortal line, "What's obvious is obviously wrong." We have expressed a contrary view for a long time, so it sounds as if we are crying wolf. But to paraphrase the old joke, just because a wolf hasn't eaten you yet doesn't mean he isn't pre-heating the oven.

I am not just bearish. It goes much further than that. The pyramid of debt, the extremity of optimism and the **b**-wave label of the advance since 2002 all portend an all-out collapse of investment prices in wave **c**. The decline in social mood during that wave will engender a crushing deflation in the galaxy-sized bubble of outstanding credit and ultimately a disastrous depression. Few of us will be able to side-step the effects of the depression, but we can all avoid the effects of falling financial prices and the deflation of the debt bubble by following the recommendations in *Conquer the Crash.*

If there is anything I would have done differently, it would have been to short the stock market in terms of real money, which would have entailed selling stocks and buying gold simultaneously. [*Note: Conquer the Crash advocated shorting stocks and owning some gold, thereby partially effecting this strategy.—Ed.*] The Dow fell 64 percent in gold terms, the NASDAQ is down over 80 percent, and both ratios made new lows last year and have barely rebounded. But dollar prices should follow suit. The last time the Dow made new all-time highs while real values were falling was January 1973, after which time stock prices were cut in half. And that was in a bear market of just Cycle degree. The current one is two degrees larger. So once this rally ends, nominal prices should fall way more than they did in 1973-4.

Symmetry

A remarkable feature of this entire period is its symmetry. As shown in Figure C-22, the Dow has spent nearly eight years forming a double top to match the double bottom of 1974-1982. Each set of turns includes one turn in real terms and one in nominal terms. The entire structure is strikingly symmetrical. I recall wondering from 1977 to 1982 why real prices were taking so long to turn up, only to have the picture resolve dramatically in 1982. When prices finally turned up for good that year, they rushed upward for 17 years in real terms. Similarly, we have won-

Figure C-22

dered from 2002 to 2007 why nominal prices have been taking so long to turn down. A symmetrical top could be the answer. When the second top is done, prices should fall at an even faster rate than they went up.

Strategy

Holding safe cash equivalents has been a reasonable position for investors over the past eight years. T-bill yields have outperformed stocks including dividends [see Figure C-23], and Swiss Money Market Claims (per *Conquer the Crash*) have provided an even greater capital gain in dollar terms. Stocks have not come close to paying for the additional risk they entail.

SEVEN-YEAR TOTAL RETURN
12/31/99 to present
Transaction costs excluded

INDEX	Total Return
CASH 3-month T-bill	+27%
S&P 500	+15%
NASDAQ Composite	-34%
Dow Jones Wilshire 5000	+24%
Dow Jones Industrial Average	+33%

Figure C-23

The Elliott Wave Theorist Interim Report, May 18, 2007

RUNNING ON FUMES

The blue chip stock averages are still going up, but their power is waning dramatically. Since April 25, when the Dow exceeded 13,000, the daily advance/decline ratio has averaged less than 1.2. In other words, there have been nearly as many stocks down on the average day as up. As the Dow has ratcheted up 1000 points since April 5, TICK readings have not exceeded +1305. This is the longest such period since March-May 2006, a much choppier and slower advance than the recent one, and it led to a drop. Normalized to the number of stocks trading, TICK has probably never been this weak on an advance of this

magnitude. The Dow Transports have not made a new high since
April 25. They still may do so, but they are lagging nevertheless.
The NASDAQ Composite peaked two weeks ago, and the broad
Value Line average topped last week. The cumulative a/d line
for the S&P 600 Small Cap index topped on April 16, and that
for the S&P topped out on May 9. Volume on the rally peaked
on May 3. This action suggests that investors' cash reserves are
mostly gone, and they are buying stocks with whatever money
they can earn or borrow.

Despite all these conditions, the Dow and S&P are
floating higher with amazing persistence. A big reason for the
persistence is that there appear to be no earnest sellers left. Even
long-time bears are throwing in the towel. This week a colleague
of ours received a request from one of the shows on CNBC beg-
ging him to appear as a bear because bearish analysts are so scarce
they can't find any. A day later, I got a similar request. They
probably found about a third of the remaining bears right there.
The ten-day average of the DSI this week again shows just a hair
under 90 percent bulls among S&P traders, right where gold was
when it topped last month. Still, the S&P seems determined to
go a few percent higher to reach or slightly exceed its 2000 high
(1552.87 intraday, basis the cash index) in wave **b** of a big flat
correction. But it seems to be taking every last borrowed dollar
to get it there.

Twenty years ago, in 1987, the Dow's valuation based on
dividend yield exceeded 1929's valuation. After a brief respite
from there to 1991, the Dow's dividend yield has ever since remained more expensive than it was in 1929. On this and many
other bases, it has been the wildest period of financial optimism
in history, by many multiples, in both duration and extent. Generally, we "know" how it's going to end, but in many real ways,
we don't. This bubble is so huge and has permeated so deeply
and broadly into society that the concrete social consequences

will have to be experienced as they unfold in order to believe they could happen. I am quite sure that if we were to forecast in detail now the social disruptions that in fact will happen over the next 15-20 years, it would be labeled fantastical. *Conquer the Crash* tried to come close, but I'm beginning to think that even my strong descriptions there are too conservative.

The Elliott Wave Theorist, June 15, 2007

Here are two ironies. (1) Credit inflation, deriving from an optimistic mood, has been holding the stock market up. Stocks have risen in dollar terms since 2002, and the dollar has been weak for most of that time. So inflation has been bullish for stocks, not bearish. (2) A slight social mood change toward the negative [evidenced by the slide in property prices and in presidential popularity] has also been motivating lenders, borrowers and legislatures to curtail the expansion of credit and debt, thus acting to turn the tide—though not yet decisively—toward deflation.

"Gimme That Bag!!"

Joe Granville used to speak of bank trust officers and their tendency to buy investments at exactly the wrong time and become "bagholders." He said that when they become pushy and demand to buy an investment from you, they are in essence screaming, "Gimme that bag!" "When they demand the bag," Joe shouted, "give it to 'em!" Well, bankers are smarter these days. Some of them know a bag when they see one, and they have learned to hand off the bag before it's too late. So who are the new bagholders? Read for yourself:

Banks Sell 'Toxic Waste' CDOs to Calpers, Texas Teachers Fund

By the way, it is fitting that people called low-grade bonds of Cycle wave V *junk*, and they call the low-grade bonds of Cycle wave **b** *toxic waste*. This difference speaks to the relative quality of these waves.

Warnings

As *Conquer the Crash* said, don't rely on your pension fund to pay for your retirement. A financial crisis of Supercycle proportion will devastate funds' holdings. For the same reason, don't expect life insurance companies to pay off everyone, either. An annuity from a safe insurer (see *Conquer the Crash*) will probably survive, and accounts at a safe bank will, too. But most institutions that rely on investment values will be severely stressed in the coming meltdown.

In California, thanks to the infinite wisdom of the legislature, it is illegal for banks to collect mortgage debt beyond the equity in a defaulting homeowner's property. The natural result has begun to occur. Schahrzad Berkland of The Berkland Group recently said in an interview, "With no skin in the game, people in foreclosure now are not even listing their homes for sale. They don't even have 6 percent equity to hire a realtor. So they live rent free for 7-9 months until evicted after auction." If you have money in California banks that are heavily invested in real estate, your money is not in the vault; it is in mortgages. You might want to get out now, before it's too late. For a list of safe depositories, see *Conquer the Crash*.

I am sometimes asked why I have such a "crazy" outlook for real estate, calling for prices to fall as much as 90 percent. I will let a subscriber answer that question. He recently sent this email:

> For what it's worth, I will recount what my father told me when real estate values were falling in the sun belt in the late 1980s. He was born in 1919 and never stopped talking about

the Depression as it made such an impression on him. I asked him one day how far the price of farmland fell in the 1930s. He answered, "Your Grandfather and I went to the auctions held on the county courthouse steps (in Illinois) and watched auctions for the best farms in this county that had been repossessed, and there were no bidders. You couldn't borrow a dime to finance a purchase, and if you had money you wouldn't part with it under any circumstances." "So," he asked me, "How much do you think they were they worth?"

Wave Form and Trend Channel

Figure C-24

Over the past year, the Dow has been climbing to the upper end of the trend channel. Figure C-24 updates this picture. By either wave count illustrated, this channel should provide a target for the end of the advance from 2002. Price and time relationships do not come into play here (at least that I can see), so wave form is our only guide. We will simply wait until prices meet the trendline or the market falls far enough to confirm that a top is in. The low Arms Trading Index (TRIN) figures and the expansion in the advance/decline ratio this week constitute evidence that the overall advance is not yet over, even if this week's rally is a B wave.

The Elliott Wave Theorist Interim Report, June 25, 2007

Stock Market Strategy Update

On May 18, we rescinded a short-covering recommendation because it was clear from internal momentum statistics that the market was ready to slip. A correction began two weeks later. The S&P futures fell 60 points in early June and 40 points here in late June. So they have, for the second time, fallen back into the range of prices on the day we last recommended a short position for aggressive speculators. The latest decline appears to be wave C of a triangle (or possibly a flat). Now is a good time to cover shorts—close to break-even—and return to a cash position until the next opportunity.

Ideally we will let the triangle end and try to catch the top of the final thrust to follow. But if the S&P cash index falls just 41 more points to below the February high at 1461.57, it will confirm that a new bear market is already underway, so aggressive speculators should adopt a fully leveraged short position at such a time. Either way, we are ready.

Investors should just keep collecting T-bill interest, which has outperformed the S&P for over seven years.

The Elliott Wave Theorist, July 13, 2007

The Big Turn

When the stock market ended wave V in 1999 in real terms and 2000 in nominal terms, the character of social action underwent a stark change. [*Note: For an explanation, read Socionomics.—Ed.*] Figure C-25 shows the dividing line between these two periods on the Dow/gold chart. Since then, the U.S. has gotten involved in a war; terrorism has increased dramatically; the President's approval ratings have reached Nixonian levels (a new low this week of 29 percent); Congress' popularity has plumbed record depths (24 percent in June); the conciliatory and apologetic tone of the dialogue among religious leaders has morphed into a tone of confrontation (radical Islam and the latest headline: "Other Christian denominations are not true

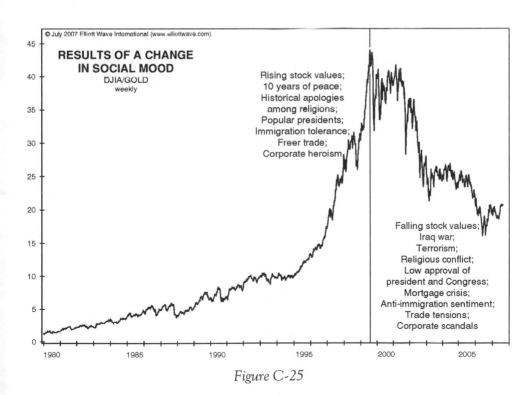

Figure C-25

churches, Pope reasserts," 7/11 AJC); populations are demanding
that authorities control immigration; governments are proposing
protectionist measures; home prices have fallen for the longest
time since the Great Depression; and bank credit instruments
are under severe price pressure due to fears of default. These
changes are not random, and they are not causing social mood to
change. They are the result of a change in social mood at Grand
Supercycle degree.

The Elliott Wave Theorist Interim Report, July 17, 2007

Even though the Dow has closed up for the past three
trading days, the average advance/decline ratio for this time is
below 1.00, indicating that more stocks fell each day on average
than rose. Weak breadth over the past five trading days relative
to Dow points gained confirms this rise as all or part of a fifth
wave. If the Dow is rising from a flat correction ending late June,
it will have one more pullback and rise on the daily chart. But if
it emerged from a triangle ending a week ago, the rally is a thrust
(see *Elliott Wave Principle*, p.51), and it is topping now.

The Dow has risen 750 points since the low associated
with our late June "cover" point. Aggressive speculators should
return to a fully leveraged short position now. We may be early
by a couple of weeks, but the market has traced out the minimum
expected rise, and that's enough to act upon.

We are sometimes asked why the market has not "reacted
to the bad news about mortgage debt prices." The very existence
of the Wave Principle means that the market does not react to
news; it moves in its own waves. News, in fact, tends to follow
the markets to which it relates. Housing stocks topped out two
years ago, indicating that optimism in that sector peaked at that
time. Today's news about mortgages is a lagging result of that

top. When stocks start down again, news relating to the stock market will get worse. Then people will say that the stock market "finally" reacted to the news about real estate loans, as if informed investors really wait weeks or months to react to the obvious. Reading waves is a challenge at times, but doing so at least keeps you focused on what matters.

The Elliott Wave Theorist, October 19, 2007

STOCKS, OIL AND INFLATION: FLASHING SIGNS OF A HISTORIC TOP

Housing Has Had It

Over two years ago in *The Elliott Wave Financial Forecast*, Steve Hochberg and Pete Kendall showed the information reproduced here as Figure C-26. Figure C-27 shows the aftermath to date. Figures C-28 and C-29 give snapshots of the initial

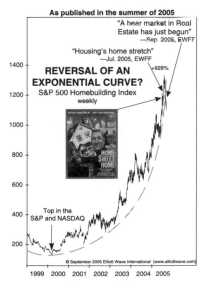

Figure C-26

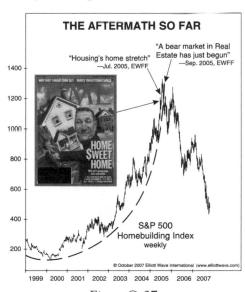

Figure C-27

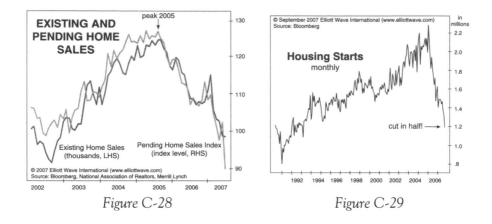

Figure C-28   Figure C-29

deterioration in the housing sector. I say initial because of the evidence in Figure C-30, which shows that people today are less able to afford a home at today's prices than they were in 2005 at 2005 prices. The housing market decline has only just begun.

Homeowners, by the way, are still bullish. A CNBC poll last week found that no less than 90 percent of U.S. homeowners expect the value of their homes to rise or stay the same over the coming year. This confidence fits the case that more price decline lies ahead.

HOUSING AFFORDABILITY
Average new home prices/disposable personal income per capita   (ratio, 3-month moving average)

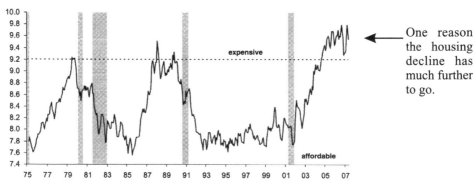

Figure C-30

Oil on Target

In 1998, EWI's *Global Market Perspective* called for a huge bull market in oil that would carry to new all-time highs. (To review that call, see pages 4 and 5 of the July 25, 2006 issue.) That run is now in its final stages.

Market psychology fits a major top, because short term measures of optimism match all-time extremes. Market Vane's Bullish Consensus is at 89%, the highest reading since the wave ① peak in September 2000, and the Daily Sentiment Index has touched an incredible 94%, in the area of the highest readings ever for any commodity. Investors everywhere have come to the conclusion that the world is running out of oil, despite the fact that the real price of oil (the oil/gold ratio; see July 2006 EWT) is lower than it was seven years ago.

Let's review the Elliott wave pattern. In March 2006, I traveled to Vienna, Austria, for the Kenos Circle Conference on oil. Figure C-31 shows the forecast I presented at that time for the price of oil. It called for oil to rally a bit further to finish

Analysis and forecast from March 2006:

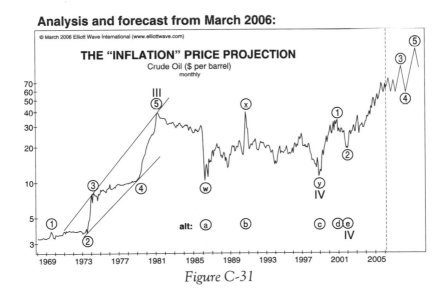

Figure C-31

Short-Term Analysis from July 2006:

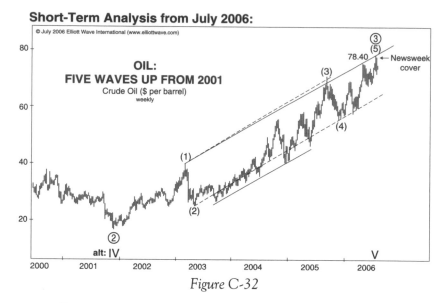

Figure C-32

wave ③, then fall sharply in wave ④, then make a new high in wave ⑤. Oil has followed every line on this forecast.

As wave ③ approached its peak, the signs of a Primary degree top were legion. On July 25, 2006, *The Elliott Wave Theorist* issued a 20-page, double issue devoted to calling the peak of wave ③ in the oil market. Figure C-32 is the Elliott wave picture presented at the time on the weekly chart showing that in the summer of 2006, oil was completing wave ③ of its big bull market from the 1998 low. The decline began right then and carried to $49.90. It was the biggest percentage decline in five years.

Today oil is near the end of wave ⑤. Peaks of fifth waves in commodities are not easy to identify. Sometimes they are blow-offs, in which prices move upward vertically and then fall just as fast as they went up. But Figure C-33 shows that the price of a barrel of crude has met the upper channel line of its Cycle-degree advance from 1998. It has gone from just above $10 a barrel, when no one cared about it, to $90, where everyone thinks it's a great investment.

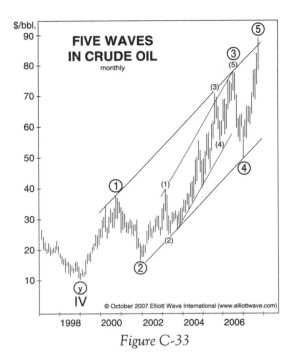

Figure C-33

This is only part of the picture. The rise from 1998 is itself a fifth wave, so the entire advance from 1933 is also ending. As Figure C-34 shows, oil is in its final wave of Supercycle degree in the bull market that began in 1933, when President Roosevelt seized Americans' gold and set the government free to monetize its debts and set the Fed free to facilitate the expansion of dollar-based credits throughout the banking system. The result has been a bull market in inflation, which the history of oil prices reflects. This chart says that the price of oil and the inflation that propelled it are reaching a historic peak. When the bull market in inflation is over, an unprecedented number of IOUs, stacked in an inverted pyramid, will collapse in value in a deflationary rush, and prices from stocks to commodities to goods and services will fall along with them.

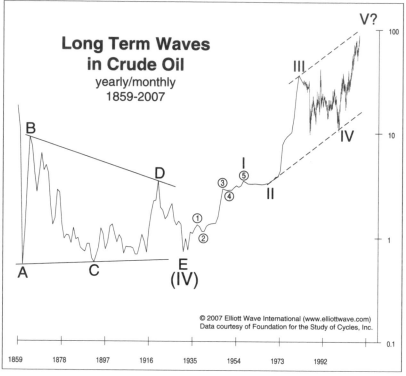

Figure C-34

Optimism in the Stock Market

The latest reading from Investors Intelligence shows 62 percent bulls among newsletter advisors, the second-highest reading over the past 21 years, a period that includes the tops of 1987 and 2000. And this is not the most extreme figure relating to investor sentiment. The *duration* of net optimism is the longest ever by many measures.

October 19 is the [20-year] anniversary of the biggest down day in the 1987 crash, so let's compare some of the technical readings at the 1987 pre-crash high with today's. Figure C-35 presents a table showing five different measures (the first two lines express the same thing) of optimism. Low valuation of dividend payouts indicate optimism, because when investors don't care

about receiving divi-
dends, it means they are
counting on capital gains
to get rich. By all these
measures, the persistence
of optimism going into
October 2007 dwarfs
that of August 1987.

Figure C-36
shows how the greatest
tops of the 20th century
compare in terms of the
duration of optimism.
The X axis records the

	Aug. 1987	Oct. 2007
DJIA Annual Dividend Yield	2.6%	2.0%
Price of $1 dividend	$39	$50
Duration Div. < 1929	3 months	13 years
Price/book value	1.73	4.04
Advisors net bullish (>97%)	156 weeks	468 weeks
Daily readings > 90% bulls	3	51

Figure C-35

length of time that bulls consistently outnumbered bears by a ratio
of at least 50/52 in Investors Intelligence's weekly readings. (I
estimate that at the tops in 1929 and 1937, bulls had outnumbered
bears continuously for about 2-2.5 years.) The Y axis records the

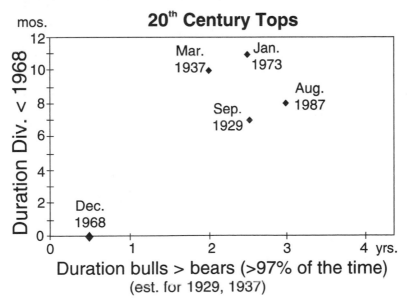

Figure C-36

length of time that the dividend yield from the Dow was less than
it was at the 1968 top, the peak with the highest dividend payout
among these five tops. As you can see, the other major tops cluster
around an area of 2-3 years for a lopsided bullish consensus and
7-11 months for extremely low dividend payout.

Now look at Figure C-37. This is the same graph but with
two added data points representing the top of January 2000 and
now. Compared to past market tops, the current juncture is nothing less than grotesque. I hope you can see some reasons why we
have expected a major top at each interim peak.

Figure C-38 is even more striking. It uses the greatest top
in U.S. history (in 1929) as a value benchmark. At the 1987
high, just before the crash, bulls had reigned for 3 years. Then,
just three months after the annual dividend yield from the DJIA
fell below that of 1929, the market crashed. At the 2000 high,
dividends had been below the 1929 level for a full six years, but
the duration for a preponderance of bulls was only 1.25 years.
That was enough for the S&P to fall in half and the NASDAQ
to collapse 78 percent.

But the situation in October 2007 dwarfs all these experiences. Advisory bulls have consistently outnumbered bears
for 9 years, by an incredible 51/52 ratio, and the dividend yield
has been below that of 1929 for 13 years. Thus, optimism is not
only historically extreme in terms of extent but also—by a huge
amount—in duration.

And remember, this graph uses the peak reading of 1929,
the greatest top of the 19th and 20th centuries, as a benchmark.
Forget comparing today's values and psychology to past bottoms.

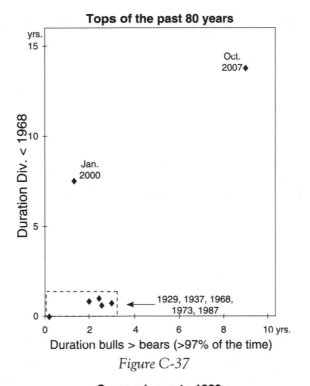

Figure C-37

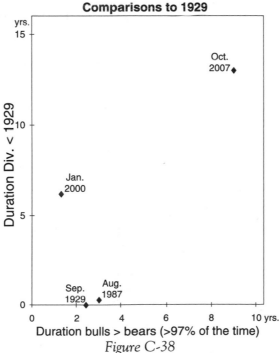

Figure C-38

Why Are Investors Bullish on Stocks, Oil and IOUs, All at the Same Time?

Explain this: The last time there was this much optimism toward oil was 1973-1974, and the stock market was falling. This time, the stock market has been rising right along with oil, and the optimism toward stocks is also extreme, by some measures the most extreme ever. (See Figure C-39.) Obviously, this is not the 1970s, when a rise in oil coincided with a collapse in stocks. But we said all along that this would not be like the 1970s. *Conquer the Crash* was the first publication (that we know of) to observe that the financial markets had begun trending together along with the ebb and flow of liquidity. So stocks and oil are rising because of the liquidity in the form of credit that has flooded the markets over the past half decade. Advocates of perpetual inflation say that this expansion will continue because the Fed can inflate at will. If that were true, then one would have to explain why the credit market is so stupid that it requires only 4 percent interest from T-bills, which are dollar-based IOUs. Inflation is raging, so shouldn't the yield on IOUs be 10, 15 or 18 percent, as in the 1970s?

Only one explanation takes all these events into account: Optimism is at an all-time extreme in extent and duration. That optimism has fueled the largest expansion in credit in history. Investors have used this credit to buy every investment. Optimism keeps lenders lending and borrowers borrowing, and it keeps investors buying stocks and borrowing to finance speculation in commodities. Until recently it kept them buying mortgages on leverage, too. Optimism also keeps interest rates low, because optimistic creditors are not afraid of default. The recent collapse in the value of sub-prime mortgages and the jump in banks' overnight lending rate were the first hints that optimism is faltering. When it reverses fully toward pessimism, interest rates on all

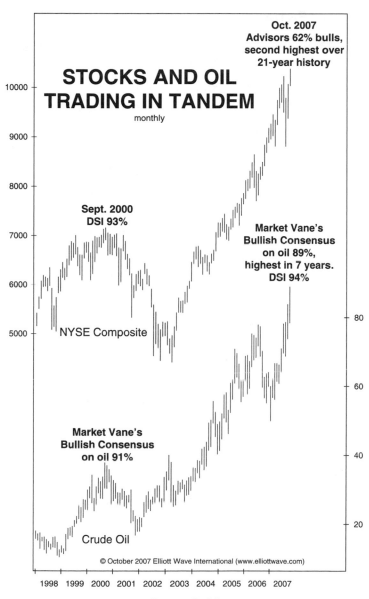

Oct. 2007
Advisors 62% bulls,
second highest over
21-year history

STOCKS AND OIL
TRADING IN TANDEM
monthly

Sept. 2000
DSI 93%

Market Vane's
Bullish Consensus
on oil 89%,
highest in 7 years.
DSI 94%

NYSE Composite

Market Vane's
Bullish Consensus
on oil 91%

Crude Oil

© October 2007 Elliott Wave International (www.elliottwave.com)

1998 1999 2000 2001 2002 2003 2004 2005 2006 2007

Figure C-39

risky debts will soar, in many cases to infinity. But rates on secure debt will fall, probably close to zero, because investors will want safety above all else.

Near Term Picture

On July 17, EWT recommended that aggressive speculators take a fully leveraged short position. That time marked the
all-time peak in several indexes, including the Dow Jones Transports (topped 7/18) and secondary averages such as the Value
Line Arithmetic index (topped 7/13). Our proxy for this type of
recommendation is S&P futures. The December futures contract
at that time (close on 7/17 to open on 7/18) was 1570.25-1572.25.
The August 26 issue outlined the bearish seasonal period that
carries through October 26. EWT made clear on page 1, "This
observation does not rule out a new high within this period."
The major averages crawled to a new high in the second week of
October. The futures contract made a new intraday high by only
7 points, closed down on that day and has fallen since. Place a
stop at 1571.25, which is break-even. If stopped, use the post-
October 12 low as a level to re-short.

Like all indicators, seasonal patterns are probabilistic.
The ending of this period has no reliably bullish implications,
because the evidence of bearish potential given throughout our
charts trumps every small-time bullish portent. In 1973 (34
years ago), the Dow and S&P bottomed on August 22, soared
until October 29, and then collapsed in November to below the
starting point of the rally. The Fed meets this year on October
31, and investors are breathlessly awaiting the next discount-rate
cut, as if it were bullish.

Investors holding interest-bearing cash equivalents have
outperformed the S&P for over seven years. Hold onto that cash
with both hands.

The Elliott Wave Theorist, November 16, 2007

The "7" Year and Stock Market Tops

A year ago EWT gave reasons for the market to peak in the "7" year of the decade and then crash. Figure C-40 updates the chart, with a new label.

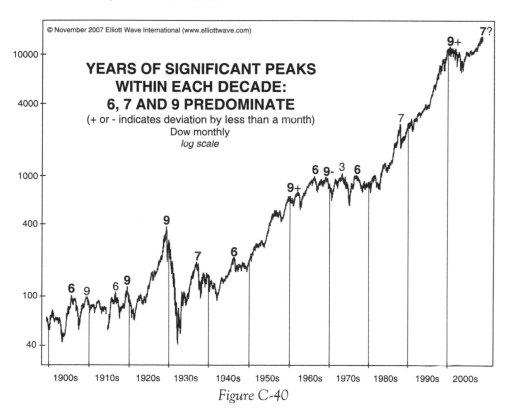

Figure C-40

The Duration of the Base Equals the Duration of the Top

EWT has been postulating that the duration of the top formation in the Dow would echo that of the bottom formation from 1974 to 1982. The June 2005 issue called for its end based on a Fibonacci ratio relationship, but the market continued rising. As shown in Figure C-41, their durations were close to equal at

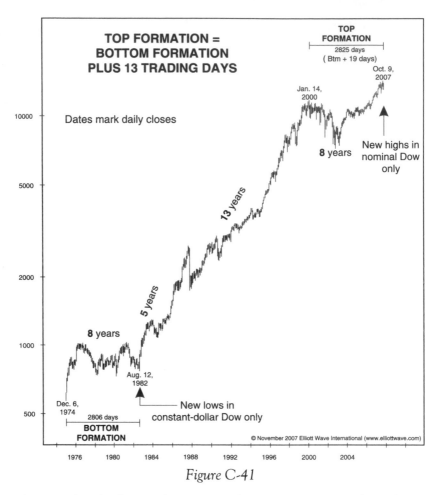

Figure C-41

the October high. At that point, the topping process lasted just 19 calendar days (a Fibonacci 13 trading days) longer than the bottoming process. This relationship is akin to many shown in *Beautiful Pictures*. While this type of analysis is experimental, to the extent that it is valid it argues in favor of the scenario under which the peak of wave **b** is already in.

The Elliott Wave Theorist, December 14, 2007

Today everyone knows three things about the future: (1) The stock market is always up in December; (2) years ending in 8 are always up; (3) pre-election years are always up. So you can bet that the vast majority on Wall Street is poised to get rich on the long side from now through the end of 2008. But if the market keeps going counter to seasonal patterns, it would go down this month and for most of 2008. A falling market this month and next year would certainly fool the majority, and it's about time the majority got fooled.

The Elliott Wave Theorist, January 17, 2008

BUST OR BUST

Everyone wants to know: Is the worst over for the stock market? The first two charts answer this question definitively.

Study Figure C-42 and tell me if you think it means that the decline is over. Tell me if it says that the S&P is on its way to 4000 (and the Dow to 36,000).

To an Elliott wave technician, this chart is affirmation for the Wave Principle's claim that history repeats, but at different degrees. It shows that 2000-2007 was a very big version of 1966-1973. These two seven-year periods saw the peak of a fifth wave, then an optimistic peak at a new high in a corrective wave (i.e. a rally in a bear market). In the former case, the S&P then fell 45 percent in less than two years. But the fifth wave in the recent period is two degrees larger than that of 1966. Likewise the extent of money managers' complacency, if we measure it by the size of the black area above the 5% line on the chart, is (as we would expect at this degree) several multiples more extreme than it was in 1973.

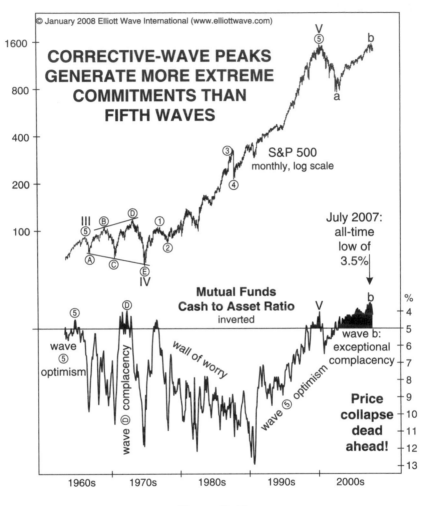

Figure C-42

This indicator implies three things: (1) forget Dow 36,000; (2) the market's selloff has not bottomed; (3) and more to the point, a huge price collapse in nominal terms—the one that will accompany extreme credit deflation—has only just begun. Of course, the majority disagrees and is happily living within the latest zone of black on the chart, meaning that they are fully invested and waiting to get rich.

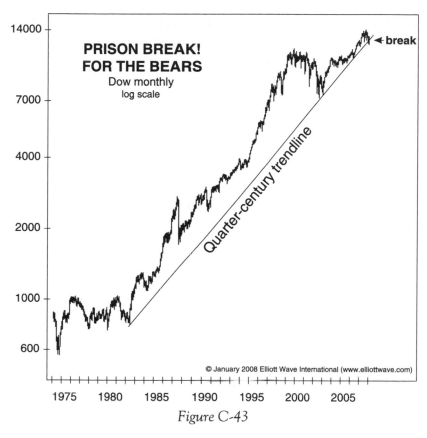

Figure C-43

Those waiting to get rich in the stock market, however, have just been kidnapped, trussed up and thrown in the trunk of a car heading to Bankruptcy City. At least that's what Figure C-43 says. Just look at this 25-year trendline, which just burst like an Army Corps levee. This line has four touch points, meaning that the market, not we, drew it. And the market just left it behind. This is news, but you won't read it in the paper. After all, there's a Fed meeting to talk about.

The extreme low reading of 3.5% cash for mutual funds shown in Figure C-42 occurred in July, the month of the high in the average stock as measured by the Value Line Arithmetic Index (and the high of the Dow Industrials and Transports combined). This is also the point at which EWT recommended a "fully leveraged short position" for speculators, which is now over 200 S&P points in the green.

Bonus Excerpt
The Elliott Wave Theorist, June 9, 2008

The Top of Wave ⑤ in Crude Oil Is Fast Approaching

I am publishing this issue a bit early in order to alert you to an opportunity developing in the oil market. Since calling incorrectly for the peak of wave ⑤ in October 2007, I have waited for the next likely juncture. As noted then about fifth waves in commodities, "some of them are blow-offs." With oil suddenly leaping as much as $10 a day, we should postulate an extended fifth wave, which in turn allows us to attempt to forecast the range for a peak.

Gold and silver have already seen their highs, so oil is due to peak soon and join them on the downside. But how do you snag a rocket-powered javelin in mid-air? Over the years I have come to the conclusion that an important key to recognizing a completed Elliott-wave bull market of Primary or Cycle degree in a commodity is to use arithmetic scale, as we did in Figure C-32. Fourth waves look normal on this scale, but they may look small on log scale. That is the case with oil right now. We can also use arithmetic scale to project the peak. Bull markets in commodities virtually always end with an extended fifth wave, as explained in Chapter 6 of *Elliott Wave Principle* (p.173):

> Also in contrast to the stock market, commodities most commonly develop extensions in fifth waves within Primary or Cycle degree bull markets. This tendency is entirely consistent with the Wave Principle, which reflects the reality of human emotions. Fifth wave advances in the stock market are propelled by hope, while fifth wave advances in commodities are propelled by a comparatively dramatic emotion, fear: fear of inflation, fear of drought, fear of war. Hope and fear look different on a chart, which is one of the reasons that commodity market tops often look like stock market bottoms.

From *Elliott Wave Principle*, p. 173

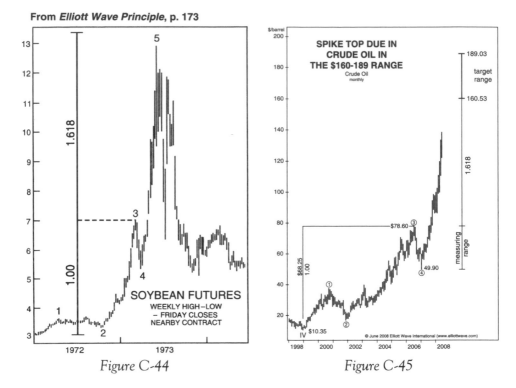

Figure C-44   *Figure C-45*

Figure C-44 shows a picture from that book, published way back in 1978. It shows how an extended wave 5 in soybeans in 1973 related by 1.618 to waves 1 through 3. In my experience, a good generalization of a normal relationship is that wave 5, when measured from the span of wave 4, will end when it reaches 1.618 times the length of waves 1 through 3. In the current situation, waves ① through ③ traveled $68.25. Therefore, wave ⑤ in crude oil should end when it is 1.618 times the shorter length, measured from the span of wave ④. This gives a target range of $160.33-$189.03 per barrel, as shown in Figure C-45.

So, one of the greatest commodity tops of all time is due very soon. Ideally, crude oil should end on a violent spike high in the $160-$189 range. [*Note: The peak occurred a month later at $147.50, and oil plummeted 78 percent in five months.—Ed.*]

Appendix D

COMMENTARY FROM THE ELLIOTT WAVE THEORIST ON THE MOUNTING PROSPECTS FOR DEFLATION, 2003-2007

DEFLATION: ONCE MORE INTO THE BREACH

The loneliness of the unequivocal and bearish deflationist is hard to overstate. When I traveled to New York last October, I was told by reporters that they knew of only one other serious deflationist, Stephen Roach of Morgan Stanley. According to The Wall Street Journal,[1] the Fed's jawboning has recently caused him to modify his stance. The only other staunch deflationist

courtesy Trend Macrolytics

I know is A. Gary Shilling, author of *Deflation: How to Survive and Thrive in the Coming Wave of Deflation* (McGraw-Hill, 1999), who still forecasts "a decade of deflation." Gary argues, however, that the deflation will be mild and beneficial, not immense and destructive. While he may turn out to be correct, he is certainly not bearish. Because of this situation, I have been unable to find a published article explaining the weaknesses in the inflationists' arguments and demonstrating that a destructive deflation is likely. If you can't find something, you have to make it yourself; thus this report. While *Conquer the Crash* anticipated and answered many of these arguments, the recent rash of commentary on the assurance of continued inflation seems to require a renewed response. Here are my answers to the arguments extant today.

"There Is No Evidence of Deflation Currently in Force"

"Deflation," headlines a financial publication, "of which there is none."[2] There are two responses to this reasonably correct assertion. First and directly to the point, the lack of deflation currently is irrelevant. The basis for forecasting is not a current indication of a trend change, because then it would not be forecasting. Economists always wait until a new trend is well entrenched and then tell you that the change occurred six months ago. A forecaster studies the precursors of trend change and then takes a stance in advance of the event. That's what EWI's deflation essays of 1998-2002 and *Conquer the Crash* have been doing. That the money supply is not contracting is of zero value in the debate of whether or not it will contract.

Second, there is a great deal of evidence that deflation is already impacting the economy selectively. The notable rises in bankruptcies, debt downgrades, delinquent loan payments, foreclosures, zero-percent loans, zero-downpayment loans, office vacancies and home equity borrowing unequivocally point to pressures from debt and over-spending, which I believe are precursors to deflation. The relentless decimation of junk bond values over the past five years portends depression, which implies deflation. The erratic but persistent fall in the Producer Price Index is a precursor to deflation. In November, the Labor Department reported that 40 percent of all goods and services were cheaper than they were a year ago. According to the Federal Reserve, the bursting of the stock bubble has wiped out more than $9 trillion of mentally perceived value, which means mentally perceived purchasing power. While only conjecture at this point, I think that the real estate bubble peaked in 2002, after four years in which total mortgage debt rose an amazing 50 percent. As happened with the stock market, the real estate market may take a year to erode slowly while people argue about what's going on, but a few years from now, a new downtrend in prices should be clearly evident.

The fact that deflation — a decrease in the overall supply of money and credit — has yet to begin simply means that the all-time record 87 percent drop in the Fed's discount rate last year freed up enough credit to fuel the housing boom and thereby keep the total volume of credit barely rising for another year. That stimulus is spent. The question remains: What do you forecast?

"Debt Is Not as High as It Seems"

A bullish economist recently argued that the level of total debt is overstated, implying that the credit bubble and therefore the threat of deflation are mild. He makes a case that "financial" debt doesn't count because adding it to the total gives double weight to other loans. If, for example, a home buyer borrows from a finance company, which in turn borrows from a bank, the latter "financial" loan doesn't count because the overall chain of transactions is really just one loan — a loan from the bank to the homeowner — through an intermediary. This assertion is offered to counter the power of a graph shown as Figure 11-5 in *Conquer the Crash* (reproduced and updated as Figure D-1). A few journalists have been seduced to treat this claim as if it were some grand, conclusive insight, admitting that they, too, "sad to say,"[3] were duped into an unwarranted concern. There are many responses to this argument.

The first answer is, "So what?" If the stewards of this and similar graphs (which include The Bank Credit Analyst, Bridgewater Associates, Ned Davis Research and the GAMCO Mathers Fund) were to factor financial debt out of the entire data series, it would, I suspect, produce much the same picture. You would still see a debt bubble in the 1920s and another one, *a larger one*, today. The implication that debt is the highest in the nation's history would be the same. The absolute level doesn't matter.

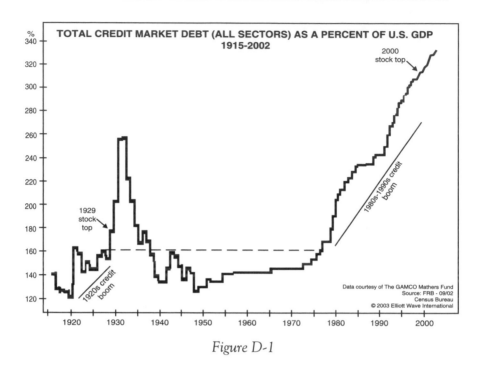

Figure D-1

Bulls resist this conclusion by asserting that financial debt today is a greater percentage of the total than it was earlier in the century, which would mean that non-financial debt as a percent of GDP would not be as high as it appears today relative to the 1920s. One problem is that they have not substantiated that assumption. Financial debt certainly existed in the 1920s, when investors, for example, could buy stock on 10 percent margin by borrowing the money from brokers, who would borrow much of it from banks, thus creating "financial" debt. Ninety percent is a lot to borrow, much more than today's 50 percent margin limit allows, and margin debt rose tenfold in the 1920s. How the numbers then would actually compare to those of today is strictly conjecture until someone makes all the proper adjustments and produces a substitute graph.

    If one were to go to the trouble of making such a graph, would it really show anything significantly different? No. If 1/3 of today's debt is financial, and, say, only 1/6 of 1929's debt was financial, then the graphed line in modern times would slip by just 1/6 of its current level, hardly enough materially to change the implications of Figure D-1.

People who give this graph short shrift seem to think that the former peak occurred in 1929, but it didn't; it occurred in the midst of the Great Depression, *after* the 1929 high. If we compare the levels of 1929 and 2000, each time the stock market topped, we find that the debt load recently is much higher, in fact nearly *double* the level in 1929, as you can see in Figure D-1. If from 2000 the ratio is to soar the same amount that it did from 1929 through the Great Depression's peak, then we will soon see the line on this graph rise past 500 percent of GDP!

There is a more subtle point to make. The very fact that countless finance companies are in the loan business tells you that debt financing has permeated the culture to a degree way beyond that of the 1920s. Many loans would not be made were it not for those finance companies. Fannie Mae and Freddie Mac, for example, make loans to people that otherwise might not be able to borrow. Banks lend to FNM and FRE in cases where they would decline to lend to the ultimate borrower. Many financiers may be middlemen, but they serve to grease the skids for bales of credit. To expand upon a point that Ned Davis recently made, if a borrower goes under, the lending intermediary may go under, in which case the bank may go under, in which case the insurance company that guaranteed the bank loan may go under. In fact, any one of these entities can go bankrupt (simply from profligacy, for example) before everyone down the line from it does, in which case, that entity's creditors will be induced to move down the line recalling credit. To ignore the pyramid of dependence in today's credit situation is to ignore a vitally important aspect of the deflationary danger. To dismiss it all as "double counting" is cavalier, to say the least.

If we were to pursue the "double counting" idea to its extremity, we could, quite cleverly, reduce the entire debt supply from $30 trillion not in the bulls' wimpy fashion to $20 trillion but to about 1/400 of that amount. Let's start with the U.S. core money supply, which is $55 billion worth of domestic greenbacks in banks and at the Fed. When a bank makes a loan, that money is deposited in (i.e., *lent to*, legally speaking) other banks, which in turn lend the money again. This "multiplier effect" is potentially infinite. (For reasons why, see Chapter 10 of *Conquer the Crash*.) Why not count all these as one loan? After all, as long as the debt is secure all the way down the chain, then it's just the same money, lent through many "intermediaries." Voila! "Don't worry; all we have is $55 billion worth of domestic debt. It's just cycled through many entities." I hope you can see that the risk of default exists all the way down the line. To conclude, I see no reason to abandon the position that *total debt is total debt, and all of it matters*.

People who offer "low debt" arguments are *bulls* on stocks, inflation and the economy. Consequently, whether consciously or otherwise, they neglect to mention many factors that are unrepresented in Figure D-1. *Conquer the Crash* listed some of them:

> This $30 trillion figure, moreover, does not include government guarantees such as bank deposit insurance, unfunded Social Security obligations, and so on, which could add another $20 trillion or so to that figure, depending upon what estimates we accept. It also does not take into account U.S. banks' holdings of $50 trillion worth of derivatives at representative value (equaling five full years' worth of U.S. GDP), which could turn into IOUs for more money than their issuers imagine.[4]

So when bullish economists attempt to debunk the debt problem, they become selective. They focus on one aspect of it and ignore many other factors. If I were as biased as such writers, I would add all of the above-implied debt to Figure D-1 and show current dollar-denominated liabilities at 1000 percent of GDP, not 300 percent. It would be an easier position to defend than that taken by the bulls, because we know unequivocally that there were negligible Social Security obligations, bank deposit insurance and derivatives in the 1920s.

The attempt to debunk the all-time historically high level of debt worldwide is akin to arguments trying to dismiss the historically extreme P/D, P/E and P/book ratios: They are selective and designed to rationalize the problem away. A curmudgeon might call them dangerous.

"Consumers Remain the Engine Driving the U.S. Economy"

Only producers can afford to buy things. A consumer *qua* consumer has no economic value or power. The only way that consumers who are not (adequate) producers can buy things is to *borrow* the money. So when economists tell you that the consumer is holding up the economy, they mean that expanding *credit* is holding up the economy. This is a description of the *problem*, not the solution! The more the consumer goes into hock, the worse the problem gets, which is precisely the opposite of what economists are telling us. The more you hear that the consumer is propping up the economy, the more you know that the debt bubble is growing, and with it the risk of deflation.

"The Fed Will Stop Deflation"

Greenspan asserts, "If deflation were to develop, options for an aggressive monetary policy response are available." He gives no examples, presumably because he feels that Fed Governor Ben S. Bernanke said quite enough on that topic the previous month.

Bernanke, an alumnus of both Harvard and MIT who is now an economist at Princeton, agrees with the vast majority of economists and pundits that "the chance of significant deflation in the United States in the foreseeable future is extremely small." He purports to explain, "The sources of deflation are not a mystery. Deflation is in almost all cases a side effect of a collapse of aggregate demand [for goods and services]." He makes no mention of why demand (by which he means bids for goods and services) can collapse, either because it is a mystery or because he wants to avoid saying so. The true source of deflation is system-wide bankruptcies induced by the contraction of a prior credit bubble. Without the preceding bubble, "demand" would never "collapse."

Bernanke is a social mechanist. He thinks that if you pull one monetary lever on the left of the macroeconomic machine, the lever on the right will go down, too. The "stability" of recent decades he attributes to "flexible and efficient markets for labor and capital" (which must have suddenly gone missing during 1835-1842, 1929-1932 and in Japan since 1990) and "the heightened understanding by central bankers and, equally as important, by political leaders and the public at large of the very high costs of allowing the economy to stray too far from price stability." Presumably, he is excluding price stability in stocks, property and Beanie Babies from that general category. Regardless, the idea that politicians and the public are enlightened about macroeconomics is nonsense. Disinflation makes central bankers look smart, when in fact, it is the natural trend of the psycho-monetary cycle and results from society-wide ignorance of macroeconomics.

Greenspan rightly warns, "Weaving a monetary policy path through the thickets of bubbles and deflations and their possible aftermath is not something with which modern central bankers have had much experience." Bernanke has had no experience with deflation at all, yet as a leader of the supposedly enlightened, he boldly presents all his answers for the threat of deflation. He spends a couple of pages advocating policies to force down long term interest rates by decree and to convert government debt from long term to short term, which taken to its ultimate conclusion means to convert T-bonds into T-notes and then into T-bills and finally into cash notes, a circuitous route to simple money printing. I'm not sure who would buy such debt paper if confidence were to erode, and Bernanke doesn't address the question. He has his hands on the levers, and he knows which ones to pull. Read about the more drastic measures for yourself (ellipses omitted; italics in the original):

> The U.S. central bank, in cooperation with other parts of the government as needed, has sufficient policy instruments to ensure that any deflation that might occur would be both mild and brief. It is true that once the policy rate has been driven down to zero, a central bank can no longer use its *traditional* means of stimulating aggregate demand[, but it] has most definitely *not* run out of ammunition. Deflation is always reversible under a fiat money system. The U.S. government has a technology called a printing press that allows it to produce as many U.S. dollars as it wishes at essentially no cost. Under a paper-money system, a determined government can always generate higher spending and hence positive inflation. Of course, the U.S. government is not going to print money and distribute it willy-nilly (although as we will see later, there are practical policies that approximate this behavior). To stimulate aggregate spending when short-term interest rates have reached zero, the Fed must expand the scale of its asset purchases or, possibly, expand the menu of assets that it buys. We can take comfort that the logic of the printing press example must assert itself, and sufficient injections of money will ultimately always

reverse a deflation. Unlike some central banks, and barring changes to current law, the Fed is relatively restricted in its ability to buy private securities directly. However, the Fed [could] offer fixed-term loans to banks at low or zero interest, with a wide range of private assets (including, among others, corporate bonds, commercial paper, bank loans, and mortgages) deemed eligible as collateral. The Fed can inject money into the economy in still other ways. For example, the Fed has the authority to buy foreign government debt, as well as domestic government debt. Potentially, this class of assets offers huge scope for Fed operations, as the quantity of foreign assets eligible for purchase by the Fed is several times the stock of U.S. government debt. The government could increase spending on current goods and services or even acquire existing real or financial assets. If the Treasury issued debt to purchase private assets and the Fed then purchased an equal amount of Treasury debt with newly created money, the whole operation would be the economic equivalent of direct open-market operations in private assets.[5]

Can you see why economists and financial writers of all types have panicked and embraced the idea that inflation is inevitable and deflation impossible? They have met the Wizard of Oz in person, and he is impressive!

He is also delusional. Can you imagine the laughingstock that the Federal Reserve System would become if its "assets" consisted of defaulted mortgages, bonds of bankrupt companies and municipalities, IOUs of shaky foreign governments and stock certificates of companies no longer in existence? Can you imagine the panic that would ensue to escape a monetary system with such assets as its reserves?

Bernanke's primary problem is that the only object he thinks exists is the monetary ledger, an inanimate balance sheet. He does not consider the responses of actual people and markets to his proposed policy actions, which will result in unintended consequences.

But the human mind is not a machine, and people are not easily predictable. For example, it is taken for granted that low interest rates are supposed to help the debt situation, right? Read this:

> Money fund yields, which currently average 1.52%, trade in line with interest rates. The rates, which are near historical lows, are driving investors out of money funds and into higher-yielding but riskier long-term-bond funds, experts say.[6]

Investors are jacking up the risk of their holdings because interest rates on safe debt issues are low, moving out of the frying pan and into the fire. According to Fitch Ratings, nearly 50 percent of the $100 billion worth of "speculative grade" debt issued from 1997 through 1999 has already gone into default. Yet desperate investors, many of whom depend upon interest income to live, are buying more of the stuff and risking their shirts. Did the Fed intend that outcome when it jammed rates lower? Are low rates helping the debt situation and the deflation threat or making it worse?

Greenspan more specifically addresses the problem of unintended consequences when he laments what to him was an unforeseen consequence of a *prudent* central bank policy over the past 20 years: "It seems ironic that a monetary policy that is successful in inducing stability may inadvertently be sowing the seeds of instability associated with asset bubbles[, i.e.,] the apparent market tendency toward bidding stock prices higher in response to monetary policies aimed at maintaining macroeconomic stability." Let's put aside for the moment that the Chairman is saying that the Fed is to be faulted only for being so darn good at its job of engineering stability, a highly debatable stance. His broader

point is crucial: *We don't know how people will react to what we do.*
Bernanke seems to think that hitting the "fast forward" button on
greenback printing presses is some kind of isolated act that would
simply add a few zeroes to the national ledger as needed, with no
psychological effects at all, no attempt by anyone to protect his
wealth in response. This sterile view of society is a policymaker's
dream and just as illusory. In fact, the financial world would go
berserk if the Fed followed Bernanke's prescriptions. Even if he
got in shape by arm wrestling Greenspan every week, he would
be exhausted from turning the crank on the printing press fast
enough to try to outrun the selling of panicked bond investors.
A falling bond market would mean rising interest rates, the opposite of what the Fed would be trying to achieve. If rates were
held down by fiat in such an environment, it would mean the
immediate end to the market for new Treasuries, creating instant
deflation. As I explain in *Conquer the Crash*, it's a Catch-22 situation. Deflation will win.

Do you really think any of the Fed's schemes will work?
Before you answer that question, you might ask yourself how its
last "sure cure" has performed. For about ten years now, the Fed
and prominent economists have repeatedly — and arrogantly
— asserted that Japan's persistent deflation resulted from the
central bank's error in *not lowering interest rates fast enough*. The
Fed assertively avoided making *that* mistake, jamming U.S. rates
down a record amount in record time in 2001-2002, to their lowest level in over 40 years. The Fed's monetary strategists applied
the one big lesson that they were so certain mattered most —
the one that was sure to work — and what has happened? The
stock market is lower, and the economy is weaker than it was at
the start of the program! Deflation is so *petulant* in ignoring the
planners, isn't it?

All these bankers are wrong about the true error committed and the actual lesson to be learned. The significant monetary

TOM TOLES / *Washington Post*

errors attending the Great Depression were not committed from 1929 to 1933. They were committed from 1914 to 1929. To admit the true error and lesson would be to condemn the very existence of fiat money and central banking. The initial error was committed by Congress in granting one bank a monopoly on the country's money. That monopoly has allowed personal greed and political ambitions to foster seven decades of easy credit. Easy credit has in turn created an unsustainable debt load throughout the society. *Nothing* can relieve that load except what has always done so: a deflationary collapse. You cannot avoid the consequences of easy credit, just as you cannot avoid the consequences of taking amphetamines for months on end. The true lesson for society is, *don't create monopoly mechanisms that foster easy credit.* I have yet to hear a decorated economist admit the actual problem. Perhaps when the dust settles, after the damage is done, it will happen.

Recent Quotes from Nobel Laureates, Fed Chairmen and Other Experts

"Ignore the Ghost of Deflation. What does not make for good contingency planning is the recent alarmism about 'deflation.' Apart from Japan, the world has not seen deflation for 70 years...."[7] — October 10, 2002

"Deflation is an overblown worry, in our opinion. The question [is] whether governments can still do to money what they have usually been able to do to it."[8] — October 25, 2002

"The good news is that monetary policy never runs out of power."[9] — October 29, 2002

"If you believe we are headed for deflation, you have conveniently filtered economic facts and history to support this notion. How can anyone believe there is going to be deflation? Even Robert Prechter comes to the conclusion that a deflationary depression is coming in his otherwise excellent book *Conquer the Crash*. Believe in Ghosts, Goblins, Wizards and Witches if you will...but don't believe in deflation occurring anytime soon."[10] — October 30, 2002

"There's a much exaggerated concern about deflation. It's not a serious prospect. Inflation is still a much more serious problem than deflation. Today's Federal Reserve is not going to repeat the mistakes of the Federal Reserve of the 1930s. The cure for deflation is very simple. Print money."[11] — November 6, 2002

"Fed officials and most private economists still think deflation is highly unlikely. Deflation doubters say the U.S. won't suffer deflation again because the Fed won't let it."[12] — November 11, 2002

"The United States is nowhere close to sliding into a pernicious deflation."[13] — December 19, 2002

NOTES

[1] Hilsenrath, Jon E. (2002, December 30). "'Reflation' Comes into Focus as U.S. Struggles to Battle Deflation." *The Wall Street Journal.*

[2] Grant, James. (2002, October 25). "Deflation, of which there is none," *Grant's Interest Rate Observer*, p. 1.

[3] Palmer, Jay. (2003, January 6). "Annual Review of Investment Books." *Barron's.*

[4] Prechter, Robert. (2002). *Conquer the Crash: You Can Survive and Prosper in a Deflationary Depression.* John Wiley & Sons, p. 106.

[5] Bernanke, Ben S. (2002, November 21). "Deflation: Making Sure 'It' Doesn't Happen Here." Speech to the National Economists Club, Washington, D.C., as posted on the Internet.

[6] Hoffman, David. (2002, October 28). "For Money Funds, Zero Sum Is No Game at All." *InvestmentNews*, p. 25.

[7] Brittan, Samuel. (2002, October 10). "Ignore the Ghost of Deflation." Published on the Internet.

[8] Grant, James. (2002, October 25). *Grant's Interest Rate Observer*, p. 1.

[9] Angell, Wayne. (2002, October 29). "Greenspan's Deflation." *The Wall Street Journal.*

[10] Douglas, Adrian. (2002, October 30). "Ghosts, Goblins, Witches, Wizards...And DEFLATION." Published on the Internet.

[11] Nobel laureate Milton Friedman, as quoted by Greg Ip. (2002, November 6). "Inside the Fed, Deflation Draws a Closer Look." *The Wall Street Journal*, p. A14.

[12] Ip, Greg. (2002, November 6). "Inside the Fed, Deflation Draws a Closer Look." *The Wall Street Journal*, p. A14.

[13] Greenspan, Alan. (2002, December 19). Speech to the Economic Club of New York, as posted on the Internet.

From the Supplement to the 2004 paperback edition of *Conquer the Crash*

Since the publication of *Conquer the Crash*, the term that was hardly given the respect of a hearing has since broken into the general consciousness. The rarely used word *deflation* has become fashionable in financial discussion, as shown in Figure D-2. It is fashionable, however, not to predict its occurrence but

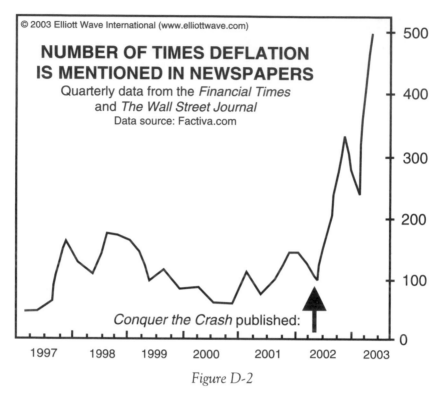

**NUMBER OF TIMES DEFLATION
IS MENTIONED IN NEWSPAPERS**
Quarterly data from the *Financial Times*
and *The Wall Street Journal*
Data source: Factiva.com

Conquer the Crash published:

1997   1998   1999   2000   2001   2002   2003

Figure D-2

primarily to *dismiss* the idea that it has any serious likelihood of occurring. The president of the Federal Reserve Bank of Dallas said in May that there is "maybe one chance out of four"[1] that deflation will occur. This comment may sound simply like another dismissal of the risk, but careful perusal of news articles shows that the odds offered by those willing to express them are down from "1 in 10,000" back in the mid-1990s (when the global rate of inflation peaked) to "at most 1 in 50" from 2001(see quotes in Chapter 13) to "1 in 4" now. This progression is highly instructive as to how conventional economists' opinions lag trends. The latest statement of odds came after a report that the Producer Price index for April fell 1.9 percent, which "was far larger than economists predicted."[2] Here are some more quotes, mostly from the past four months:

"Not one economist [of 67 surveyed] said it was 'very likely' the economy would slip into deflation, and only 6% said it was 'somewhat likely.' About 95% said deflation was "not very likely" to happen."[3]

"Fed policy-makers have mounted a virtuoso performance over the past six weeks to influence financial markets without even cutting rates. That should allay any worries that the Fed is in danger of running out of ammunition to stimulate the economy with interest rates already so low."[4]

"The whole deflation story has been over-hyped...the economy does not lack for monetary fuel. Once money starts circulating through the economy at a more normal pace, the central bank won't be worrying about deflation."[5]

"The United States has too many good things going for it to make a forecast of deflation credible." "I don't believe that the United States is at the brink of significant and sustained deflation."[6]

"It is most unlikely that any future deflation will be as long or severe as it was in the Depression.... The Fed can conduct heterodox monetary policy, expanding the money supply by buying such things as long-term bonds. And ultimately, such a policy will stop the deflation."[7]

"In remarks broadcast to bankers in Berlin, Greenspan characterized the probability of crippling deflation as 'low'.... [He] said policymakers were...willing to 'lean over backwards' to contain deflationary forces."[8]

"There is little reason to believe that a monetary contraction is imminent. Few who are discussing this appear to have much understanding of what they are talking about. A renewal of price inflation, not deflation, should be our greatest concern."[9]

"Inflation is a Bigger Danger Than Deflation."[10]

"The best way to beat deflation is to aggressively increase liquidity by pumping up high-powered money. The Federal Open Market Committee did this in 1998 and 1999 [and] it can do so again."[11]

"Who's Afraid of Big Bad Deflation?" "Stocks Do Best Near Zero Inflation."[12]

"The idea that we are looking at a general deflation is wrong. There is simply no indication in the data of deflation."[13]

"[The] president of the Federal Reserve Bank of San Francisco...said, 'The chances of really experiencing declining prices is quite small.' He also said that the Fed has done research on whether deflation is a possibility, and its simulations have shown the probability is 'quite low' in 2003 and 2004."[14]

"Myth #5: We Are Staring Deflation in the Face. Inflation, as ever, is the sleeping dragon.... Deflation is still a fairy tale bogeyman at this stage — a Troll with which to frighten the children into silence and compliance."[15]

"Deflation Fears Are Irrational."[16]

Deflation Scare is Losing Air
Advisers, investors no longer concerned
Deflation Scare Is a Thing of the Past

Fears of deflation have been deflated.

Investors — virtually in a matter of weeks — have forgotten about the threat of deflation, and financial advisers are crossing it off their list of worries.

"It appears that the deflation-is-dead camp has won," says Keith B. Hembre, director of economic research for

U.S. Bancorp Asset Management Inc. in Minneapolis. "It's a crowd psychology kind of thing."

A survey by the National Association for Business Economics in Washington backs the deflation-is-dead thinking. None of the respondents to the May survey, all of whom were responsible for making macroeconomic predictions, predicted a decline in the consumer price index during the next two years.

"I would venture to say that, if anything, the position [against deflation] would have solidified" since May, says Tim O'Neill, president of the association and chief economist of the Toronto-based BMO Financial Group (formerly Bank of Montreal).

It's not going to happen here, says Nancy Kimelman, chief economist of SEI Investments in Oaks, Pa. "I have full faith in the American financial system to stop deflation in its tracks, and I think we're doing it."

Hers is a view widely held by financial advisers and others who are investing with abandon for the first time in years.

Brian Kohute, chief financial officer of the HJ Financial Group in Plymouth Meeting, Pa., says he is one of those people.

"We thought the risk of deflation was very heavy in the first half of the year," says the adviser, who oversees the $110 million his firm manages. "That's really changed" in the past few weeks.[17]

So, as they say, the more things change, the more they stay the same. Perhaps all these people will turn out right, but I think that the beliefs expressed above are simply an expression of the underlying social ebullience that is manifest in the stock market rally and economists' optimistic consensus. The progression of increasing attention paid to the deflation question, coupled with the continual denials that deflation will happen, appear to be part of a social psychological progression toward a credit crisis.

Something has to give, and *that something will be prices*. Global inflation, as measured by prices, has already declined from more than 30 percent per year in 1990-94 (*At the Crest* sounded a warning of the coming trend in 1995) to about 3 percent. Monetary trends are not a matter of *weeks*; they are a matter of decades, and this one isn't over. When the Dow turns down again and breaks 7000, it will signal the onset of a more intense phase of the deflationary progression.

Is the Fed really *fighting* deflation by aggressively lowering its interest rates? Everyone thinks so, but the result of deflation — its primary outward symptom — is lower prices. And what has the Fed been doing? It has spent over a year *lowering the price of renting money*. Within that period, in fact, the Fed has lowered prices more than anyone! It has participated in the initial phase of the deflationary process as if it were a merchant on the street discounting its wares to a disinterested public. It did so in response to slack demand for its product — credit — just as the auto manufacturers and others are doing with their products. Deflationary psychology brings about lower prices, and the Fed is lowering its prices.

The true power is not at the Fed but in the trend of social mood. Currently, the total credit supply is still rising, but commercial and industrial loans have fallen since 2001. In other words, lenders are exhibiting deflationary psychology in being unwilling to finance productive enterprise. Yet, ironically, they are quite willing to finance consumption via home, auto and credit-card loans. This dichotomy is untenable, as production is what ultimately pays for consumption. The speeding vehicle of debt-financed consumption is about to hit the brick wall of credit-starved (non)production.

The Next Phase

As recounted above, people are finally talking about deflation (if only to dismiss it). The next word that should begin to slide into the lexicon is *depression*. I would like to feature quotes from authorities on the low likelihood of depression, but we find literally no professional economists, academics or Wall Street strategists even discussing the possibility. It is too remote even to mention! The term "depression" is where the word "deflation" was a few years ago, i.e., outside the general consciousness. Although no one is using that term now, soon it will be everywhere. The first phase will be widespread insistence that it can't happen, which will be the next clue that it is. The two "d" words in the subtitle to this book were anticipatory, published at a time when the likelihoods of their happening were (and still are) considered — as one economist said at the time about deflation — as remote as "being eaten by piranhas." Keep your toes on the riverbank.

Notes

[1] Ip, Greg. (2003, May 19). "Having Defeated Inflation, the Fed Girds for War on Falling Prices." *The Wall Street Journal.*

[2] Kirchhoff, Sue. (2003, May 16). "Deflation Fears May Rise as Economy Fights for Traction." *USA Today.*

[3] Hagenbaugh, Barbara, and Barbara Hansen. (2003, June 23). "Economists Expect Cut; Many Don't Advise It." *USA Today.*

[4] Associated Press. (2003, June 23). "To stop Deflation, Federal Reserve May Drop Interest Rate Again."

[5] Baum, Caroline. (2003, June 18). "Houston, Deflation Launch Has Been Scrubbed." *Bloomberg News.*

[6] Fed Vice Chairman Roger Ferguson, quoted in *The Wall Street Journal*, May 19, 2003 "Having Defeated Inflation, Fed Girds for New Foe: Falling Prices," by Greg Ip and Jon Hilsenrath; and by the Associated Press, June 14, 2003, "Price Drops Could Lead to Deflation."

[7] Shiller, Robert J. (2003, June 12). "The Technology Deflator." *The Wall Street Journal.*

[8] Kirchoff, Sue. (2003, June 4). "Greenspan Upbeat About Economy." *USA Today.*

[9] American Institute for Economic Research. (2003, May 26). "Deflation." Research Report.

[10] Lee, Tim. (2003, May 26). "Inflation is a Bigger Danger Than Deflation." *Financial Times* online.

[11] Cosgrove, Michael. (2003, May 21). "The Fed's Complacency." *The Wall Street Journal*.

[12] Headlines in *The Wall Street Journal*, May 16, 2003.

[13] George Von Furstenberg, Indiana University, formerly on the Council of Economic Advisors, quoted in *The Atlanta Journal-Constitution*, May 10, 2003, "Fed deflation warning creates waves," by Michael E. Kanell.

[14] De Rosa, David. (2003, May 7). "Will U.S. Catch Japan's Deflation Bug?" *Bloomberg News*.

[15] Corrigan, Sean. (2003, May). "Myths of the Crash." *The Free Market*. Ludwig von Mises Institute.

[16] Bugos, Ed. (2003, February 19). "Deflation fears are irrational." *Goldenbar Report*, on the Internet.

[17] Southall, Brooke. (2003, September 1). "Deflation scare is losing air." Investment News (excerpt). To be fair, the article quoted one economist who still urges caution about dismissing the possibility of deflation.

[Note: Here in September 2009, sentiment is even more strongly biased against the prospects for deflation. 52 of the 53 economists just polled by The Wall Street Journal (on September 9) predict a rising CPI through the end of 2010, and all of them predict an expanding GDP for the next four reported quarters. On the bearish side, the expectation among high-profile financiers quoted in the media is no longer just for inflation but for hyperinflation.—Ed.]

The Elliott Wave Theorist, February 20, 2004

SECULAR DEFLATION AND THE END OF A CYCLICAL REFLATION

Jaguar Inflation

I am tired of hearing people insist that the Fed can expand credit all it wants. Sometimes an analogy clarifies a subject, so let's try one.

It may sound crazy, but suppose the government were to decide that the health of the nation depends upon producing Jaguar automobiles and providing them to as many people as possible. To facilitate that goal, it begins operating Jaguar plants all over the country, subsidizing production with tax money. To everyone's delight, it offers these luxury cars for sale at 50 percent off the old price. People flock to the showrooms and buy. Later, sales slow down, so the government cuts the price in half again. More people rush in and buy. Sales again slow, so it lowers the price to $900 each. People return to the stores to buy two or three, or half a dozen. Why not? Look how cheap they are! Buyers give Jaguars to their kids and park an extra one on the lawn. Finally, the country is awash in Jaguars. Alas, sales slow again, and the government panics. It must move more Jaguars, or, according to its theory — ironically now made fact — the economy will recede. People are working three days a week just to pay their taxes so the government can keep producing more Jaguars. If Jaguars stop moving, the economy will stop. So the government begins *giving Jaguars away*. A few more cars move out of the showrooms, but then it ends. *Nobody wants any more Jaguars. They don't care if they're free. They can't find a use for them.* Production of Jaguars ceases. It takes years to work through the overhanging supply of Jaguars. Tax collections collapse, the factories close, and unemployment soars. The economy is wrecked. People can't afford to buy gasoline, so many of the Jaguars rust away to worthlessness. The number of Jaguars — at best — returns to the level it was before the program began.

The same thing can happen with credit.

It may sound crazy, but suppose the government were to decide that the health of the nation depends upon producing credit and providing it to as many people as possible. To facilitate that goal, it begins operating credit-production plants all over the country, called Federal Reserve Banks. To everyone's delight, these banks offer the credit for sale at below market rates. People flock to the banks and buy. Later, sales slow down, so the banks cut the price again. More people rush in and buy. Sales again slow, so they lower the price to one percent. People return to the banks to buy even more credit. Why not? Look how cheap it is! Borrowers use credit to buy houses, boats and an extra Jaguar to park out on the lawn. Finally, the country is awash in credit. Alas, sales slow again, and the banks panic. They must move more credit, or, according to its theory — ironically now made fact — the economy will recede. People are working three days a week just to pay the interest on their debt to the banks so the banks can keep offering more credit. If credit stops moving, the economy will stop. So the banks begin *giving credit away*, at zero percent interest. A few more loans move through the tellers' windows, but then it ends. *Nobody wants any more credit. They don't care if it's free. They can't find a use for it.* Production of credit ceases. It takes years to work through the overhanging supply of credit. Interest payments collapse, banks close, and unemployment soars. The economy is wrecked. People can't afford to pay interest on their debts, so many bonds deteriorate to worthlessness. The value of credit — at best — returns to the level it was before the program began.

See how it works?

Is the analogy perfect? No. The idea of pushing credit on people is far more dangerous than the idea of pushing Jaguars on them. In the credit scenario, debtors and even most creditors lose everything in the end. In the Jaguar scenario, at least everyone ends up with a garage full of cars. Of course, the Jaguar scenario is impossible, because the government can't produce value. It can, however, reduce values. A government that imposes a central bank monopoly, for example, can reduce the incremental value of credit. A monopoly credit system also allows for fraud and theft on a far bigger scale. Instead of government appropriating citizens' labor openly by having them produce cars, a monopoly banking system does so clandestinely by stealing stored labor from citizens' bank accounts by inflating the supply of credit, thereby reducing the value of their savings.

I hate to challenge mainstream 20th century macroeconomic theory, but the idea that a growing economy needs easy credit is a false theory. Credit should be supplied by the free market, in which case it will almost always be offered intelligently, primarily to producers, not consumers. Would lower levels of credit availability mean that fewer people would own a house or a car? Quite the opposite. Only the timeline would be different. Initially it would take a few years longer for the same number of people to own houses and cars — *actually* own them, not rent them from banks. Because banks would not be appropriating so much of everyone's labor and wealth, the economy would grow much faster. Eventually, the extent of home and car ownership — *actual* ownership — would eclipse that in an easy-credit society. Moreover, people would *keep* their homes and cars because banks would not be foreclosing on them. As a bonus, there would be no devastating across-the-board collapse of the banking system, which, as history has repeatedly demonstrated, is inevitable under a central bank's fiat-credit monopoly.

Jaguars, anyone?

The Elliott Wave Theorist, August 24, 2005
(written at the peak of credit expansion in the real estate sector)

The Credit Supply Is About To Begin a Major Deflation

The June 28 issue of "Bullion Buzz" quotes investment guru Jim Rogers as saying, "Anyone who thinks there will be deflation does not understand twenty-first century central banking. There may well be a deflationary collapse later, but before that happens the government will print money until the world runs out of trees." Of course, Jim is a legendary market analyst, but it is rare to hear him take a stand against the minority view. In this case, his words can pertain to only about half a dozen people in the United States, with the other 299,999,994 of them siding with Jim. They are, moreover, putting their money where their mouths are, buying stocks, commodities, gold and property and borrowing money at an unprecedented rate on the conviction that it will consistently lose value. Usually the crowd is wrong, and this is a big crowd.

At this point, dollar-denominated debt has reached $37.3 trillion. The economy has little basis on which this ocean of debt will be repaid. With investment markets poised to fall across the board, the United States, and probably most of the world, is on the cusp of a great deflation. The credit supply will contract, and despite ubiquitous professional and popular belief to the contrary, there is nothing that the Fed can do about it. (See Chapters 11 and 13 in *Conquer the Crash*.) By the time the central bank gets around to printing money as opposed to offering credit, the devastation will have run its course.

The Elliott Wave Theorist, November 17, 2005

The Coming Change at the Fed

The consensus appears to be that the long term expansion in the credit supply will continue or even intensify under the Fed chairmanship of Ben Bernanke. One reason many people share this belief is their recollection of Bernanke's November 2002 speech, "Deflation: Making Sure 'It' Doesn't Happen Here," in which he likens the Fed's printing press option to dropping money from helicopters. There are reasons to believe, however, that the outcome will not be as the majority expects.

One reason that Bernanke is likely to preside over a deflation in credit is that everyone believes the opposite. Investors have poured money into commodities, precious metals, stocks and property in the belief that if anything is certain, it is death, taxes and inflation. When the majority of investors thinks one way, it is likely to be wrong. This is basic market analysis.

But how can the majority be wrong this time, when Bernanke had vowed to shower the banking system with liquidity given any deflationary threat? Of course, people *always* ask such questions as a trend matures, whether the market is oil in 2005 ("How can oil go down when world production has peaked for all time?"), gold in 1980 ("How can gold go down with all this inflation?"), stocks in 2000 ("How can stocks go down in a New Economy?"), the dollar in 2004 ("How can the dollar go up when we have this huge trade deficit?") or inflation ("How can we have deflation? Bernanke won't allow it."). There is always a "fundamental" reason to believe that the trend will accelerate; that's what gets people fully committed. We truly need not provide any other answer, but we can.

A more complex answer begins with the understanding that analysts constantly confuse *credit* creation with money creation. In fact, just today an essay became available on the

Internet that includes a presumptuous edit of a statement by
the dean of Austrian economics, Ludwig von Mises. In *Human
Action* (p.572), Mises said, "*There is no means of avoiding the final
collapse of a boom brought about by credit expansion.*" This statement
is true and undoubtedly reads as intended. Yet the author of the
article felt compelled to explain von Mises, with the following
insertions: "There is no means of avoiding the final collapse of a
boom brought about by [*bank*] credit [*and therefore money*] expansion." First, a credit boom does not have to be financed by banks.
As Jim Grant recently chronicled, railroad companies financed
one of America's greatest land booms, which, as Mises predicted,
went bust. Second, credit is not money. Economists speak of "the
money supply" as if they were referring to money, but they are not;
for the most part, they are referring to credit. The actual supply
of dollar-denominated money, legally defined in today's world,
is Federal Reserve Notes (FRNs), i.e. greenback cash [and Fed
reserves, which on demand would have to be paid in greenback
cash]. That money provides a basis for issuing credit. Credit may
seem like money because once extended, it becomes deposited
as if it were cash, and the depositor's account is credited with that
amount of money. But observe: the account is only *credited* with
that amount of money; the *actual* money upon which that credit
is based is not in the account. Every bank account is an I.O.U.
for cash, not cash itself. Needless to say, the $64.3 billion in cash
in U.S. bank vaults and at the Fed is insufficient backing for the
38 trillion dollars worth of dollar-denominated credit outstanding, not to mention at least twice that amount in the implied
promises of derivatives. The ratio is about 1 to 600. This ratio
has grown exponentially under the easy-credit policies of the Fed
and the banking system.

When credit expands beyond an economy's ability to pay
the interest and principal, the trend toward expansion reverses,
and the amount of outstanding credit contracts as debtors pay
off their loans or default. The resulting drop in the credit supply

is deflation. While it seems sensible to say that all the Fed need do is to create more money, i.e. FRNs, to "combat deflation," it is sensible only in a world in which a vacuum replaces the actual forces that any such policy would encounter. If investors worldwide were to become informed, or even suspicious, that the Fed would follow the 'copter course, it would divest itself of dollar-denominated debt assets, causing a collapse in the value of dollar-denominated bonds, notes and bills. This collapse would be deflation. It would be a collapse in the dollar value of the outstanding credit supply.

Contrary to popular belief, neither the government nor the Fed would wish such a thing to happen. The U.S. government does not want its bonds to attain (official) junk status, because its borrowing power is one of the only two powers over money that it has, the first being taxation. The Fed would commit suicide if it were to hyper-inflate, because Federal government bonds are the *reserves* of the Fed. That's why it is called "the Federal Reserve System." U.S. bonds are the source of its power. As long as the process of credit expansion is done slowly, as it has been since 1933, people can adjust their thinking to accommodate the expansion without panicking. But by flooding the market with FRNs, the Fed would cause a panic among bond-holders, and their selling would depress the value of the Fed's own reserves. The ivory-tower theory of unlimited cash creation to combat a credit implosion would meet cold, harsh reality, and reality would win; deflation would win. Von Mises was exactly right: "There is no means of avoiding the final collapse of a boom brought about by credit expansion." Observe that he said "*no* means." He did not say, "No means other than helicopters."

Bernanke's plan, according to articles, is to aim for a 2% annual inflation rate. "Bernanke has called that the Goldilocks idea: not too hot, not too cold. The just-right spot...."[1] He is convinced that such a policy is all the economy needs to keep it steady. Clearly, Bernanke is a firm believer in the idea that the economy is a machine, whose carburetor simply needs fine-tuning to get it to run smoothly. Economists, deep believers in the potency of social directors, are convinced that "monetary policy... moves the entire economy."[2] There is no room for "animal spirits" as far as this idea is concerned. Because of this proposed targeting plan, Bernanke is expected to act "More openly. More methodically. More predictably."[3] Well, Ben might aim to do those things, but society, the economy, the credit supply and the stock market do not behave in such a manner. When you think you have them under your thumb, they have *you*.

Like most economists, Bernanke doesn't accept the idea of the causal power of waves of social mood. He therefore believes, for example, that the Fed engineered the boom of the 1980s and 1990s. He also thinks, as do most economists, that the Fed's freshman errors in the early 1930s caused the Great Depression. Essayist Fred Shostak reminds us that at the Conference to honor Milton Friedman's 90th birthday on November 8, 2002, Bernanke promised the Friedmans that the Fed now understands how to keep the machine in tune. He said, "I would like to say to Milton and Anna: Regarding the Great Depression. You're right, we did it. We're very sorry. But thanks to you, *we won't do it again*."[4] That's quite a promise, and it might have some validity if the underlying premise of the Fed's power were correct. But social mood *will* "do it again," and there is nothing that Bernanke can do about it. He reiterated this guarantee in his acceptance remarks at a press conference on October 24, saying, "I will do everything in my power to ensure the prosperity and stability of the U.S. economy."[5] "Everything in my power" equates to nothing when it comes to reversing social trends.

Like the entrenched belief in continued inflation, there is a widespread expectation of smooth sailing under Bernanke. Summing up the prevailing view, an economist says, "Bernanke is universally admired and respected by people who have seen him on the inside of that institution. The bottom line is that this is excellent news for the Fed and for the economy."[6] A nationally known economist adds, "We need a Fed chairman who is steady, solid and sticks to basics. Ben Bernanke is the right person at the right time."[7] This general conviction will set up the vast majority to be fooled and ruined. There is a vocal minority who views him as a potential disaster, but the only danger they see under his leadership is excessive inflation. With virtually everyone prepared for either good times or severe inflation, bad times and deflation will catch them all off guard.

It is not the case that Fed chairmen are either fools or geniuses, as their records appear to imply. They do, however, preside over eras that make them appear to be one or the other. I am firmly of the opinion that Ben Bernanke, well educated by Harvard and MIT though he is, and fine fellow though he may be, is doomed to suffer a historically bad image as chairman of the Federal Reserve. If for some reason he leaves the post prematurely, his immediate successor(s) will suffer that fate. The trend in social mood will continue to determine the chairmen's degree of success, not the other way around.

As to Bernanke's qualifications, I must demur from the accepted view that he understands the economy and markets at some genius level. On August 31, 2005, Reuters issued this statement:

> Bernanke said the bond market's reaction to the hurricane, pushing market-set interest rates lower, showed more concern about the potential hit to growth than to the risk of a broad inflation surge due to soaring energy prices. "I think that is a vote of confidence in the Federal Reserve," the former Fed governor said. "People are confident that inflation will be low despite these shocks to gasoline and oil prices. Looking forward...reconstruction is going to add jobs and growth to the economy," he added.

In four short sentences, Bernanke, in my humble opinion, expresses six erroneous ideas:

1. The bond market did not *react* to the hurricane. There is no evidence that any market reacts to natural disasters. This idea is a myth that derives from the natural human tendency to default to mechanical models of social causality.

2. Markets have never translated natural disasters into "concern about the potential hit to growth." You cannot pick out hurricanes, tornadoes, floods, city fires or blackouts on a chart of stocks, bonds, oil or anything else.

3. The idea that any two-point move in the bond market is "a vote of confidence in the Federal Reserve" is ludicrous. One would then have to believe that every two-point setback during the year is a vote of non-confidence in the central bank.

4. People are not "confident that inflation will be low." They are buying homes at a record pace, certain of price gains. Investors are bullish on oil, gold, silver, commodities and REITs. The public is convinced that gasoline prices will stay up.

5. "Shocks to gasoline and oil prices" do not make inflation rise. Price rises due to shortages have nothing to do with inflation, much less do they have a causal inflationary role in general as Bernanke implies by the word "despite." Inflation is due to the expansion of money and/or credit, period.

6. The destruction of any useful item, even a screwdriver, much less the mass destruction of infrastructure, does not "add jobs and growth to the economy." It *detracts* from the economy. The French economist Frederic Bastiat

exposed this erroneous idea over a century and a half ago. (To learn more, just type "Bastiat, broken window fallacy" into Google search.)

Bernanke will surely reign in a bear market, when almost every decision he makes will be seen as dumb. But as this example shows, he also seems to hold some erroneous ideas.

NOTES

[1] Kanell, Michael. (2005, October 25). "Bernanke Likely to Set Target for Inflation, Work to Hit It." *Atlanta Journal-Constitution*, p. A10.

[2] Ibid.

[3] Ibid., p. A1.

[4] As quoted in Shostak, Frank, "What Should We Expect from Bernanke Now That He Is the Fed's Chairman?" www.brookesnews.com/053110bernanke.html, 10/31/05.

[5] Shell, Adam. (2005, October 25). "Markets Applaud Bernanke's Nomination." *USA Today*.

[6] Kanell, Michael. (2005, October 25). "Bernanke Likely to Set Target for Inflation, Work to Hit It." *Atlanta Journal-Constitution*, p. A10.

[7] Laffer, Arthur. (2005, October 26, 2005). "Ben Bernanke is the Right Person at the Right Time," *The Wall Street Journal*.

The Elliott Wave Theorist, June 16, 2006

For a long time there have been signs of an *impending* deflation. Now there are signs that deflation has arrived. Japan is leading the way. Its monetary base has fallen dramatically since the beginning of the year (15 percent in the past two months according to USA Today). Stock markets around the world have suddenly fallen 10 to 50 percent. Commodities that were soaring have reversed violently. Real estate is now in a "buyers' market," when there are buyers. The investment binges of the past three years are not the story; they are the *precursor* to the story. The big story is in the subtitle to *Conquer the Crash—How To Survive and Prosper in a **Deflationary** Depression*. The biggest event that the history books will record is not the jumps in investment markets from 2003 to 2006 but the across-the-board collapse that is about to follow.

In 2004, Pete Kendall and I wrote an article for Barron's in which we argued that all investment markets had begun moving together, not contra-cyclically as they had in the past. We theorized that late in the credit and economic cycle, liquidity is the motor of all investment markets. We showed a graph of the major markets, including stocks, junk bonds and precious metals, and called them "all the same market." Of course, two years ago people thought that our claim was crazy because markets would have to be crazy to move all together. But markets are crazy, and predicting such events requires understanding that markets are impulsive and patterned, not rational, and that they go through similar expressions of the same cycle of psychology over and over. The extent and duration vary, but the essence is always the same.

The flip side of markets going up together is that when the reversal comes they all go *down* together. We have been predicting this event for way too long, but it finally seems to be upon us. The wild speculation supported by the expanding, inverted pyramid of credit is exhausted. Five-wave movements of major proportion are completed and behind us. Parabolic moves have ended. Valuations that prompted thieves to focus on stealing copper wire recall the days in late 1979 when people hoarded pennies. Such activities are signs of an extreme overvaluation. If it were just a matter of pricing in inflation, then there would be no point in stealing; everything would be going up proportionately. I would like to point out here that silver at $9.50 is still down over 80 percent from its peak in January 1980. It is perhaps the single worst investment of the past 26 years, despite a quarter century of continuing credit inflation. Is the silver market crazy? Not this time. I think it is pricing in (unconsciously by mood, not consciously by reason) the coming depression. The silver bugs who spent the past three years writing essays on how silver is in short supply worldwide and needs to go to $200/oz. have once again trapped their clients into taking massive losses. The public doesn't buy copper, but it does invest in hedge funds, and the hedge funds are long copper big time. We'll soon see how that one turns out. I still believe that the metals will be a super buy at the bottom of the developing depression. But if you bought into the latest run-up, you won't be able to afford to buy any of them at the low. Cash is going to be king, so make sure you have some.

The problem today is that not some individuals or corporations or governments but the entire system is saturated with credit. Worse, much of the credit is propping up other credit, and this n^{th}-generation credit is propping up the financial markets. When the financial markets go down, IOUs will come due. Conversely, when IOUs come due, markets will go down. People who must finance debt to maintain their standard of living will soon be selling *everything and anything* to stay afloat. When people on the edge are strapped, they will sell their investments to pay the interest on their debts. If they won't do it themselves, their creditors will do it for them. Banks are already repossessing homes at a furious pace. In Georgia, April foreclosures were up 300 percent from April 2005. This is only the beginning.

A reader asks, "Can we get stagflation instead of deflation?" *No, we can't.* This is not the 1970s; it's the 2000s. By the guideline of alternation alone we know that this cycle will not act like the last cycle. Nor is it acting like the last cycle. There is a blatant difference between now and the '70s: while commodity prices have had big run-ups, *so have stocks; so have bonds; so have junk bonds.* This condition alone is so anomalous to the 1970s that it should put the army of replay advocates on warning.

Pundits tell us, "We are in a hyperinflation, like 1920s Germany." *No, we are not.* In the early 1920s, the Allies told Germany to pay reparations that Germany couldn't afford. It found a practical solution in printing marks. The inflation of the past 73 years is not primarily currency inflation but credit inflation. Credit can implode in a deflationary depression; currency cannot. Once currency is printed, it's out there for good. Some people argue that the Fed will print currency at a hyperinflationary rate. But that's a guess at best, and so far all we have seen is the same old game of facilitating credit. Perhaps the Fed ultimately will resort to runaway currency printing, but before then it will try to keep the monetary system afloat and the government's bonds— its own reserves—valuable. This is the period in which deflation will strike. After it is obvious that credit stimulation has failed, hyperinflation may be a "last resort," but I stress the word *may*. In the 1930s, it was no resort at all; the Fed opted to stay healthy instead. So before hyperinflation even might become a threat, you should be able to get wealthy betting on the downside. Even if you don't wish to speculate in that direction, you can get wealthy simply by maintaining your money and then employing it at the bottom. But in a system-wide collapse, this task will not be easy. That's why I wrote a whole book about how to do it.

Because of the tremendous, unprecedented build-up in credit, the deflation will probably be swift. So many debtors are on the margin of survival today, and so many others are right behind them, that once the weakest hands default, the dominoes will fall fast. When it hits, the whole system will succumb. Banks will fail. Insurance companies will fail. Many values that people think they own—in the form of mutual funds, stock portfolios, bond portfolios, commodity-index funds, bank accounts, insurance contracts, real estate, etc.—will evaporate.

Economists are convinced that the Fed can "fight" inflation or deflation by manipulating interest rates. But for the most part, all the Fed does is to follow price trends. When the markets fall and the economy weakens, the price of money falls with them, so interest rates go down. When the markets rise and the economy strengthens, the price of money rises with them, so interest rates go up. The Fed's rates fell along with markets and the economy from 2001 to 2003. They have risen along with markets and the economy since then. Regardless of the Fed's promise to keep raising rates, *you can bet that the price of money will fall right along with the markets and the economy.* Pundits will say that the Fed is "fighting" deflation, but it will simply be lowering its prices in line with the others. It is highly likely that the next eight years or so will test the nearly universally accepted theory—among bulls and bears alike—that the Fed can control anything at all. The Great Depression made it look like a gang of fools, as will the coming deflationary collapse. We have predicted unequivocally that the new Fed chairman will go down as Hoover did: the butt of all the blame, and if you are reading the newspapers you can see that it's already started. "When Bernanke Speaks, the Markets Freak" (San Jose Mercury News, June 10, 2006); "Bernanke is being blamed for spooking Wall Street" (USA Today, June 7); "Bernanke to blame for volatility" (Globe and Mail, Canada, June 13, 2006). The new chairman had a brief honeymoon (which we also predicted), but it's already over. By the way, I heard his commencement speech at MIT last week, and in it he spoke eloquently of the value of technology and free markets. But he also opined that economists have successfully applied technology to macroeconomics. We believe that the collective unconscious herding impulse cannot be tamed, directed or managed. In our socionomic view, the Fed cannot control the mood behind the markets, but rather, *the mood behind the markets controls how people judge the Fed.* We'll ultimately find out who's right.

Many institutional investors think they are safe because they are in various ways "insured." Investment-insurance schemes, typically involving options hedging, will fail spectacularly. In this Supercycle bear market, prices will fall so hard at the center of

the decline that portfolio managers who sold puts and calls as a
hedge will have to scramble to buy back the puts, which will soar
in price far more than the calls will fall in price. Many managers
will have to sell underlying assets to afford to buy back their puts,
which will pressure the market further. The stock market never
crashes *up*, so this is a one-way risk. Back in 1997 Kate Welling
(www.weedenco.com) conducted an interview with Andrew
Smithers, who spelled out quite clearly why the financial markets
might be able to accommodate individual risks via insurance
schemes but never *systemic* risk. (Thanks to Tony Cherniawski of
The Practical Investor for reminding us.) When rock climbing, it
might be possible to have a single buddy as death-fall insurance,
but if 50 climbers are all roped together, the system is in danger
and so are all the climbers. When everyone buys insurance against
financial loss, the insurers can't possibly pay. I am disgusted with
the insurance and banking industries for selling contracts that
they cannot possibly honor in a system-wide collapse. They still
think that only one bank might fail, or only one broker or trader.
Many weak bonds received AAA ratings in the 1990s because
the issuers purchased "insurance." What a joke. The supposed
insurance will be so much dank air in a depression. Why? Well,
where do you think the insurers have invested their assets? It's
in all the same investments in which their leveraged clients are
invested! They own real estate, consumer loan packages, stocks
and bonds. What will they use to pay off clients in a crash? As
CTC says, do not rely on any form of insurance to pay off in a
depression. Yes, bears wrote some good stuff back in 1997. That's
also when we published "Bulls, Bears and Manias," which is available as a chapter in *Market Analysis for the New Millennium* (see
www.elliottwave.com/books). Nine-year-old essays by bears are
not only still valid but they are also more applicable than ever.
And don't think there has been a great stock market advance
since that time. The S&P 500 index is essentially unchanged
from July 1998 to now. And that's in *dollar* terms! In real terms,
of course, it's far lower.

How did we get to this dangerous point? The answer is that Grand Supercycle-level optimism fueled credit expansion. Creditors have to be optimistic to expect debtors to repay, and debtors have to optimistic to think that they can repay. Record debt requires record optimism. We already know that governments in collusion with central banks have fueled bank credit. But banks fuel consumer credit, and debt has permeated society out to the very edges of viability. *Marginal debtors are the very bedrock of the whole system.* The double irony is that (1) marginal debtors are about to expand their numbers, and (2) it won't help the system but will kill it, because most of the marginal debtors will morph into bankrupt debtors.

The Elliott Wave Theorist, March 23, 2007

The Biggest Mistake

The most important thing to understand about the financial environment is that credit is not money. Stock enthusiasts say that "liquidity" will keep the boom going; precious metals and commodity bugs say that "inflation" will continue to rage; and real estate investors rely on "creative financing" to keep prices rising. Every one of these investment stances depends upon inflation, and every proponent for them is convinced that inflation is an endless, one-way process. Currency inflation can continue indefinitely, but extensive credit inflation never does; it always implodes. The American economy—indeed most of the world economy—suffers primarily not from currency inflation but credit inflation.

The financial markets are signaling an end to credit inflation. Most bonds are rated junk. The leading commodities—oil, copper, gold and silver—have topped. Real estate is crashing. Banks are tightening mortgage requirements. The stock market has turned down. All these investments had benefited from the most aggressive and extensive credit inflation in history. Now they are beginning to respond to the first days of the biggest contraction in credit ever. But hardly anyone understands this process. Most economists call the current situation a "Goldilocks" economy, where everything is just right. This is an irresponsible position, but it is also inevitable because by definition optimism accompanies major stock market peaks. A vocal minority sees the severe dislocations in debt, deficits and speculation. But instead of warning of a collapse in prices these economists advocate owning commodities, precious metals, real estate, oil company shares, mining shares and other resource stocks, all of which are to rise in the environment of perpetual inflation that they envision. In other words, there is almost no one who advocates holding safe, interest-bearing cash equivalents as protection from the developing credit implosion and a source of profit while everything else goes down. The only book I know of to advocate this position is *Conquer the Crash*.

Credit inflation is the expansion and even the pyramiding of IOUs. Investors issue IOUs to buy stocks, corporations issue IOUs to expand business, consumers issue IOUs to buy houses and cars, and governments issue IOUs as if they were throwing beads from a Mardi Gras float. The longer the process continues, the more IOUs come to be regarded as assets, meaning that borrowers then use them as collateral for more borrowing. As investment prices rise, they, too, become collateral for more loans. And on it goes, until it doesn't. When the house of (credit) cards begins to fall in on itself, the trend turns from inflation to deflation. That's when creditors turn their focus from lending to collecting and when debtors turn their focus from borrowing to repaying. But by this time there are too many IOUs, and debtors cannot service them, much less repay them. Falling asset values and economic contraction thwart efforts to honor the loans. Debtors begin to default. When that happens, the game is up.

Credit deflation is the most devastating financial event of all. It is rare, and that is why it confounds so many analysts. The wrong vision leads to confusion. Under the Goldilocks vision, no one can understand why stocks would fall. Under the inflationary vision, no one can understand why real estate or commodities would fall. An article in the Financial Times (March 6) says of the latest sell-off in gold, "The performance of gold has been the most difficult to explain. Traditionally, the precious metal is considered a safe haven in times of uncertainty and risk aversion and it normally rises when equity markets fall. In fact gold prices have fallen more than 7 per cent over the past week." What's wrong with this view is that the supposed "tradition" is baloney. Gold doesn't reliably go up when other things are going down. Gold has been following the stock market on the upside for three years. If a coincident advance was not an anomaly, why is a coincident decline? In fact, gold and silver have been going up and down with the Dow even on a daily and intraday basis. This is not inconsistent action; the only inconsistency is with the theory that gold and silver are always contracyclical and therefore effective disaster hedges. Sometimes they are, and sometimes they aren't, but one thing is for sure: They are not deflation hedges, and deflation is what we face.

The following excerpt, from a March 8 article in the Toronto Star, expresses the difference between currency inflation and credit inflation. You can feel the looming default disaster throughout this description:

> The city's debt level is skyrocketing and Toronto is falling further and further behind on much-needed repairs, city council was told yesterday as members approved this year's capital budget. "It's difficult for many people to fathom how deep in debt we are, how much deeper in debt we're going, and how at the end of this plan we have (room for) no further debt that we can take on," Councillor David Shiner said yesterday.

Still, following a day of acrimonious debate, councillors endorsed a $1.432 billion budget that includes everything from a $3.7 million program to calm neighborhood traffic and add bike lanes, to $2.9 million for a new meeting room at city hall and more office space for Mayor David Miller's staff. Miller called it a "city building" budget. But several councillors said the city is flirting with big trouble by more than doubling its debt and failing to dig into a huge backlog of repair projects ranging from eroding roads to Toronto Zoo improvements.

City officials said Toronto's debt was $1.7 billion in 2005 but will increase to more than $2.6 billion this year and is expected to balloon beyond $3.1 billion by 2011. This year, the city will spend 12.6 per cent of its property tax revenues on debt servicing. That figure is expected to rise to 15.4 per cent by 2011. Shiner said the city's debt servicing will cost every Toronto household roughly $2,352 over the next five years. "Many people don't know how they're going to afford that, and we don't have a plan to pay for it," he said.

But Miller told reporters at the end of the day, "It's a very good budget."

This is a microcosm—and a conservative one at that, involving no leverage or derivatives—of what's happening everywhere. The size of today's credit bubble is so huge that it dwarfs, by many multiples, all previous bubbles in history. The developing deflation will be commensurate with the preceding expansion, so it will also be the biggest ever. Staying in traditional investments—stocks, real estate, commodities and most corporate and municipal bonds—will surely prove to be a deadly decision. It's not the "Goldilocks" 1950s. It's not the inflationary 1970s. And it's not a "business as usual" extension of the 1980s-1990s bull market. It's 1929 times ten. Those who can't see the difference

will suffer the consequences. Those who see it — this means *you*
—will survive and prosper.

The Role of the Fed

Most people envision the central bank as a currency
inflation machine, a "printing press." But most of the time, the
central bank is not inflating by way of its press. It does create currency inflation when it monetizes government debt. It facilitates
credit inflation when it panics and lowers its lending rate to below
market levels. As bad as these practices are, their extent pales
in comparison to the fact that the Federal Reserve System is a
structure that allows banks to engage in credit inflation. Without
the Fed, they couldn't get away with it. The Federal Reserve's
paper-money monopoly actively fosters inflation, but once that
system is in place, most of the time the Fed plays a passive role
in fulfilling the demands of banks for credit, which fulfills the
demands of borrowers for credit. Many economists say that the
Fed manages the rate of inflation at X percent a year, but this
view leads to two errors. First is the belief that once inflation
happens, it is permanent. But it is not; credit expansions lead to
collapse. Second is the belief that the Fed is in control. It seems
to be in control, and that illusion makes investors complacent
about the prospects for deflation; in fact, it makes them militantly
deny even the possibility. But the Fed is not in control, and the
coming crash will prove it.

The Illusion of Control

Mike Whitney's website, The Market Oracle, reports that
the Plunge Protection Team has put on its superhero outfits:

> The Working Group on Financial Markets, also know as the
> Plunge Protection Team, was created by Ronald Reagan to
> prevent a repeat of the Wall Street meltdown of October

1987. Its members include the Secretary of the Treasury, the Chairman of the Federal Reserve, the Chairman of the SEC and the Chairman of the Commodity Futures Trading Commission. Recently, the team has been on high-alert given the increased volatility of the markets and, what Hank Paulson calls, "the systemic risk posed by hedge funds and derivatives."

Financial powers concocted similar schemes in the collapse of 1929. The question is whether this gang of four and their bags of credit can actually change the direction of the stock market. I don't think so, but we'll find out eventually. It will be good to keep in mind some of the market's history with respect to crashes. I have a rare item: a book of graphs of the Dow's daily ranges going back 100 years. It shows that when the market crashed in September and October, 1929, the Dow did not go straight down. It had huge intraday rallies, most of which were reversed by day's end. I suspect the same kind of action during wave c. When the inevitable breathtaking rallies occur, I'm sure we will hear that the PPT is behind them. And maybe it will be. But the rallies will come at the right junctures in the wave pattern, and they won't change the major trend. (For more on the PPT, see pages 367-368 of *The Wave Principle of Human Social Behavior*.)

The Elliott Wave Theorist, April 30, 2007

Investors Are Buying More with IOUs Than with Money

When I wrote *Conquer the Crash*, outstanding dollar-denominated debt was $30 trillion. Just five years later, it is $43 trillion, and most of the increase has gone into housing, financial investments and buying goods from abroad. This is a meticulously constructed Biltmore House of cards, and one wonders whether it can stand the addition of a single deuce. Its size and grandeur are no argument against the ultimate outcome; they are an argument *for* it.

Figure D-3 depicts just one isolated aspect of the debt bubble as it relates directly to financial prices. In 1999, the public was heavily invested in mutual funds, and mutual funds had 96 percent of their clients' money invested in stocks. At the time I thought that percentage of investment was a limit. I was wrong. Today, much of the public has switched to so-called hedge funds (a misnomer). Bridgewater estimates that the average hedge fund in January had 250 percent of its deposits invested. This month the WSJ reports funds with ratios as high as *13 times*. How can hedge funds invest way more money than they have? They *borrow* the rest from banks and investment firms, using their investment holdings as collateral. So they are heavily *leveraged*. And this is only part of the picture. Much of the money invested in hedge

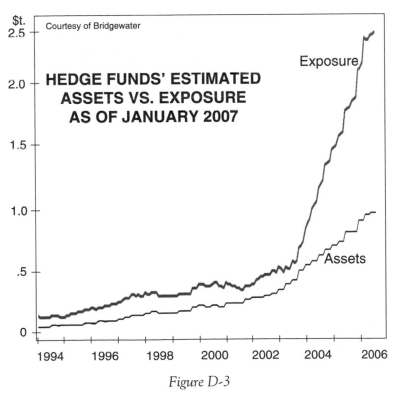

Figure D-3

funds in the first place is borrowed. Some investors take out mortgages to get money to put into hedge funds. Some investment firms borrow heavily from banks and brokers to invest in hedge funds. As for lenders, the WSJ reports today, "…the nation's four largest securities firms financed $3.3 trillion of assets with $129.4 billion of shareholders' equity, *a leverage ratio of 25.5 to 1.*" So the financial markets today have been rising in unison because of leverage upon leverage, an inverted pyramid of IOUs, all supported by a comparatively small amount of actual cash. This swelling snowball of borrowing is how the nominal Dow has managed to get to a new high even though it is in a raging bear market in real terms: The expansion in credit inflates the dollar denominator of value, and the credit itself goes to buying more stocks, bonds and commodities. The buying raises prices, and higher prices provide more collateral for more borrowing. And all the while real stock values, as measured by gold, have quietly fallen by more than half! Seemingly it is a perpetual motion machine; but one day the trend will go into reverse, and the value of total credit will begin shrinking as dollar prices collapse.

The investment markets are only part of the debt picture. Most individuals have borrowed to buy real estate, cars and TVs. Most people don't *own* such possessions; they *owe* them. Credit card debt is at a historic high. The Atlanta Braves just announced a new program through which you can finance the purchase of season tickets. Can you imagine telling a fan in 1947 that someday people would take out loans to buy tickets to a baseball game? Instead of buying things for cash these days, many consumers elect to pay not only the total value for each item they buy but also a pile of additional money for interest. And they choose this option because they *can't afford* to pay cash for what they want or need. Self-indulgent and distress borrowing for consumption cannot go on indefinitely. But while it does, the "money supply"—actually the *credit* supply—inflates. But it is all a *temporary* phenomenon, because debt binges always exhaust themselves.

As far as I can tell, virtually everyone else sees things differently. Countless bulls on stocks, gold and commodities insist that the process is simple: the Fed is inflating the "money supply" by way of its "printing press," and there is no end in sight. The Fed is indeed the underlying motor of inflation because it monetizes government debt, but the banking system, thanks to the elasticity of fiat money, manufactures by far the bulk of the credit—*credit*, not cash. If you don't believe credit can implode and investment prices fall, then why did the housing market just have its biggest monthly price plunge in two decades, and why is the trend toward lower prices now the longest on record? If you don't think credit and cash are different, then why are the owners of "collateralized" mortgage "securities" beginning to panic over the realization that their "investments" are melting in the sun? Lewis Ranieri, one of the founders of the securitized mortgage market, recently warned that there are now so many interests involved in each mortgage that massive cooperation among lawyers, accountants and tax authorities will be required just to make simple decisions about restructuring a loan or disposing of a house, i.e. the collateral, underlying a mortgage in default. In the old days, the local bank would suss things out and come to a quick decision. But now the structures are too complex for easy resolution, and creditors are hamstrung with structural and legal impediments to accessing their collateral. The modern structures for investment are so intricate and dispersed that a mere recession will trigger a systemic disaster. When insurance companies and pension plan administrators realize that they can't easily and cheaply access the underlying assets, what will their packaged mortgages be worth then? And what will happen to the empty houses as they try to sort things out? This type of morass relates to *debt*. Cash is easy; either you have it or you don't.

The gold and silver markets know the difference between money inflation and credit inflation. Gold has made no net progress in the past year and in fact for the past 27+ years. Silver is languishing, still trading 75 percent below its high in *dollar* terms, making it by far the worst investment of the past quarter century. Flat-out currency inflation would have a powerful tendency to show up immediately in gold and silver prices. Credit is another matter. Gold prices reflect the fact that an increase in debt is not the same as an increase in cash. New cash is here to stay; debt expansion can morph into contraction. Thriving creditors, moreover, do not want metals; they want interest. And credit is voracious, eating up debtors' capital at a rate of 5 percent a year. When the debtors become strapped, they sell other assets, including gold, to get cash to pay their creditors. Eventually, creditors with falling income due to default will join the ranks of those with less money to buy things. But most investors don't see it our way; in April, for the second time in wave **b**, the DSI reached 90 percent bulls among traders in both gold and S&P! When else in history has it happened? Try *never*. Although the past few years show that there can be periods of exception, markets usually do not reward a lopsided bulk of investors with the same outlook.

But there is a much more important event for believers in perpetual inflation to explain: the trend of *yields* from bonds and utility stocks. In the 1970s, prices of bonds and utility stocks were *falling*, and yields on bonds and utility stocks were *rising*, because of the onslaught of inflation. But in the past 25 years bond and utility stock prices have gone *up*, and yields on bonds and utility stocks (see Figures D-4 and D-5) have gone *down*. Once again, this situation is contrary to claims that we are experiencing a replay of the inflationary 19-teens or 1970s. Those investing on an inflation theme cannot explain these graphs. But there is a precedent for this time. It is 1928-1929, when bond and utility yields bottomed and prices topped (see Figure D-6) in an environment of expanding credit and a stock market boom. The Dow

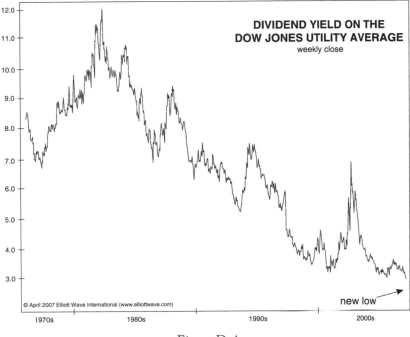

DIVIDEND YIELD ON THE
DOW JONES UTILITY AVERAGE
weekly close

© April 2007 Elliott Wave International (www.elliottwave.com)

new low

1970s   1980s   1990s   2000s

Figure D-4

Jones Utility Average was the last of the Dow averages to peak in 1929, and today it is deeply into wave (5) (see Figure D-7) and therefore near the end of its entire bull market. All these juxtaposed market behaviors make sense only in our context of a terminating credit bubble. This one is just a whole lot *bigger* than any other in history.

Some economic historians blame rising interest rates into 1929 for the crash that ensued. Those who do must acknowledge that the Fed's interest rate today is at almost exactly the same level it was then, having risen steadily—and in fact way more in percentage terms—since 2003. So even on this score the setup is the same as it was in 1929. Remember also that in 1926 the Florida land boom collapsed. In the current cycle, house prices nationwide topped out in 2005, two years ago. So maybe it's 1928 now instead of 1929. But that's a small quibble compared to the

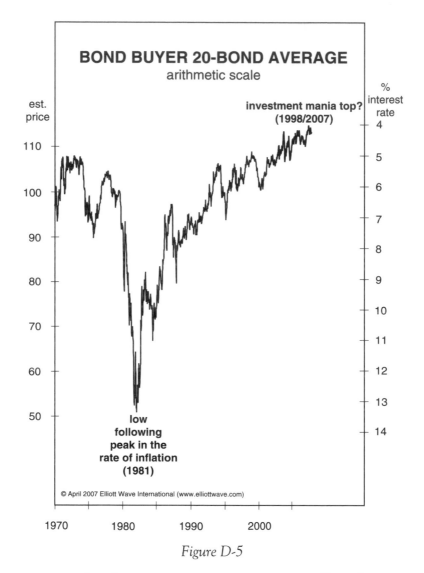

Figure D-5

erroneous idea that we are enjoying a perpetually inflationary goldilocks economy with perpetually rising investment prices.

As to whether the Fed can induce more borrowing by lowering rates in the next recession, we will have to see, but evidence from the sub-prime and Alt-A mortgage markets as

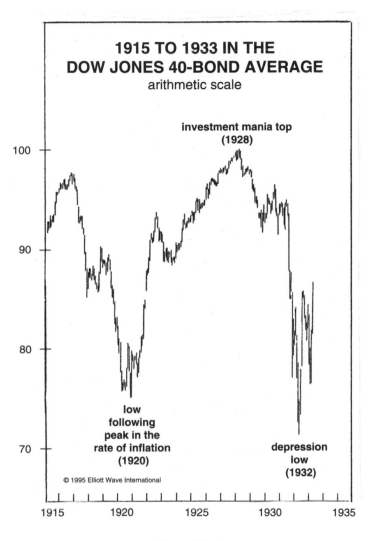

Figure D-6

well as ratios like the one in Figure D-3 suggest more strongly than ever that consumers' and investors' capacity for holding debt is maxing out. I see no way out of the current extreme in credit issuance aside from the classic way: a debt implosion.

Figure D-7

The Elliott Wave Theorist, July 13, 2007
(written at the all-time peak in DJI plus DJT)

Today the mortgage market is leading the charge in our scenario. The latest news reports tell not only of the devastation to debt portfolios but also of the worthlessness of the rating services for protecting investors and even their complicity in covering up the collapse in the true value of many mortgages.

Conquer the Crash was finished in March 2002. Look at Figure D-8 and notice that the fewest debt downgrades of the decade occurred that year. As CTC said, as an investor you cannot wait until problems are obvious to act; by then it's too late. You have to anticipate problems and then get out of the way before they happen.

As for the price of mortgage debt, Figure D-9 tells the story, thanks to the diligence of Markit Group Ltd., whose work has brought some transparency to this field. The lower line denotes the price of subprime mortgages, and the middle line shows prices of "alt.-A," the mid-grade mortgage paper. The top line prices prime mortgages, the ones whose payers have some equity and a good

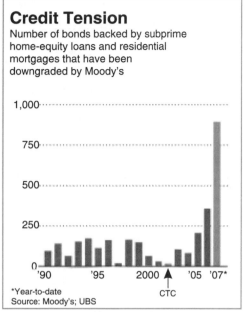

Credit Tension

Number of bonds backed by subprime home-equity loans and residential mortgages that have been downgraded by Moody's

*Year-to-date
Source: Moody's; UBS

Figure D-8

source of income. But these graphs rely on dealers for prices, and many of these mortgages are not trading. So even these data do not show the true extent of losses. There is a big lag between what everyone in the industry suspects is the real price and what happens to the index. As Pete Kendall says, "It's a surreal world where prices are lagging actual values."

The rating services fulfilled their usual role [in failing to warn of the danger]. But readers of *Conquer the Crash* are not surprised, and *we didn't own any such debt*.

Some readers of *Conquer the Crash* took exception to this statement, from Chapter 9:

> [F]inancial values can disappear into nowhere.... The "million dollars" that a wealthy investor might have thought he had in his bond portfolio or at a stock's peak value can quite rapidly become $50,000 or $5000 or $50. *The rest of it just disappears.* You see, he never really had a million

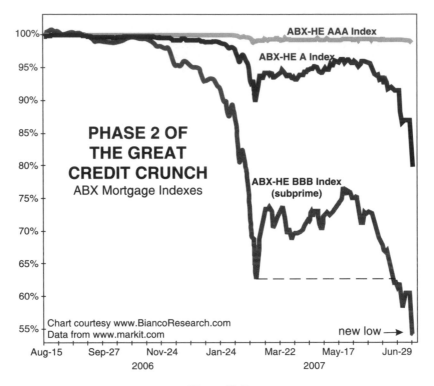

Figure D-9

dollars; all he had was IOUs or stock certificates. The idea that it had a certain financial value was in his head and the heads of others who agreed. When the point of agreement changed, so did the value. Poof! Gone in a flash of aggregated neurons.

This warning is being borne out today. Read this except from a Bloomberg news report of July 11:

> As delinquencies on home loans to people with poor or meager credit surged to a 10-year high this year, no one buying, selling or rating the bonds collateralized by these bad debts bothered to quantify the losses. Now the bubble is bursting and *there is no agreement on how much money has vanished*: $52

billion, according to an estimate from Zurich-based Credit Suisse Group earlier this week that followed a $90 billion assessment from Frankfurt-based Deutsche Bank AG.

Do you see that line, *"money has vanished"*? It's not really money; it's financial value, but it didn't move from one asset to another. It just disappeared.

The Elliott Wave Theorist, August 26, 2007

Deflation Has Arrived

Deflation is a contraction in the nominal value of outstanding credit. Much dollar-denominated credit has been falling in value recently. The contraction began in sub-prime mortgages and is spreading to other IOUs. The *availability* of credit—the willingness of investors and creditors to lend—is also contracting. Banks have withdrawn credit lines from hedge funds and would-be home buyers. The past month has finally exposed the massive risks that have existed in highly leveraged hedge funds and mortgage securities. Make no mistake: A mortgage loan of 100 percent on the value of a house bought for speculation is leverage, in fact infinite leverage. Creditors are fast realizing that the value of the collateral, previously believed to equal the value of the loan, is less than they thought. (See later housing discussion.)

The subtitle of *Conquer the Crash* is *How to Survive and Prosper in a **Deflationary** Depression.* Deflation always brings declines in *nominal* values, i.e. prices of investments and eventually of goods and services. The "deflationary" part is finally beginning, and the "depression" part will follow. If you have not prepared for the latter development, please read the second half of *Conquer the Crash* and do what it says.

Can't Buy Enough...of That Junky Stuff, or, Why the Fed Will Not Stop Deflation

We hear it every day: "What about the Fed?" The vast majority of investors and commentators seems confident that the Fed's machinations make a stock market collapse impossible. Every hour or so one can read or hear another comment along these lines: "the Fed will provide liquidity," "the Fed is injecting money into the system," "the Fed will be forced to bail out homeowners, homebuilders, mortgage companies and banks," "the Fed has no choice but to inflate," "the government cannot allow deflation," "the Fed will print money to stave off deflation" and any number of like statements. None of them is true. The Fed is not forced to do anything; the Fed has not been injecting money; the Fed does have choices; the government does not control deflationary forces; and the Fed will not print money unless and until it changes its long-standing policies and decides to destroy itself.

A perfect example of one of these fallacies recently exposed is the widespread report in August that the Fed had "injected" billions of dollars worth of "money" into the "system" by "buying" "sub-prime mortgages." In fact, all it did was offer to stave off the immediate illegality of many banks' operations by *lending* money against the collateral of *guaranteed* mortgages but only temporarily under contracts that oblige the banks to buy them back within 1 to 30 days. The typical duration is 3 days. Observe three important things:

(1) The Fed did not give out *money*; it offered a temporary, collateralized *loan*.

(2) The Fed did not *inject* liquidity; it offered it.

(3) The Fed did not lend against worthless sub-prime mortgages; it lent against *valuable* mortgages issued by Fannie Mae (the Federal National Mortgage Association), Ginnie Mae (the Government National Mortgage

Association) and Freddie Mac (the Federal Home Loan Mortgage Corporation) [all of which are de facto 100 percent government-guaranteed]. The New York Fed is also accepting "investment quality" commercial paper, which means highly liquid, valuable IOUs, not junk.
As a result:

(1) The Fed took almost no risk in the transactions.

(2) The net liquidity it provided—after the repo agreements close—is zero.

(3) The financial system is still choking on bad loans.

(4) Banks and other lending institutions must sell other assets to raise cash to buy back their mortgages from the Fed.

These points are crucial to a proper understanding of the situation. The Fed is doing nothing akin to what most of the media claim; like McDonald's, it is selling not so much sustenance as time, in this case time for banks to divest themselves of some assets. But in the Fed's case, that's all it's selling; you don't get any food in the bargain.

In the early 1930s, as markets fell and the economy collapsed, the Fed offered loans only on the most pristine debt. Its standards have fallen a bit, but not by much. Today it will still lend only on highly reliable IOUs, not junk. And it doesn't even want to own most of those; it takes them on only temporarily as part of a short-term repurchase agreement.

The Fed's power derives from the value of its holdings, which are primarily Treasury bonds, which provide backing for the value of the Fed's notes. What would a Federal Reserve Note be worth if it were backed by sub-prime mortgages? The real value of U.S. Treasury debt is precarious enough as it is, but at least it has the taxing power of the government behind it. But if the Fed bought up the entire supply of sub-prime mortgages, its notes would lose value accordingly. So will the Fed bail out mortgage companies, as the optimists seem to think? No, it won't. Those who think the Fed will buy up junk with cash delivered by helicopter are dreaming.

Ironically, of course, the Federal Reserve System and the federal government—both directly and via creations such as privileged mortgage companies and the FDIC—have *fostered* all the lending and the junk debt that resulted. But these entities want only to benefit from the process, not suffer from it. As we will see throughout the bear market and into the depression, the Fed is self-interested and will not brook losses in its portfolio. Those who own the bad loans, and perhaps some foolish government entities that try to "save" them, will take losses, but the Fed won't.

One might imagine various schemes by which the government would guarantee such mortgages, but if it did, the mortgages would in effect become Treasury bonds. The problem, as others have pointed out, is that government guarantees on bad debt would simply encourage more of it. Unless the government decides to freeze the mortgage lending industry, which would have its own devastating repercussions, it cannot pull off a bailout scheme.

What must the banks do with their "grace period" of a few days that the Fed's repo agreements provide? They have to *raise the cash to buy back the IOUs that the Fed agreed to hold for them.* How does a bank raise money? By selling assets. Thus begins the downward spiral: Contracting credit causes asset sales, which cause collateral values to fall, which causes lenders to curtail lending, thus contracting overall credit, which causes assets sales, and so it goes. Thus, the Fed is not staving off deflation; at best, it may have helped—momentarily—to make it more orderly. But the selling of assets has begun regardless.

One of the Fed's just-accessed "tools" is its authority to suspend various lending restrictions. As Fortune (August 24) just reported, a week ago the Fed, in an unprecedented move suggesting growing panic, suspended the limit on the percentage of capital that Citigroup and Bank of America can lend to their affiliated brokerage firms. With that permission, these banks immediately raised their loans from the previous maximum of 10 percent of their total capital to an enormous 30 percent, and they have permission to go higher if they want. Observe that the Fed did not lend to the brokers. It merely authorized these banks to do it. The banks, though obviously desperate to shore up their brokerage divisions, just as necessarily believe that their loans will be paid back, which means that they are bullish on the stock market and most other financial markets. But what will happen when markets fall further and the banks' depositors get wind of the fact that their money has been lent to speculators with leveraged market positions? The Fed, which greased the loan scheme by financing the loan to these banks (not the brokers) through its discount window, now has a claim on these banks' assets. It will be utterly fascinating to see what the Fed decides to do when these big banks finally call the Fed and say that if it calls in its loans, they will go bankrupt. I'm betting that the Fed, perhaps after a few more frantic calls to other creditors for help, will eventually call in the loans anyway.

Does the Fed have secret tools to stave off deflation? Yes, to the same extent that Hitler, hiding in a bunker in 1945, had secret weapons to stave off the Allies. The Fed has only one tool: to offer credit, and its arsenal is depleted because it will offer credit *only on terms good to itself*. And borrowers will borrow only if they think they can pay back the debt after selling assets. You can bet that the Fed is lending only to banks that it believes have the necessary assets to survive its loans' repayment provisions. If not, well, it will be the FDIC's problem. The Fed is not engineering a system-wide bailout; it is just rearranging deck chairs.

Interest rates are higher than they were in 2002. Many people say that the Fed therefore has lots of room to bring rates down and keep the economy inflated. Do lower interest rates cause recovery? No, they simply reflect a crashing market for credit. The market makes interest rates rise and fall, and the Fed's rates typically just follow suit. Sometimes central banks force the issue, as when the Fed in the final months of 2002 lowered its discount rate to 0.75 percent, staying a bit ahead of the decline in T-bill yields. But its systematic rate drops didn't stop the S&P from losing *half its value in 31 months*. When the Japanese central bank lowered rates virtually to zero in the 1990s, doing so likewise did not prevent Japanese real estate prices from imploding and the Nikkei from proceeding through its *biggest bear market ever* by a huge margin. Rates near zero, then, did not constitute a magic potion. Zero was simply the price of loans at the time; nobody wanted them. So the "room" the Fed presumably has may or may not matter. If the market decides to take rates to zero or below, the Fed will simply follow and then have no power.

The Fed does not "inject" liquidity; it only offers it. If nobody wants it, the inflation game is over. The determinant of that matter is the market. When bull markets turn to bear, confidence turns to fear, and fearful people do not lend or borrow at the same rates as confident ones. The ultimate drivers of inflation and deflation are human mental states that the Fed cannot manipulate. The pattern of the stock market's waves determines the ebb and flow of these mental states, and now that a bear market has begun, nothing will stop the trend toward falling confidence and thus falling asset prices, credit deflation and economic depression.

The truth is that the Fed's supposed tools of adding liquidity, such as the limit suspension just granted to the big New York banks, are formulas for total disaster. The terrible secret is that every one of the Fed's tools is nothing but a mechanism to make matters worse. Just because it has taken 74 years to get to the point at which this fact is once again about to become obvious does not mean that it wasn't true all along. The Fed is short-sighted, and its schemes to foster liquidity for short term crises have served, and are continuing to serve, to ensure the ultimate collapse of most of the nation's banking system. The storm clouds are getting dark, so that time may have arrived.

The market is certainly poised for a panic. Confidence has held sway for 2½ decades, during which time investors have become utterly unconcerned with risk. They hold a number of misconceptions that foster such complacency. The day the Fed lowers one of its rates or engineers a major temporary loan and the stock market goes down anyway is the day that investors will become utterly uncertain of what they believe about market causality, and panic will have no bridle. Sadly, Ben Bernanke will be blamed for the debacle, when all he will have been guilty of is serving an immoral monopoly, bad timing and failing to understand the forces at work. The third item pertains to almost everyone.

The Fed Is Not Smart Enough To Stop Deflation, Even If It Could

The dab of grease on the gears in the form of the recent discount-rate cut did not come as part of the Fed's normal policy. According to a Bloomberg article of August 17, the surprise discount rate cut was "an extraordinary policy shift." In other words, *the Fed did not know what the hell was going on.* It was caught off guard and had to react. In fact, right through July the Fed's spokespeople were all saying that the number one threat to the economy was inflation! Like virtually all futurists, the Fed's economists extrapolate trends to derive forecasts. They never look at underlying indications of coming trend *change*. That's fine; it helps those of us who at least try to do so. But the idea that the

Fed comprises a group of masterminds who "get it" at some deep
level and can thereby control things is miles off the mark. For
more on this theme, see the "Potent Directors Fallacy" discussion
in *The Wave Principle of Human Social Behavior*.

A Deflationary Spiral

When the sub-prime mortgage market crashed, other
bonds, including supposedly safe municipal and corporate bonds,
also fell. Most commentators believe that forced liquidation is
the only reason that perfectly good investments fell in price. As
one report dated August 24 said, "There's really no credit-related
reason behind the decline." But *Conquer the Crash* is on record
predicting that a large portion of currently outstanding corporate
and municipal debt will become worthless. Every trend has to
begin somewhere, and its ultimate outcomes are never evident
at the start of a move. By the end of the price decline in these
bonds, when a bit of glue on the back of them will aid their use
as wallpaper, observers will finally postulate why the bear market
started in the first place. Even if most of the recent price declines
are due to forced sales, those sales in turn are decreasing the total
value of investments, which in turn will curtail individuals' and
companies' economic activity, which will lead to an economic
contraction, which will stress the issuers of such bonds to the
point that they will be unable to make interest payments or
return principal. In other words, whether investors understand
it now or not, the forced sale of bonds is itself enough reason to
sell them also on the basis of default risk.

Despite my description, this process is not linear. Every
step of the way seems to have an immediate causal precursor,
but like credit inflation, credit deflation is in fact an intricate,
interwoven *process*, whose initial impetus is a *change in social mood*
from optimism toward pessimism. If you are still on the fence
about this idea, ask yourself: What changed in the so-called "fun-

damentals" between June and August? The answer is: *absolutely nothing*. Interest rates did not budge; there were no indications of recession; there were no changes in bank lending policies; there were no chilling government edicts. *The only thing that changed was people's minds*. One day sub-prime mortgages were a fine investment, and the next day they were toxic waste. There was no external cause of the change; it was an endogenously caused and regulated change, as all aggregate financial changes are. According to socionomic theory [see www.socionomics.net], the stock market is a sensitive indicator of such changes in mood. This is why EWT has continually said that the financial structure will hold up *as long as the stock market rises*. A downturn occurred in mid-July, and its consequences in terms of negative social mood are becoming swiftly evident. Remember, C waves (see *Elliott Wave Principle*, Chapter 2) are when optimistic illusions finally disappear and fear takes over. Sounds like now.

The Home Investment Illusion

What is the financial status of a home? Many people say they "invest" in their homes. But a home is not an investment. It is an item that loses value through deterioration even if no one lives in it. A home is expensive to finance, expensive to maintain and expensive to buy or sell. Ironically, *it is also very costly to realize the loss of value on a home*. According to The Boston Globe (8/24/07), "Foreclosing on a house and selling it in an auction costs $50,000, on average, in New England, and that amount is on top of the funds the lender needs to pay off the loan itself." Under such circumstances, can anyone say with a straight face that you owned an "investment"? Even a desired home costs money, but an unwanted home is nothing less than a giant albatross of decay and expense.

A home may seem to have some investment advantages, but all of them are artificial, having been created by govern-

ment: (1) you get a tax break, and (2) prices tend to rise through
inflation. But any purchase or investment that the government
supports artificially will eventually hurt the intended beneficia-
ries. Thanks to government subsidies and inflation, the housing
market grew disproportionately, and now too many people are
stuck in homes they cannot afford.

As house prices fall, financially sound mortgage payers will
find that their mortgage payments constitute a higher and higher
percentage of the value of the house, becoming ridiculously high.
Then when the economy contracts, even these conscientious payers may find themselves out of a job and unable to continue the
mortgage payments, even if most of the house is paid for. They
were responsible people (within their limits of knowledge), but
they will lose their homes anyway.

Now ask yourself again, would the Fed want to own
mortgages on homes it would likely have to repossess and then
refurbish, re-sell or rent out? No way.

The Elliott Wave Theorist, October 19, 2007

Falling Interest Rates in This Environment Will Be Bearish

You cannot pick up a newspaper, turn on financial TV or
read an economist's report without hearing that the Fed's latest
discount-rate cut is bullish because it indicates the Fed's decision
to "pump liquidity" into the system. This opinion is so completely
wrong that it is hard to believe its ubiquity.

First of all, the Fed does not "decide" where it wants
interest rates. *All it does is follow the market.* Figure D-10 proves
it. Wherever the T-bill rate goes, the Fed's "target rate" for federal funds immediately follows. That's all there is to it. If you
refuse to believe your eyes, then listen to the former chairman;
Alan Greenspan is very clear on this point. On September 17, a
commentator on CNBC asked, "Did you keep the interest rates

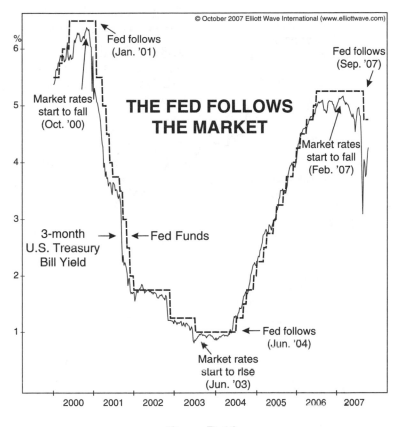

© October 2007 Elliott Wave International (www.elliottwave.com)

THE FED FOLLOWS THE MARKET

Fed follows (Jan. '01)

Market rates start to fall (Oct. '00)

Fed follows (Sep. '07)

Market rates start to fall (Feb. '07)

3-month U.S. Treasury Bill Yield → ←Fed Funds

Fed follows (Jun. '04)

Market rates start to rise (Jun. '03)

Figure D-10

too low for too long in 2002-2003?" Greenspan immediately responded, "The *market* did." Rates were not "too low" or the period "too long," either, because the market, not the Fed, made the decision on the level and the time, and the market is never wrong; it is what it is. If investors in trillions of dollars worth of U.S. Treasury debt worldwide had demanded higher interest, they would have gotten it, period.

Second, *falling interest rates are almost never bullish.* All you have to do to understand this point is look at Figure D-11. Interest rates fell persistently through three of the greatest bear markets in history: 1929-1932 in the Dow, 1990-2003 in the Japanese Nikkei, and 2000-2002 in the NASDAQ. The only

Figure D-11

comparably deep bear market in the past 80 years in which interest rates rose took place in the 1970s when the Value Line index
dropped 74 percent. Economists all draw upon this experience,
but they ignore the others. Today's environment of extensive
investment leverage and an Everest of debt in the banking system

is far more like 1929 in the U.S. and 1989 in Japan than it is like the 1970s. Why is a decline in interest rates bearish in such an environment? *Because it means a decline in the demand for credit.* When people want less of something, the price goes down. The recent drop in rates indicates less borrowing, which means that the primary prop under investment prices—the expansion of credit—is weakening. That's one reason why stock prices fell in 2000-2002 and why they are vulnerable now. This is the *opposite* of "pumping liquidity"; it's a slackening in liquidity.

The Big Bailout Bluff

Last week, a consortium of the USA's three largest banks—Citigroup, Bank of America and JP Morgan Chase—agreed to create a super fund (called M-LEC) of $80 billion "to buy distressed securities from SIVs [Structured Investment Vehicles]." Of course, like the Fed's loans for only the very best paper, the super fund will buy only high-quality mortgages, not the sub-prime or Alt-A stuff.

Do you think this plan will work? First let's examine what the SIVs did to get themselves in trouble. As AP (10/16) reports,

> The SIVs used short-term commercial paper, sold at low interest rates, to buy longer-term mortgage-backed securities and other instruments with higher rates of return. With the seizure of the credit markets, many SIVs had trouble selling new commercial paper to replace upcoming obligations on older paper.

Their plan, in other words, was the equivalent of a perpetual motion machine: "Money for Nothing," as the song title goes. But the world does not work like that. Oversized interest rates often mean that the investment is in fact sucking money out of principal. Sometimes investors can get away with the gambit for awhile, but eventually *somebody* pays the bill. The collapse in sub-prime mortgages and in the commercial paper that supported them has simply adjusted the value of the principal to make up for the outsized returns that these investors got over the past five years. But guess what: The money that banks owe on their commercial paper didn't change. Sounds like trouble. And here is what are they are doing about it:

> This time around, the banks hope to not only prevent credit problems from spreading, but also are bailing themselves out. (AP, 10/16)

This idea is the equivalent to trying to levitate yourself by pulling on your legs. These banks are going to offer more commercial paper to buy mortgage assets; in other words, they are going to borrow more short-term money in order to buy long-term assets from themselves! That is, if they can borrow the money in the first place. One of the casualties in the rout was the commercial paper market; investors are realizing that it backs a lot of lousy mortgage debt, so they are backing away from investing in the commercial paper that backs the mortgages.

The last time banks colluded to hold up an entire market was October 1929. It didn't work.

On July 9, 2007, the CEO/Chairman of Citigroup said, "When the music stops, in terms of liquidity, things will be complicated." Now wait a minute. We keep hearing that the Fed will shore up all their debts with perpetual liquidity, so how do you explain this comment? Answer: The bankers know better. Liquidity, formerly the solution, is now the problem, and the bankers know it.

The only solution that bankers, regulators, politicians and the Fed can think of is to do more of what they did to get into the problem in the first place: create more debt. They know of no other response. When the big bankers met via conference calls, "Besides hearing from senior executives from each of the big banks, the group also sought ideas from others." In other words, they are flailing for a solution to a problem that has no solution aside from taking measures to make it worse. I still think there is no better analogy to a system-wide credit binge than a person who keeps going only by gulping down amphetamines. He will collapse if he stops taking them, but if he keeps taking them he will ultimately die. Bankers always choose to ingest more speed. Their choice is to collapse now or die later. They always choose later. But they cannot avoid the inevitable result.

The Elliott Wave Theorist, December 14, 2007

HIGH NOON FOR THE FED'S CREDIBILITY

On one end of the dusty street stand five outlaws: the Federal Reserve, the Bank of Canada, the Bank of England, the European Central Bank and the Swiss National Bank. On the other end of the street stands the monster that they created and nurtured in their global lab. The outlaws have opened with a barrage of bullets. But the only bullets they have are made of the monster's very substance: debt. Every bullet that hits him only makes him stronger. And now the monster is beginning to draw his gun, and it's a bazooka. He is taking aim. The monster is about to overcome his makers.

Last Chance Saloon

The world's "big five" central banks—the Federal Reserve, the Bank of Canada, the Bank of England, the European Central Bank and the Swiss National Bank—have just made the announcement of their lives. Apparently working all night on Tuesday-Wednesday, the Fed arranged all these players' cooperation in order to come up with a plan to bolster confidence among the world's creditors and borrowers. The Wall

Street Journal (12/13) calls it "the biggest coordinated show of international financial force since Sept. 11, 2001." As a result, before Wednesday's U.S. stock-market opening, this consortium of money monopolists announced to the world that it would provide billions of dollars worth of "liquidity" in the form of low-cost, one-month loans to qualified banks with high-quality collateral, essentially presenting them free passes to make money in the LIBOR market and elsewhere. In this one blazing statement broadcast worldwide, it seems that the dream/nightmare of believers in perpetual inflation has come true: With unlimited fiat credit at their disposal, the world's central banks are proudly coordinating a drive to create more inflation.

But the *seems* is different from the *is*. If these central banks had pledged to exchange their IOUs indiscriminately and permanently for any and all other debts, they would indeed have created permanent inflation. But this new plan is just another repo deal, in which the borrowing banks still have to pay back the money, with interest, in 28-30 days. What's more, weak debt is not acceptable collateral; these central banks are willing to hold only the good stuff, and then only for a month. As EWT has argued many times, there has been no indication whatsoever that the Fed is about to begin swapping its IOUs for subprime mortgages or any other junk paper. They will accept only good debt, and only for 30 days. Very little has changed.

Nevertheless, this is probably the single most important central-bank pronouncement yet. *But it is not significant for the reasons people think.* By far most people take such pronouncements at face value, presume that what the authorities promise will happen and reason from there. But the tremendous significance of this seismic engagement of the monetary jawbone is that *if this announcement fails to restore confidence, central bankers' credibility will evaporate.*

At least that's the way historians will play it. But of course, the true causality, as elucidated by socionomics, is that *an evaporation of confidence will make the central bankers' plans fail.* The outcome is predicated on psychology. If wave c of the bear market has begun, nothing the Fed does will engender confidence. On the contrary, everything it does will be interpreted, in the trend toward negative social mood, as something bad. The Fed's failures will not create fear; fear will create the Fed's failures.

Increasing fear manifests in certain behaviors. For one thing, bankers become fearful of lending. Recent surveys show a dramatic change in bankers' willingness to lend. Many of them have raised the size of required down payments on a house from zero to 20-30 percent. On the other side, investors become fearful of borrowing. For example, hedge funds that have amassed huge portfolios of bad mortgages were powerfully leveraged, some as much as 30 to 1. A small increase in fear has already induced many of them to pare back their leverage. Depositors' fear is also a factor. Just a few weeks ago the Local Government Investment Pool run by the Florida State Board of Administration, which held the assets of many state government organizations, had such a run that it suspended withdrawals. Does anyone think that its current and former depositors will blithely add more money to this fund just because the Fed says it can make more credit available? Well, it *could* happen. But if the trend is now toward greater fear in society, it won't. One of the most entertaining articles in recent memory is one from Bloomberg on December 4, about the fund in Florida. The portion underlined will be suitable for framing:

> On Nov. 30, an advisory panel of local governments in the Florida pool held a conference call with members of the State Board of Administration. The SBA put out a "Preferences Survey" for discussion, and Question No. 1 was

"What percent of your current holding would you withdraw in December 2007, if it meant you would receive 99 cents on the dollar?" The next three questions were exactly the same, except with 98 cents on the dollar, 95 cents on the dollar and 90 cents on the dollar. <u>The municipal officials on the call would have none of it. They want 100 cents on the dollar. Anything less, they said, would be unacceptable.</u>

News flash for these investors: *You can't tell the market what you will or won't accept. It tells* **you**. Another line in the article expresses the problem correctly, failing only in expressing the futility of a solution:

> They were a pretty conciliatory and reasonable bunch. They kept saying that what was needed was to restore <u>confidence</u> and <u>trust</u> in the fund.

Good luck changing the mood of the crowd.

Just look at how psychology, not conventional wisdom, expressed its dominance on the very day of the dramatic announcement: It seemed obvious to everyone what should happen in response to the knowledge that more central-bank credit was available. Gold and silver should soar. Oil should double overnight. Stock markets around the world should leap to the skies in anticipation of Dow 1,000,000. But did any of the obvious things happen? No. The opposite happened.

But not right away. Investors, saturated with blind faith in the inflationary powers of central bankers, caused the S&P futures contract to gap up a huge 34.5 points. Six minutes later, the temporary euphoria was over, and the market started to sell off. Shockingly, stocks of banks, which the Fed's announcement was designed to help most, led the reversal and by noon were down on the day. Although the averages closed up, the bank stocks didn't. The very next morning (yesterday), gold and silver, which had barely moved on the great Fed announcement, cracked below their early December uptrends, as the U.S. dollar took off in its biggest two-day rally since June to extend what is now the biggest rally in a year.

As Gomer Pyle used to say, "Su-prise, su-prise!" *But we at Elliott Wave International are not surprised at these events.* We have been surprised only by how long it has taken to get here. The only question remaining is how long it will take the bulk of the financial world to realize that the Fed is running out of ammo.

If the stock market has one more high coming, the Fed will temporarily look smart again. But a break of the August low will lead to the perception that the Fed's machinations have stopped working. When that happens, the reasoning that supports investors' faith in perpetually rising investment prices will melt, and those wrapped up in the credit balloon will rush to the exits. Fearful borrowers will scramble for dollars to pay off their loans. Fearful lenders will refuse to roll over loans and demand dollars as final payment. The only way to satisfy these urges will be to *sell stuff.*

Would you be surprised to learn that Wednesday's news and wild market action have a precedent? They do. In the stock market collapse of September-November, 1929, consortiums of banks announced several times that they were pooling resources to prop up stock prices. They failed. But today's central banks are many multiples bigger than the biggest banks of 1929, and they have unlimited credit and no real-money standard. They are nothing less than super-banks, which can create credit from nothing; *all a customer has to do is ask for it.*

Ah, but that's the problem. Someone has to ask. The expansion of credit depends on willing and able borrowers. Debtors have to trust the future well enough to borrow—and pay back with interest—the credit the central banks have to offer. The root of today's systemic dilemma is not *mechanical,* as the monetary engineers believe, but *psychological*. Bernanke thinks he can pull switches to prevent deflation. But you can't pull switches on a crowd. It pulls switches on you.

It is true that today's lending institutions dwarf those of 1929. But this is not a solution; *it's the problem*. They are the very reason that the market top of 1999-2007 is many multiples larger, in both extent and duration, than the 1929 top. People have their logic backwards. Bigger banks don't save markets from bubbles and crashes; they just make bubbles and crashes bigger.

When the Fed's credibility withers in the environment of a bear market, the monster will have overpowered his makers, and the gunfight will be over.

A Mystery: If Money is Loose, Why Are the Debt Markets in Distress?

Is money tight or loose? Most people would laugh at this question and say that, with the Fed being so "accommodating," money is obviously loose. But that is not my view. The Fed has always followed the T-bill rate when setting its discount rate and Fed funds target. From its February 2007 high, the U.S. T-bill rate has fallen 2.33 percentage points, but the Fed has lowered rates only one percentage point. Aside from the lower rates in its new repo auction scheme, it is still charging more than a full point above the T-bill rate, which is more than it normally would charge for its loans. The reasons are instructive.

The first reason for the slow rate reduction is that professional and public opinion is angry at the Fed for having fostered, through its role as lender of last resort, the bubble of loose money that supported the real estate mania and its sour resolution. So the Fed has decided that it wants to appear conservative and responsible by lowering rates slowly, even though the market rate for T-bills calls for a faster reduction. In other words, the Fed is sensitive to criticism and is therefore subject to outside opinions.

This is not the way monetary engineering is supposed to work, is it? The public's emotions and opinions are not supposed to affect the Fed's decisions. But they do. That's just one of the problems with monetarism.

The second reason for the slow rate reduction is that inflation has raged up to this point, so many among the Fed's governors, quite naturally, fear inflation. But past and future trends are two different things. Inflation has raged, but deflation is next. Yet it takes a historian, not an economist, to see it coming. The Fed, then, is reacting to the past. Today's announcement of the biggest monthly jump in the Consumer Price Index in over two years is the kind of news that fans inflation fears even after they are no longer valid. The CPI lags all other indicators of inflation. To make policy based on the CPI is to be behind the curve. Home prices are already falling, and if the U.S. dollar and precious metals have reversed trend, they will be leading indicators of the real problem: deflation. So the Fed is basing its conservatism on old news, keeping money tight and not realizing that it is doing so.

But hey, I'm all for it. Whatever hastens the debt implosion so we can get past it and—one would hope—rebuild a valid (i.e. free market) monetary system is welcome.

Another Mystery: With Inflation Raging and the Dollar in Free-Fall for Six Years, Why Are T-Bill Rates So Low?

I met with a group of smart analysts a few months ago, and the one thing they agreed made no sense was the low interest rates on U.S. Treasuries. Many investors and analysts believe that the market has been inexplicably blind for several years and that these rates must soar. Well, sometimes markets do seem to ignore the obvious only to move in the anticipated direction later. But at other times, it is the participants who don't get it. I think this is one of those times.

One answer to the mystery is that we are in the "winter" portion of the Kondratieff economic cycle, which is when interest rates on good debt fall to their lows. That's what has been happening in Japan since 1990, and it is happening here, albeit more slowly.

But most people are not satisfied with cyclical explanations, so let's try another tack. I think the market "understands" that the inflation of recent years is not so much currency inflation as credit inflation. This is a crucial difference, because credit can disappear. I think the market is priced for an approaching debt implosion. Even though the dollar can't buy much now, surviving dollars will soon buy more, and anyone who has the foresight to keep his money *in debt that does not fail* will be wealthy in a kingdom of paupers. So 4%-5% rates on Treasuries provide a perfectly good return on IOUs that will almost surely survive the credit collapse. When much of this debt, which is falsely perceived as money, disappears, remaining dollars will be valuable. Soon even a one percent return will be welcome, as it was in 2002-3 and as it has been in Japan.

Conquer the Crash is on record forecasting that interest rates will trend *lower*—probably to near zero—for bonds that will remain AAA, and *higher*—in many cases to infinity—for bonds that are at risk of default, a category that includes most currently outstanding consumer, corporate and municipal debt. I believe this process has already begun. T-bill rates fell hard in 2007, and shortly thereafter rates on sub-prime mortgages soared and in cases of default have already reached infinity. So I do not think the market has been "wrong." I think it agrees with my book.

Appendix E

*F*ULL *C*IRCLE

Updating Chapter 1 of *Conquer the Crash*

Chapter 1 of *Conquer the Crash* showed that the rising wave V from 1975 through 1999 was weaker than the rising wave III from 1943 through 1965 in terms of the economic activity they engendered. Now we can show that wave **b** from 2003 through 2007 was weaker still. Figure E-1 provides a visual depiction of these upward waves in their historical context. Figures E-2 and E-3 update the associated economic figures. The relentless deterioration of economic health in this series of rising waves over many decades portends a reversal into depression, as happened at the end of the previous periods of prosperity ending in 1720, 1835 and 1929.

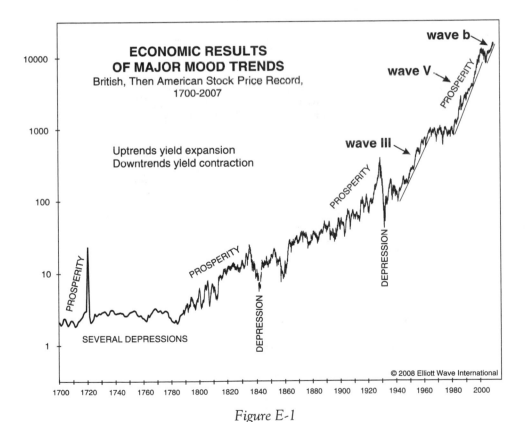

Figure E-1

Balance Sheet Items at the End of Wave III vs. Wave V vs. Wave b
(scales at left)

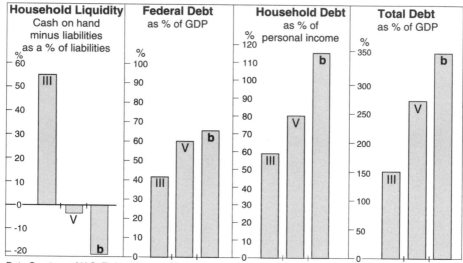

Data Courtesy of U.S. Federal Reserve Board
Household liquidity data courtesy of contraryinvestor.com

© 2008 Elliott Wave International

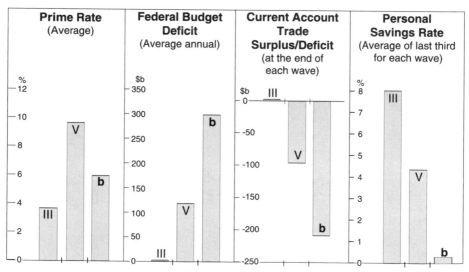

Data Courtesy of Ned Davis Research and Federal Reserve Board

Figure E-2

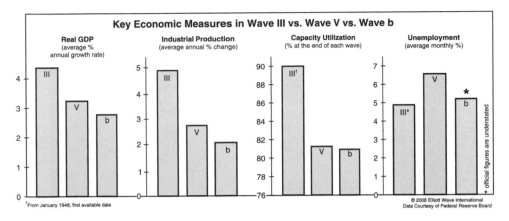

Figure E-3

A Decade of Optimism with No Net Progress

The Value Line Geometric Average peaked in April 1998 and has never exceeded its price at that time. This index had risen for 24 years, since 1974. Naturally, 1998 is when investors *began* a streak of nearly uninterrupted optimism. From October 1998 through March 2008, stock market advisors, as tracked in weekly polls by Investors Intelligence.com, were net bullish for 481 out of 490 weeks. In other words, for nearly 9½ years, the average year contained 51 out of 52 weeks in which bulls outnumbered bears. One would have to go back to the late 1920s even to postulate a time when such a ratio might have existed even for as long as three years. These figures are commensurate with the Elliott-wave case presented in Chapters 3 and 4 of *Conquer the Crash* that the stock market peak being formed was the greatest in nearly 300 years, if not longer.

Figure E-4 shows the action of the S&P 500 during this time when optimism reigned so powerfully. It is ironic yet entirely natural that buy-and-hold investors made no profits at all during this period. The S&P 500 returned 3.84% during this time, while a simple investment in U.S. Treasury bills returned 30.22%. Bears were ignored or derided over this decade, but in fact they proved to be investors' only lifeboat in a sea of optimistic advisors.

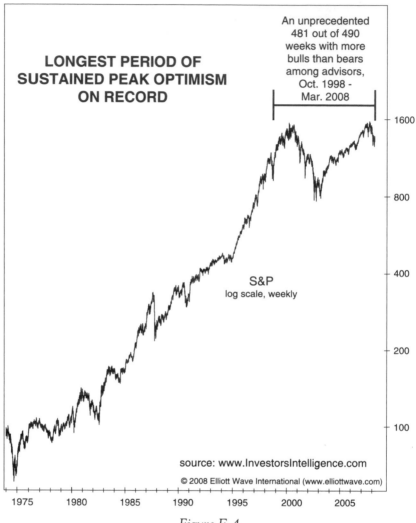

Figure E-4

A 30-Year Perspective

[*This section appeared in the paperback printing for 2004. It is reproduced here with Figure E-7 updated through 2007.—Ed.*]

    Elliott Wave Principle (1978) forecast both a great bull market in stocks and a great bear market to follow. It is instructive to travel back in time to see how different things were then and how dramatically the social mood of the time contrasts with today's relentless optimism. Figure E-5 shows a picture of the DJIA as of 1978, when *Business Week* was reporting as follows:

    — "More and more economists are forecasting recession."[1]

    — "If the dollar continues to plummet, the pressure may prove unstoppable."[2]

    — "The mood of the consumer and of business executives indicate a deterioration in expectations about prospective business conditions."[3]

    — "The public's...fear of inflation has never been greater than it is today."[4]

Naturally, most investors expected stocks to fall. What would *you* have forecast for the stock market at that time?

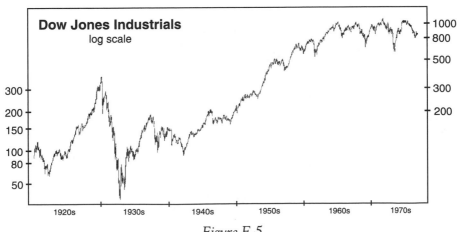

Figure E-5

Figure E-6

Figure E-7

Elliott Wave Principle depicted what the authors thought would be a reasonable shape for wave V and its aftermath. This chart is reproduced in Figure E-6. It was derived by inverting the 1929-1937 period and adding it to the low that had just occurred in March of 1978. Our graph called for the DJIA to climb from the 1974 low in "five Primary waves with the fifth extending," carrying beyond the upper trendline of the channel at Supercycle degree, and then to fall below 400. This forecast shows that Elliott wave analysts knew back in those early days the wild upside experience that lay ahead. The first half of that forecast took much longer and went far higher than originally anticipated, but otherwise this picture was a good guide to the future. Per Figure E-7, the rising portion of the projection ended in 2007. The second half appears to be underway.

Outlining an entire stock-market cycle is not the only round trip that Elliott wave analysis made possible. Way back in November 1979, a year after *Elliott Wave Principle* was published, inflation was raging and precious metals were two months from their peaks in an explosive ten-year rise. That's when *The Elliott Wave Theorist* forecasted a dramatic shift in the monetary trend. It also outlined a scenario for the approaching second half of the monetary cycle that began in the 1940s. Here is the commentary from that time:

> The evidence I have available argues persuasively that at the very least we are reaching an interim peak in the inflationary spiral. Elliott counts suggest important tops in silver, gold, the commodity market indexes and short term interest rates.
>
> The incredible conjunction of "fives" in different markets all seem to point to the same conclusion: *The world is about to begin a phase of general disinflation.* **As I see it, a pattern of several disinflationary years leading to a deflationary trend**

later on would be a perfect scenario for the Elliott outlook for stocks. A gradual disinflation would [correspond with] an optimistic mood in the country and lead to the conclusion that we may have finally licked the inflation problem. This sentiment would support a bull market in stocks for several years until the snowballing forces of deflation began to take over. At that point, a major deflationary crash would be impossible to avert, and the Grand Supercycle correction would be underway.

— *The Elliott Wave Theorist*, Special Report, "Commodities, Interest Rates and Inflation: A Major Top?" November 18, 1979

Despite the long time it took to play out, this monetary trajectory has never been in doubt. The projected disinflationary period finally ended in 2005-2008, and the "snowballing forces of deflation" are taking over.

NOTES

[1] *Business Week.* (1978, March 8). "The Talk Grows of a Coming Recession."

[2] *Business Week.* (1978, March 20). "The Dollar Fades as a Reserve Currency."

[3] *Business Week.* (1978, May 8). "Business Outlook."

[4] *Business Week.* (1978, May 22.) "How Inflation Threatens the Fabric of U.S. Society."

Media and Misc. References

Chapter 1

Seigler, Mark V. (1998, June). "Real output and business cycle volatility, 1869-1993: U.S. experience in international perspective." *Journal of Economic History.*

Chapter 3

Elliott, Ralph Nelson. (series of books and articles published from 1938-1946). Republished: (1994) *R.N. Elliott's Masterworks—The Definitive Collection*, Prechter, Jr., Robert Rougelot. (Ed.) Gainesville, GA: New Classics Library.

Mandelbrot, Benoit. (1988). *The Fractal Geometry of Nature.* New York: W.H. Freeman.

Frost, Alfred John and Prechter, Robert Rougelot. (1978). *Elliott Wave Principle—Key to Market Behavior.* Gainesville, GA: New Classics Library.

Prechter, Robert Rougelot. (1999). *The Wave Principle of Human Social Behavior and the New Science of Socionomics.* Gainesville, GA: New Classics Library.

Prechter, Robert Rougelot. (1982, October 6 and November 8). *The Elliott Wave Theorist.*

Chapter 4

Prechter, Robert Rougelot. (2001, September 11). "Elliott Waves and Social Reality." *The Elliott Wave Theorist.*

Chapter 5

Elliott, Ralph Nelson. (1946). *Nature's law.* Republished: (1994) *R.N. Elliott's Masterworks—The Definitive Collection*, Prechter, Jr., Robert Rougelot. (Ed.) Gainesville, GA: New Classics Library.

Jasen, Georgette. (1994, May 13). "Darts Beat Pros but Losses Are the Rule." *The Wall Street Journal.*

Jasen, Georgette. (1996, July 10). "Pros Lose Out to Chance, Industrials." *The Wall Street Journal.*

Jasen, Georgette. (1997, February 11). "Investment Pros Defeat Darts, but Can't Top Surging Market." *The Wall Street Journal.*

Jasen, Georgette. (1997, April 9). "Pros Beat Darts, but in a Losing Contest." *The Wall Street Journal.*

Jasen, Georgette. (1998, May 13). "Pros Beat Darts, but Picks Trail Dow Jones Industrials." *The Wall Street Journal.*

Jasen, Georgette. (1998, November 5). "Darts Draw Blood as Pro Losses Far Exceed Those of Industrials." *The Wall Street Journal.*

Prechter, Robert Rougelot. (1983, August 18). "The Superbull Market of the '80s—Has the Last Wild Ride Really Begun?" *The Elliott Wave Theorist.*

Kendall, Peter Mark. (1998, September 16.) "Wave V Fundamentals and Their Implications." *The Elliott Wave Theorist.*

Chapter 6

Prechter, Robert Rougelot, editor. (2002). *Market Analysis for the New Millennium.* Gainesville, GA: New Classics Library.

Glassman, James K. and Kevin A. Hassett. (1999, March 17). "Stock Prices Are Still Far Too Low." *The Wall Street Journal.*

Birger, Jon. (2002, March). "Faith Stocks." *Money.*

Chapter 7

Siegel, Jeremy J. (1999, April 19). "Manager's Journal: Are Internet Stocks Overvalued? Are They Ever." *The Wall Street Journal.*

Siegel, Jeremy J. (2000, March 14). "Big-Cap Tech Stocks Are a Sucker Bet." *The Wall Street Journal.*

Glassman, James K. and Kevin A. Hassett. (1998, March 30). "Are Stocks Overvalued? Not a Chance." *The Wall Street Journal.*

Dornbusch, Rudi. (1998, July 30). "Growth Forever." *The Wall Street Journal.*

Angell, Wayne D. (1999, February 3). "The Bubble Won't Burst." *The Wall Street Journal.*

Glassman, James K. and Kevin A. Hassett. (1999, March 17). "Stock Prices Are Still Far Too Low." *The Wall Street Journal.*

Ip, Greg. (1999, August 30). " Does Tech 'Explosion' Alter Market's Nature?" *The Wall Street Journal.*

Ip, Greg. (1999, September 13). "New Paradigm View for Stocks is Bolstered." *The Wall Street Journal.*

Gilder, George. (1999, December 31). "The Faith of a Futurist." *The Wall Street Journal.*

Kadlec, Charles W. (2000, April 18). "Market Mayhem. Don't Worry, the Great Prosperity Still Coming." *The Wall Street Journal.*

Ford, Constance Mitchell. (2000, January 3). "Economists Are Euphoric About the Prospect for 2000—Nearly All Surveyed Believe Expansion Will Become Longest on Record." *The Wall Street Journal.*

Ford, Constance Mitchell. (2001, January 2). "Euphoria Dominating Last Year Turns to Prudence in 2001." *The Wall Street Journal.*

Hilsenrath, Jon E. (2002, January 4). "Economic Forecasters Expect Moderate Recovery in 2002." *The Wall Street Journal.*

Hughes, Siobhan. (2002, February 22). "Economists Optimistic. Survey Says Recession Likely Is Already Over." *The Atlanta Journal-Constitution.*

Hager, George. (2002, February 28). "Recessionette' Might Be at an End." *USA Today.*

Fox, Justin. (2002, March 18). "The Profitless Recovery." *Fortune*.

Barnes, Angela. (2002, January 10). "Managers Bullish on Equity Markets. Expect Double-Digit Return, Survey Finds." *The Globe and Mail* (Toronto).

Prechter, Robert Rougelot. (1995). *At the Crest of the Tidal Wave*. Gainesville, GA: New Classics Library.

Leonhardt, David. (2002, March 12). "After Sept. 11, Diverging Attitudes about the Market." *The New York Times*.

Prechter, Robert Rougelot. (2001, September 11). "Elliott Waves and Social Reality." *The Elliott Wave Theorist*.

Altman, Daniel. (2001, December 29). "Positive Reports Hint at Swift Recovery." *The New York Times*.

Meyers, Mike. (2002, January 6). "Better Times Coming." *Star* (Minneapolis).

Torres, Carlos. (2001, December 29). "Hope Soars in U.S." *Rocky Mountain News*.

Sommar, Jessica (2002, March 1). "Recovery at Last." *New York Post*.

Hagenbaugh, Barbara and George Hager (2002, March 8). "Fed Chief Declares Recession at an End." USA Today.

Pethokoukis, James. (2002, January 14). "Business Bounces Back. How to Cash in. That Old Blue-Sky Feeling." *U.S. News & World Report*.

Curl, Joseph. (2002, January 1). "Bush Predicts 2002 Will Be 'a Great Year'." *Washington Times*.

Chapter 9
Bolton, A. Hamilton. (1957, February 11). Personal letter to Charles Collins.

Chapter 11
Federal Reserve System. (2001, December 31). "Flow of Funds Accounts of the United States." Washington, D.C: Board of Governors of the Federal Reserve System.

The Federal Reserve Bank of St. Louis. "FRED, an Economic Time Series Database." http://www.stls.frb.org/fred/.

Chapter 12
Prechter, Robert Rougelot. (1979, November 18). "Commodities, Interest Rates and Inflation: A Major Top?" *The Elliott Wave Theorist*.

Kondratieff, Nikolai. (1926). "The Long Waves in Economic Life." Republished: (1935, November). *Review of Economic Statistics*.

Chapter 13
Norton, Rob. (1997, September 8). "Why not to Worry about Deflation." *Fortune*.

Wiseman, Paul. (1991, January 17). "Deflation? Not Yet. Some Prices Are Tumbling but Not All." USA Today.

Reisman, George and Robert Klein. (1999, November 15). "No Inflation? Look Again." *Barron's*.

American Institute for Economic Research. (2002, February 25). "Deflation?" *Research Reports.*

Luskin, Donald L. (2001, November 19). "Deflation: The Basics." *The Luskin Report.*

Quinn, Jane Bryant. (1998, February 16). "In Praise of Deflation." *Newsweek.*

Shilling, A. Gary. (1998, August 26). "Deflation Is Nothing to Fear." *The Wall Street Journal.*

Nevallier, Louis. (1998, August 27). Interview CNBC.

Kanell Michael E. (2001, November 17). "Sliding Oil Prices a Break for Drivers." *The Atlanta Journal-Constitution.*

Cooper, James C. and Kathleen Madigan. (2001, November 16). " That's not Deflation Ahead, Just Slower Inflation." *BusinessWeek.*

Miller, Karen Lowry. (2001, December 10). "Beware the Bugaboo. What's Worse Than Inflation? Its Opposite." *Newsweek.*

Blackstone, Brian. (2001, April 16). "Fed's Parry: US Economy Growing at Slight Positive Rate." *Dow Jones Newswires.*

Miller, Rich. (1998, January 7). "Prices under Pressure. Deflation Could Slam Brakes on Economies." *USA Today.*

Birger, Jon. (2002, January). "Can Washington Save Wall Street?" *Money.*

Abelson, Alan. (1999, August 30). "Werner Visits Wall Street." *Barron's.*

Chapter 16
Birger, Jon (2001, December). "The Rock." *Money.*

Chapter 19
Van Dusen, Christine (2001, December 29). "Despite Woes, Banks Well-Capitalized." *The Atlanta Journal-Constitution.*

Weiss, Martin. (2002). *Ultimate safe money guide.* New York: John Wiley & Sons.

Chapter 20
The Dick Davis Digest. (2000, January 31 and 2001, January 15). "Top Stock Pick Special." Fort Lauderdale, FL: Dick Davis Publishing.

Chapter 22
Roosevelt, Franklin D. (1933, April 5). "Executive Order 6260." *Federal Register.*

Chapter 26
Prechter, Robert Rougelot. (2001, August). "On the Cresting Wave—a Q&A with Robert Prechter." *The Elliott Wave Theorist.*

Chapter 27
Lambert, Michael J. and Kristin D. Stanton. (2001, September). "Opportunities and Challenges of the U.S. Dollar as an Increasingly Global Currency: a Federal Reserve perspective." *Federal Reserve Bulletin.*

New York Times. Article unavailable.

Appendix C

Laffer, Arthur. (2005, October 26). "Ben Bernanke Is the Right Person at the Right Time," *The Wall Street Journal.*

Newman, Alan, "Still on Overdrive," Internet, Cross-currents.net.

Appendix D

American Institute for Economic Research. (2003, May 26). "Deflation." Research Report.

Angell, Wayne. (2002, October 29). "Greenspan's Deflation." *The Wall Street Journal.*

Associated Press. (2003, June 23). "To Stop Deflation, Federal Reserve May Drop Interest Rate Again."

Baum, Caroline. (2003, June 18). "Houston, Deflation Launch Has Been Scrubbed." *Bloomberg News.*

Bernanke, Ben S. (2002, November 21). "Deflation: Making Sure 'It' Doesn't Happen Here." Speech to the National Economists Club, Washington, D.C., as posted on the Internet.

Brittan, Samuel. (2002, October 10). "Ignore the Ghost of Deflation." Published on the Internet.

Bugos, Ed. (2003, February 19). "Deflation Fears are Irrational." *Goldenbar Report,* on the Internet.

Corrigan, Sean. (2003, May). "Myths of the Crash." *The Free Market.* Ludwig von Mises Institute.

Cosgrove, Michael. (2003, May 21). "The Fed's Complacency." *The Wall Street Journal.*

De Rosa, David. (2003, May 7). "Will U.S. Catch Japan's Deflation Bug?" *Bloomberg News.*

Douglas, Adrian. (2002, October 30). "Ghosts, Goblins, Witches, Wizards...And DEFLATION." Published on the Internet.

Grant, James. (2002, October 25). "Deflation, of Which There Is None," *Grant's Interest Rate Observer,* p. 1.

Greenspan, Alan. (2002, December 19). Speech to the Economic Club of New York, as posted on the Internet.

Hagenbaugh, Barbara, and Barbara Hansen. (2003, June 23). "Economists Expect Cut; Many Don't Advise It." *USA Today.*

Headlines in *The Wall Street Journal,* (2003, May 16).

Hilsenrath, Jon E. (2002, December 30). "'Reflation' Comes Into Focus as U.S. Struggles to Battle Deflation." *The Wall Street Journal.*

Hoffman, David. (2002, October 28). "For Money Funds, Zero Sum Is No Game At All." *InvestmentNews,* p. 25.

Ip, Greg. (2002, November 6). Quoting Nobel laureate Milton Friedman. "Inside the Fed, Deflation Draws a Closer Look." *The Wall Street Journal*, p. A14.

Ip, Greg. (2003, May 19). Quoting Fed Vice Chairman Roger Ferguson, "Having Defeated Inflation, the Fed Girds for War on Falling Prices." *The Wall Street Journal*.

Kirchhoff, Sue. (2003, May 16). "Deflation Fears May Rise as Economy Fights for Traction." *USA Today*.

Kirchoff, Sue. (2003, June 4). "Greenspan Upbeat about Economy." *USA Today*.

Lee, Tim. (2003, May 26). "Inflation is a Bigger Danger Than Deflation." *Financial Times* online.

Palmer, Jay. (2003, January 6). "Annual Review of Investment Books." *Barron's*.

Prechter, Robert. (2002). *Conquer the Crash: You Can Survive and Prosper in a Deflationary Depression*. John Wiley & Sons, p. 106.

Shiller, Robert J. (2003, June 12). "The Technology Deflator." *The Wall Street Journal*.

Southall, Brooke. (2003, September 1). "Deflation Scare is Losing Air." Investment News (excerpt). To be fair, the article quoted one economist who still urges caution about dismissing the possibility of deflation.

Von Furstenberg, George (2003, May 10) Indiana University, formerly on the Council of Economic Advisors, quoted in *The Atlanta Journal-Constitution*, "Fed Deflation Warning Creates Waves," by Michael E. Kanell.

Appendix E

Business Week. (1978, March 8). "The Talk Grows of a Coming Recession."

Business Week. (1978, March 20). "The Dollar Fades as a Reserve Currency."

Business Week. (1978, May 8). "Business Outlook."

Business Week. (1978, May 22.) "How Inflation Threatens the Fabric of U.S. Society."